PENGUIN BOOKS

Praise for *Emotion by Design*

'Reading this book made me smile in my soul, proving that
creativity, community and empathy have created one of the
greatest brands of our lifetime'
Mary Portas

'A brand isn't a logo, it's a story. In this guidebook-plus-memoir,
Greg helps us see how a commitment to our creative practice
can make any story better'
Seth Godin

'*Emotion by Design* is Greg Hoffman's transformative and intensely
personal journey building one of the world's most important,
groundbreaking brands. It's a must-read if you work with creatives,
and if you want to unlock their unique genius to build authentic
brands and waves of support across your entire company'
Laszlo Bock, author of *Work Rules!*

'Not only does *Emotion by Design* offer a gripping insight
into the creation of some of the most iconic marketing in
history, it is also a powerful love letter to the power of a
sense of purpose in doing our work'
Bruce Daisley, author of *The Joy of Work*

'This is the ultimate playbook to unleash creativity in any team –
and in turn effect real, transformative change for you
and your company'
Jake Humphrey, author of *High Performance*

D0898555

'An unforgettable account of a man and a business that never had to try to be someone else's idea of cool – because they had already defined it themselves'
Rory Sutherland, Vice-Chairman of Ogilvy and author of *Alchemy*

'Great story, amazing career, so inspirational . . . What a book. I couldn't put it down'
Chris Evans

ABOUT THE AUTHOR

When Greg Hoffman joined Nike as a design intern in 1992, he had little idea he would end up as the most senior marketer at the world's most renowned brand. But over the next twenty-eight years, Hoffman would help lead some of the most famous campaigns in history – from the 'Find Your Greatness' campaign during the London 2012 Olympics to the 'Risk Everything' campaign at the 2014 FIFA World Cup. His work would take him from Nike's Oregon headquarters to stadiums, courts and arenas around the world. And he would ultimately be appointed Chief Marketing Officer, responsible for the Nike Swoosh's brand recognition everywhere on earth.

Hoffman retired from Nike in 2020. He has been cited as one of the US's leading creatives by *Fast Company*, *Business Insider* and *AdAge*. He lives in Portland, Oregon.

EMOTION
BY
DESIGN.

Creative Leadership Lessons
from a Life at Nike

Greg Hoffman

PENGUIN BOOKS

PENGUIN BOOKS

UK | USA | Canada | Ireland | Australia
India | New Zealand | South Africa

Penguin Books is part of the Penguin Random House group of companies
whose addresses can be found at global.penguinrandomhouse.com

First published in the US by Twelve Books in 2022
First published in the UK by Cornerstone Press in 2022
Published in Penguin Books 2023
001

Copyright © Greg Hoffman, 2022

The moral right of the author has been asserted

Printed and bound in Great Britain by Clays Ltd, Elcograf S.p.A.

The authorised representative in the EEA is Penguin Random House Ireland,
Morrison Chambers, 32 Nassau Street, Dublin D02 YH68

A CIP catalogue record for this book is available from the British Library

ISBN: 978–184–794356–9

www.greenpenguin.co.uk

MIX
Paper from
responsible sources
FSC® C018179

Penguin Random House is committed to a
sustainable future for our business, our readers
and our planet. This book is made from Forest
Stewardship Council® certified paper.

To my wife and children,
Kirsten, Rowan, and Ayla:
Thanks for always dreaming with me.

CONTENTS

INTRODUCTION:
THE ART OF SPORT

I'm looking at a projection screen that's flanked by more than a hundred flags from nations around the world. The international atmosphere is fitting, because this is Nike's Sebastian Coe Building, named for the British runner who won the gold medal in the 1500 meters at both the 1980 and 1984 Olympic Games. One of Coe's quotes comes to me now: "Competing is exciting, and winning is exhilarating, but the true prize will always be the self-knowledge and understanding that you have gained along the way." At the end of a twenty-seven-year journey from design intern to chief marketing officer of the Nike brand, I feel those words. It's February 2020 and this is my retirement celebration.

On the screen, I see "GH," my initials. I am surprised—and honored—that it's been designed in a way that's reminiscent of the athlete logos we created over the years for the likes of LeBron, Tiger, and Serena. I got my start at Nike in 1992 designing logos for products, athletes, and anything else Nike sent my way. Now, my persona was a logo, bringing it all full circle, and right off the bat my emotions are making their way to the surface.

The evening is full of reminiscences and a word or two of advice (from me) to the people with whom I have worked and who have been my family for nearly three decades. One of the more moving moments is when the new head of creative for the brand, my old friend and protégé Gino Fisanotti, presents me with a gift. It's a large framed portrait of Colin Kaepernick by the photographer Platon.

You may not know Platon by name, but you likely have seen his work: His signature black-and-white photographs of celebrities, world leaders, athletes, and artists are critically acclaimed for capturing the essence of the person behind the title or reputation. In a single image of, say, Muhammad Ali, you see the human in the boxing legend. In that way, Platon's portraits don't look like the heavily art-directed, idealized work one usually attributes to professional photographers. Rather, they are meant to appear like Platon shot his subject in a stolen moment, a brief second where the image slips and the all-too-real person emerges, especially in the eyes. His high-contrast photographs, set against a white background, presents the person and the personality in the rawest way.

That sort of creative genius doesn't just happen; it must be *designed* to happen. Like all great art, a Platon portrait is meant to evoke an emotion, but that emotion isn't accidental. There is a deliberateness in the process, no different from a writer weaving a story. I can't really tell you how Platon does it; how he's able to tell a story through his portraits and elicit a response from his audience that exposes some truth about the human experience. But I can tell you how we, as brand marketers, can strive to achieve it.

My passion for fine art on the level of Platon is matched only by my love of sport. At first glance, these appear to be two separate interests, but when we look below the surface of sport we see that it has the ability to stir the purest and most visceral of our emotions; agonies and ecstasies played out on the field and in the stands for us all to feel. As Nelson Mandela once said: "Sport has the power to change the world. It has the power to inspire, it has the power to unite people in a way that little else does."

As I looked at Platon's portrait of Kaepernick, I once more felt the power of art to convey an impression that is both timely and timeless. The portrait was part of a marketing campaign—my last campaign at Nike—but it was also art, designed to be more than a simple photograph. It is imbued with Kaepernick's personality and passion. At the same time, this portrait is a statement of purpose for Nike: the ability of sport to change the world. The portrait hangs proudly in my home office today because it represents not only great art, but also great brand marketing. Indeed, it is a reminder to me that art and marketing can fulfill the same ends, and often should try to fulfill the same ends.

And, lastly, looking at the portrait, I am reminded about the journey that made it possible. A journey that started roughly five months earlier.

. . . . . .

In August 2019, I went to see Platon in his studio in New York City. Our friendship dated back to 2013, when I, then head of Global Brand Creative for Nike, invited him to speak at one of the company's "brand camps." In addition to being a master photographer, Platon is also a master storyteller who has this amazing ability to weave mesmerizing narratives through his singular images. I had the honor of introducing Platon to the audience and interviewed him onstage about his process and some of his most famous portraits. Out of that, our friendship began. The next time we worked together was when I asked him to shoot the Brazil National Football team for Nike, which had sponsored the team and designed its uniforms in 2014, after its Confederations

Cup victory. The resulting photographs were iconic Platon, mostly black-and-white images of the players themselves, set against a white background, but with the added splash of yellow highlighting the jerseys: The players are presented as individuals, but the yellow ties them together as a team. Perhaps the true stroke of genius for Platon's work in Brazil was that he went far beyond what my brief—or work outline—had defined as the project, and ended up shooting not just the athletes but also the passionate Brazilian fans. The finished photographs put both groups side by side. The result was something that transcended mere sport, because his photographs showed how sports and culture are so closely entwined. To ignore the latter in favor of the former is to miss *why* sports resonates with so many millions around the world.

But when I walked into Platon's studio that August day, I didn't come with any plan. We talked as friends, and then Platon mentioned that he was donating his photographs of African-American leaders who had been civil rights champions to the Smithsonian's National Museum of African American History and Culture. It is an impressive list of heroes, from Muhammad Ali to Harry Belafonte to Elaine Brown. An insight flashed in my mind.

"You're missing someone," I said.

"Who?" he asked.

"Colin Kaepernick."

Platon replied that he couldn't get access to someone like Colin. I could help with that. When I left Platon's studio, I called Gino, who at that time was starting to plan marketing around a new limited-edition Air Force 1 shoe for Colin. Gino, thinking it over, said that a series of Platon portraits of Kaepernick might be a great way to help launch the new sneaker and tell a larger story. And so, the Kaepernick "True to 7" campaign began to become a reality. I flew back to the Nike campus and met with Gino to talk specifics. The idea was simple: Tie the campaign—which featured not only a shoe but also a jersey—to Colin's "seven values" that informed his belief system through a series of iconic Platon black-and-white portraits. The campaign launched in December 2019. To help promote the campaign, Colin had posted on his Twitter page: "For those true to themselves on and off the field. Proudly, unapologetically and against all odds. This is only the beginning."

·······

And now, one of those Platon portraits hangs in my house, a gift from Gino, whose support, insight, and devotion to our work with Colin was instrumental in making my last Nike project one of the most memorable.

The story of our work with Colin began two years before my visit with Platon, during a lunch get-together at Nike Headquarters in Beaverton, Oregon. That is a topic for another chapter, but it means that the Platon portrait represented more than the "True to 7" campaign. It was a physical representation of a creative journey that had begun years earlier, during a moment when we listened to Colin to learn what *he* wanted to say. Platon had never been a part of our designs, not until I met with him at his New York studio. But the creative process doesn't follow a linear path, and often moments of inspiration come upon you in unlikely places—if you're open to them. The entirety of our work with Colin Kaepernick was based off the insight that his message, by exposing hard truths about racial injustice, was inextricably tied with sports and the experience of Black Americans. But beyond the social impact of Colin's message are the lessons the "True to 7" campaign can teach brands. For Colin (and for Nike) there was no distinction between the personal and the professional. He was the same person on the field as he was off, and it was Nike's responsibility to reveal this person and his passion to the world. Had we focused only on Colin's message, we would have missed its relevance to sport. Likewise, had we focused only on sport, we would have undercut Colin's message. The two—the personal and the professional—had to be one.

A lot of the inspiration for this book came from the work with Colin, and from the journey I took during those final years of my Nike tenure, where so many of the lessons and insights I had formed during the previous two and a half decades had come together. The creative philosophy that I wholeheartedly speak to my audiences today, in my capacity as a brand advisor for start-ups and more established companies, was encapsulated with the creative collaboration with Kaepernick, Gino, Platon, and the talented Nike brand team, and forms the basis of this book. Put simply, a brand gains a competitive advantage through its ability to construct powerful emotional bonds with its consumers. I believe this connection can be consistently achieved by cultivating a strong creative culture.

I call this **Emotion by Design**—the ability to create stories, images, and experiences that make people feel that even their most audacious dreams are possible to achieve. Over the years, I forged this philosophy within a creative culture where ideas were dominant. Now my passion is in instilling this creative marketing and branding philosophy in others, for a key point about Emotion by Design is that *it can be practiced and applied by all types of business leaders and teams*. The success of this creative methodology isn't dependent on large resources. An agency of five employees can generate phenomenal success with its branding just as effectively as a company of thousands. Millions of dollars aren't required to make consumers feel. The emotional connections that form a bond between brand and consumer don't depend on the size of the brand or its resources; they depend on the power of the story and the depth of the connection.

I also want to refute the notion that not everyone is creative. While the application of ideas—the art directing, the copywriting, the app design, the film directing, to name a few—is reserved for those with expertise in these fields, the conception of those ideas isn't—and shouldn't be—limited to "creatives." Everyone has an imagination; everyone has aspirations and dreams. The trick is instilling a culture and an environment where those imaginations are given space—and are given voice. Too many brands and companies stifle the innate talent of their teams by harnessing their creative energies to preconceived notions and personal biases. These companies at times try to channel their creative minds into highly structured processes and modes of thought—and risk ending up with a brand that can be uninspiring and unconnected with their consumer bases.

Which is why brands must embrace a mindset that invites outside voices into their creative process and encourages these voices to draw upon their unique experiences to inform their work. Diversity and inclusion should be a goal in its own right, but it amazes me that even today, so many companies don't see *why* a diversity of experiences, thought, backgrounds, ideas, and values is a prerequisite to build a creative force that can change the world. Creativity grows from the insights we discover that others miss. We find these insights through the diversity of experience in our teams, as well as from our own passion for exploring beyond what we know.

This book is a celebration of creativity and a call to arms for brand builders to rediscover the human element in forming consumer bonds. In the chapters that follow, readers will go on a journey of creativity through insights drawn from my Nike experience and beyond, and whose lessons can be applied across the continuum of marketing disciplines. From building stories of greatness for LeBron to drawing inspiration from Kobe's boundless curiosity and imagination to a concert for the Air Force 1 sneaker to creating a movement about movement with Kevin Hart to motivating new generations of athletes through Just Do It. Readers will experience the art within marketing and the Emotion by Design that it creates.

Building a world-class brand today is a fine balance between art and science. Data has given us more knowledge about our consumers than we could have ever imagined. We now have the ability to be more effective, more timely, more tailored, and more productive with our content and storytelling. But while data and analytics has given us more in one sense, it's also taken from us as well. We are less creative, we are less innovative, and we take fewer risks. It's not a question of priority, but of balance. When in harmony, art and science can achieve amazingly effective results. The information and data these lines of code present to us are amazingly useful, and allow us to eliminate friction and inconveniences from the consumer experience. But the scales are not balanced. The result in many cases is that brands have come to prioritize transactional relationships with consumers, when they should be building human relationships.

In this book, I will convey the lessons and principles I have forged from thirty years in this field. I will examine how a lot of my creative process and principles took their inspiration directly from the arena of sport's greatest collaborators—its athletes, coaches, and teams. My hope is that readers will be able to see how these creative processes and principles possess a universal application for brands large and small. Above all, this book strives to be a useful plan for business, marketing, and creative professionals, whether you are a team of one or a group of one thousand. The insights in this book, when applied, can empower you as a leader, your team, and your brand to achieve a level of creative excellence that builds lasting bonds with your consumers.

A Note on Structure

Before we begin, I want to explain the structure of this book to help readers understand what it attempts to do. The book is presented in a way that gives the reader a playbook for unleashing creativity within your team. And when I say "creativity," I'm referring to the kind of paradigm-shifting creativity that stirs emotions and connects us to one another. The chapters are organized so that the foundational elements are provided first, followed by the application of those elements.

The book draws heavily on the innovative work from my career within the world of sports, giving readers in many cases a closer look at what that creative teamwork looked and felt like to produce some of the most memorable and iconic marketing campaigns of our time. I was fortunate in beginning my tenure at Nike during a time of radical creative collaboration for the brand. This culture and community endured throughout my career even as Nike experienced phenomenal growth and had to mature beyond its less structured beginnings. Within the teams where I worked there existed an ethos that encouraged imagination and ideation. There also existed a culture of resourcefulness that meant you were often given responsibility over a project even if you didn't have the requisite experience. All of us had the sense that we were *building* something special, and I don't mean just the company. I mean that we felt as if our work was connecting with consumers in a way that produced real human moments. Our films, our campaigns, our products *mattered* to people. Nike was becoming the definitive brand in sports footwear and apparel, and this bestowed upon us a feeling of responsibility. If what we were doing mattered to people, then we had an obligation to get it right for them. When a brand achieves that level of consumer engagement, then in many ways you are no longer selling something; you are part of the culture. This, of course, also means that you must *protect* what you have built and ensure that the level of excellence consumers have come to expect continues. No small task, and for this reason I hope that this book gives readers the tools to create a culture within their own organizations that is able to continually produce excellent branding, storytelling, and experiences that build and maintain those powerful emotional bonds with their audience.

With the notable exception of chapter 1, every chapter follows a similar structure and presents a unique element that will produce a stronger brand. The end of each chapter will also include a list of principles that highlight and condense that chapter's ideas and themes. Chapter 1 gives readers a better understanding of who I was when I first joined Nike, and thus is very biographical, while the other chapters are presented thematically. The stories I have chosen to illustrate a lesson or idea in specific chapters are the best stories I could tell in that moment. But the creative process never is so orderly, and stories I have chosen for one chapter could easily have applied to another. For this reason, readers will notice the repetition of certain ideas—empathy, insight, and creative collaboration, to name a few—popping up in several stories. And that's because all those elements went into those creative endeavors. Chapter 2 presents several of these themes in a "foundational" way; in other words, without these traits present in your organization, it's hard to find inspiration and innovate with purpose.

Finally, I want to highlight the closing themes of the book here at the beginning. As brand marketers, we have the amazing opportunity to use our insights, our tools, and our imaginations to say something about the world around us. We must remain true to our brand's purpose, but we should not ignore those opportunities to create impactful, world-changing moments. The stories we put out into the world can only build a stronger bond with our consumers when they are tied to the same aspirational motivations that reside in every person. Reach for those horizons. Cynicism is our opponent, and we must constantly fight against it. In short, be part of something greater. Strive for achieving a higher purpose. Leave a legacy of greatness.

EMOTION
BY
DESIGN

CHAPTER 1

MY JOURNEY INTO THE ARENA

My friend saw that I was struggling and handed me a glass of water. It was true my mouth was dry, but that was nothing compared to my nerves. The extrovert who loves sports, competition, and hip-hop just wasn't showing up that day; today, it was the introvert artist. The art, my art, wasn't the problem. The problem was telling the story of my art—more accurate, my designs—to the audience in front of me. The dozen or so sets of eyes that belonged to my professors, my classmates, and other designers whose work and craft I respected and which had guided and informed my own, were turned on me, waiting to be impressed, to be amazed, to decide if I was truly one of them. One set of eyes in particular I felt boring into me, judging and weighing whether I had what it takes to enter this elite world of design. On the line was nothing less than the dream I had four years earlier, when I entered the Minneapolis College of Art and Design.

I was in the middle of presenting my senior thesis, an exploration between the visual arts and the liberal arts through the medium of design: a story of the contrasts and parallels between those worlds as told through my imagery. This was highbrow stuff, a journey in design meant to be taken in by the creative community. But if the journey is to be taken, then it must first be accepted as worthwhile, as meeting the highest standards, not by following the rules, but by pushing beyond everything that had come before. And the set of eyes I most needed to take this journey with me belonged to Laurie Haycock Makela, head of the Walker Art Center in Minneapolis, which is one of the most respected and most visited contemporary art museums in the world.

A month or so earlier, I had applied for one of the highly coveted Walker internships in the design department. Despite my heightened anxiety the day of my senior thesis presentation, I didn't lack confidence in my talent. I knew I was tracking toward being one of the top designers in my class, and so I wasn't surprised when Laurie called to let me know I was one of the finalists for the spot. She also suggested that I invite her to my presentation. Of course when the head of the Walker "suggests" you do something, it's not really a suggestion at all. My senior thesis wasn't only a presentation of the talent I had honed while at MCAD; it was now an interview.

Joining the Walker, even as an intern, would have been the culmination of many dreams and efforts since I was a child. Born of a Black father and white mother, I was adopted by my white parents and grew up in a nearly all-white suburb of Minneapolis called Minnetonka. Surrounded by the natural beauty of the land, and feeling more than a little like an outsider with my mixed heritage, I turned inward and mined my imagination. By the time I was five, I was accustomed to hearing from my parents and teachers: "You are a great artist!" My parents invested in summer drawing classes—having the middle school art teacher over to the house for dinner—new drawing and drafting tables, and even creating a drawing wall in the small bedroom I shared with my two brothers. The wall became the mural of my imagination.

In grade school, I began to experience a lot of direct racism. I wasn't equipped to deal with it, as I didn't have anyone to learn from and look to who had similar experiences—so I turned to my art. Drawing allowed me to put my daydreams on paper and escape from reality. By the time I reached high school, I was immersed in different dimensions of the art and design world, which weren't exactly normal interests for a Black kid in the early 1980s. But I found comfort in this passion, which allowed me to make sense of the world by reimagining what was possible. I also found my identity (though not all of it) in this confluence of art and design and I wanted more.

These were lofty ambitions for a kid from Minnesota, even if I had access to one of the best institutions for my talents in the Minneapolis College of Art and Design. During orientation, I heard a not-uncommon statement by one of our advisors: "Look around," he said, indicating my fellow freshmen. "Only ten percent of you will be practicing design as a career." He was right, of course, but I heard those words as a challenge. This elite world of design was my calling, and I'd be damned if I wasn't going to join its ranks. Ten percent was still stiff competition, and I was determined to outwork and outhustle them. By the end of my time at MCAD, I could say I did both, and my eyes were now set on the future, specifically the Walker, which offered one of the most coveted yearlong internships for young designers. The Walker Art Center was the embodiment of what I adored: cutting-edge design that broke boundaries and pushed the definition of what was possible. Tasked with visually communicating the latest art exhibitions, Walker designers got as much latitude for self-expression as the artists themselves. It's the kind of design that doesn't really exist anymore in today's digitally driven world. Back then, designers at the Walker made trends, just as much as the artists whose work was housed within its walls. To showcase that art, through posters, catalogs, and exhibitions, required a level of design that was as equally revolutionary. To enter that world was to be on the verge of entering the elite arena of design.

Now, all that stood between me and the attainment of my dream was a senior thesis that brought in such esoteric thinkers as Carl Jung and Laurie Haycock Makela. I gulped the glass of water given to me by my concerned friend and forged ahead...

. . . . . .

"I think you should do it," my friend told me. It was the spring of my senior year at MCAD, a month or so before I was set to present my senior thesis, and "it" referred to a minority internship program being offered by Nike. "I'm going to go for it, and you should, too," he said.

"No, man, that's your thing," I replied. I wasn't just being nice either. My friend was what today we would call a "sneaker head," the type of person who dreams about sneakers and designs shoes in his notebook in his spare time. While my mind was focused on bringing esoteric psychology into my design work, he loved thinking up cool new shoe designs. We were both at MCAD but were obviously on different tracks. Nike most certainly was his thing; mine was the Walker, which I had already applied to.

But it wasn't like his suggestion to apply to Nike came out of nowhere. Since I was a child, I had loved sports and competition. As a kid, I didn't turn only to art to find my identity, I also drew inspiration from the performances and personalities of Black athletes of the '70s and '80s. Immersing myself in sport became a daily ritual. Collecting football and baseball cards was beyond an obsession. I had a large paper route so I could make some spending money, but more important, I could pore over the sports section and memorize the Major League baseball batting averages and home run leaders, who back then were dominated by African-American ballplayers.

The culture these athletes helped create—which was really a reflection of the urban Black culture that I had very little experience with—had started to infiltrate the mass market. The days of Bill Russell and Converse All-Stars were slowly but surely giving way to Michael Jordan and Nike. I mention Nike specifically because much of how I consumed these new superstars was through the medium of marketing. Away from the court or field, athletes were swiftly becoming aspirational icons of cool—and the marketing images and ads had become generators of the same exhilaration and emulation that one would get watching these athletes perform. I was taken in by these artistic displays, not realizing at the time that the emotions they gave me were the emotions they had been *designed* to give me. It was design on a wholly different level from what I would learn when I entered college.

Now, let's turn the clock to 1992. Everywhere you looked, you saw it—that unmistakable rebellious Nike spirit. You could pop on the television, and there would be tennis star Andre Agassi, clad in neon green apparel, smashing the ball while the Red Hot Chili Peppers played in Nike's Rock 'n' Roll Tennis commercial. Turn the channel again, and you'd hear the lyrics "and we all shine on" from John Lennon's "Instant Karma," serving as the anthem for Nike's latest Just Do It commercial.

That spring of 1992, Nike was on fire. It was the twentieth anniversary of the company, and with ambassadors of the brand like Jordan, Charles Barkley, Jerry Rice, and Ken Griffey Jr., Nike was everywhere, as was its iconic trademark, the Swoosh. With more than $3 billion in annual revenue, Nike might no longer have been a small Oregon upstart; however, its rebellious attitude and revolutionary spirit were still intact and spreading rapidly across the world. To own a pair of Nikes wasn't just the height of cool; it said something about how you looked at sport and life: You played to win, but you did it with style.

Time and again, Nike was at the intersection of sports and culture. They weren't just responding to it, they were creating and leading it. As Jordan was in hot pursuit of his second NBA championship with the Chicago Bulls, Nike released the coveted Air Jordan VII sneaker and the commercial hit of the Super Bowl, "Hare Jordan." In the ad, Michael teamed up with Bugs Bunny to defeat a team of bullies on the basketball court. On top of that, the brand opened its second Niketown retail store in Jordan's backyard of Chicago. They had revolutionized sneakers, and now the Niketown concept was redefining the shopping experience.

Nike's innovation was fueling its dominance across basketball, running, tennis, and cross-training. The launch of the all-new Air Huarache line of footwear was in full bloom. Flipping through any magazine at the time, you would undoubtedly come across its ad that asked in big, bold type, "Have You Hugged Your Foot Today?"—a promise about how comfortable this innovation was on your feet. Turn a few more pages, and you would see another ad showcasing Nike's new outdoor sports line called All Conditions Gear, led by the Air Deschutz sport sandal, with its tagline, "Air Cushioning Meets Air Conditioning." Nike's voice was as innovative as the products themselves.

Like every other competitive, sports-loving kid of the era, I was fully immersed in this new culture created by Nike, without entirely realizing why. What's odd is that I never really saw what Nike did with its marketing—it's mastery of images and emotions—as *design*. Design was what I did; it was what I was in school for, it was what I would go to the Walker to do. In other words, design was more than some commercial selling shoes. And then that spring my world turned upside down: In the 1980s and 1990s, *Print* magazine was the number one graphic design publication in the country, and of course I eagerly awaited each new issue. Its Spring 1992 issue had a story on the Nike Image Design team, with a picture showing the team waist-deep in the man-made lake that was at the center of the new Nike headquarters in Beaverton, Oregon. The man in the center of the photo, flanked by twenty other designers, was Ron Dumas, head of the Image Design team and creator of the Jordan "Wings" poster—which showed a life-size Jordan in his Bulls uniform with outstretched arms, one hand palming a basketball, above a quote from William Blake: "No bird soars too high if he soars with his own wings."

I knew the poster well, since I had it in my college apartment. In that moment, after reading the article, I suddenly realized something that I'm almost embarrassed to admit to today: There were *designers* behind these images and ads that had had (and continued to have) such a profound effect on me. It sounds absurd for the designer I was then, but I had never given much thought to the people behind Nike's marketing. Now, here they were, staring me in the face, waist-deep in water. The feeling I had in that moment was a bit, I imagine, like an astronomer discovering a new planet in space: It's been there the whole time, but you're only now seeing it.

Now, my friend has told me there's an opportunity to work in this mysterious world that I just now knew existed. I went home and sat in my sparsely appointed college apartment, staring at the Jordan "Wings" poster on my wall, Michael staring back, with the Blake quote calling to me. Michael's intense gaze, coupled with this quote about striving for greatness, convinced me: I would apply for the internship.

. . . . . .

In early April, I learned that my senior thesis presentation had gone over well with those who mattered most, especially with Laurie. Soon after, I heard that I had been accepted to the Walker Art Center internship, which would start on September 1. The Nike internship was over the summer, which meant I could do both—if I was accepted to both. But despite my excitement for the Nike opportunity, my vision and dreams remained with the world of the Walker. It represented the pinnacle of everything I had learned and honed while at MCAD, whereas Nike seemed to me like a fun way to spend the summer.

Then I get the call from Nike, offering me the spot. As it happened, my classmate, the sneaker head who had also applied for the internship, was in the room at the time Nike called. He was happy for me, even if I could feel his disappointment. The call came from Chris Aveni, then one of the heads of the Nike Image Design team. It was a quick, almost curt call: The internship began in the first week in June, where there would be a day and a half of orientation. If I couldn't make the start date, which was a week after my graduation, then the internship would go to someone else. There was no question that I would accept the offer then and there.

Looking at my friend, and overcoming the guilt I felt, I said I could make it. How, I didn't know. After graduation I was broke and had no way of getting to Oregon. Thankfully, my parents decided to loan me their Ford Econoline van, the kind with the fold-out bed, poker tables, blinds in the windows, and airbrushed color gradients on the sides. I wasn't about to complain about these garish design features and the bumper stickers, even if it went against what I stood for as an aspiring designer. For a family of seven on a teacher's salary, loaning me the van for the summer was a huge sacrifice for my parents.

I drove the van twenty-seven hours across the country from Minneapolis, over the Badlands of South Dakota, between the Rocky Mountains, and onto Highway 84 through the breathtaking Columbia River Gorge. I finally arrived in Beaverton, and drove straight to the Nike office parking lot. All I knew about Oregon was this address. The problem was that this was a Thursday; the internship didn't start until the following Monday, and I didn't know another soul in the area. So I slept in the van in the parking lot for the next three nights while looking for an apartment that wouldn't charge me first month's rent up front, because I had only $300 to my name and a maxed-out credit card.

The days allowed me to get a good look at my new workplace, my *brand-new* workplace. The new Nike campus had been a work in progress for more than a year, with new buildings opening on a rolling schedule. Each building was named after an iconic athlete who'd had an impact on the brand, from Michael Jordan and John McEnroe to Joan Benoit Samuelson, the first women's Olympic marathon champion. It was a combination of museum, park, and office, all in one. To a sports-obsessed kid like me, it was like my mecca. I was never going to be a professional athlete, but this was pretty darn close. More important, Nike recognized that creating an inspiring, physical work environment would yield greater collaboration, productivity, and innovation. While many companies follow this model today, Nike's unique insight was that to ignite creativity, it helped to work in creative spaces. It was as if Nike's ethos was reflected in the architecture and environment, a place where creatives could thrive in a domain dedicated toward inspiring their talents. To *feel* inspired by your surroundings, and to use that emotion to inform your work, set a new standard in corporate culture. As any pair of Nikes is more than a pair of shoes, so too was the Nike headquarters more than a collection of buildings to house employees. The buildings themselves were part of the story, generating an immersive experience that to my twenty-two-year-old eyes and heart was beyond anything I had imagined.

The beating heart of the campus was the state-of-the-art Bo Jackson Fitness Center. Three years earlier, my emotional connection with the brand had deepened with the launch of the memorable Bo Knows campaign and the introduction of cross-training to the world. This commercial had a profound effect on me. My parents had bought me a sand-filled weight lifting set when I was thirteen, so by the time the campaign came around, I was years into a daily ritual that combined cardio and weights. The Bo Jackson Fitness Center would become my home away from home that summer.

On Monday I joined seventeen other interns of color from across the company for a brand orientation, and I quickly realized I was the only one from out of state. The rest were all local kids, straight from Oregon. The orientation was hosted by Jeff Hollister, the third employee at Nike and a close friend and teammate of Steve Prefontaine, the legendary University of Oregon and Olympic distance runner and the first athlete Nike ever sponsored.

Jeff talked about the history of the company in vivid detail, the brand's values, and the maxims that defined the Nike team culture. We learned what it meant to *lead from the front*, Prefontaine's approach to running races. When Jeff translated that to the brand and business world, it meant if you want to be an innovator, you need to defy the conventional tactics, and take the lead from the start and let the competition react. It was only the beginning of what would become a steady stream of leadership principles born from sports and applied to brand building. That day we left with the voice of Pre through his famous quote, "To give anything less than your best, is to sacrifice the gift."

From the very beginning, Nike was subverting my expectations. True, I would likely receive a slightly less...*motivational* talk when I joined the Walker in September, but the concepts that Jeff mentioned—and which Pre personified—could have been ripped from the Walker itself: defying convention, pushing boundaries, going beyond what was possible. There was a culture here, I remembered thinking, a culture of excellence.

And what a culture it was. This was the early 1990s, and this was Oregon, the focal point for so many countercultural trends then just picking up speed. On the radio, bands like Pearl Jam, Nirvana, and Soundgarden had introduced a new style of music known as grunge—a kind of rebellion against the glam metal and hair bands of the 1980s (whose power ballads were a constant presence in the halls of my high school). This new wave of music defined a generation with its biting irreverence and sense of irony—which also fairly accurately defined the people and ethos I met in the Image Design office. There was almost a conscious determination in the office to reject the traditional trappings of corporate life: While I came from a world where "business casual" was owned by brands like Banana Republic and Ralph Lauren (a style I most heartily embraced) this office was dominated by shorts and sandals, at times even bare feet and open, half-buttoned shirts. On my first day of work, in a Ralph Lauren button-up, I was told: "We need to teach you how to dress." Yes, it was a culture all its own—brashness with a wink. Almost the entire design office was homegrown: born and raised in Oregon with a strong affinity for outdoor adventure sports. The department had a formidable intramural softball team called the Short Order Cooks—so named because of the last-minute requests that always ended up on the design team's desk. Some of the guys in my office even belonged to a band called the Bookhouse Boys.

In tone, if not in spirit, I realized I was very far away from the world of MCAD and the Walker. At twenty-two, I was the youngest member of the Nike Image Design team and the only intern in the design office, and I walked in there absolutely unprepared for what I was about to experience. These were people who took the whole "work-life balance" part of the job seriously. They were great designers but that wasn't all they were; some were outdoor enthusiasts, most loved music, and they brought all these hobbies, interests, and passions into the office with them, like someone bringing in a picture of their family. I quickly learned that an inordinate amount of time was spent planning and executing practical jokes on others in the office. To pull just one example, some of the guys designed a wall clock for a specific person in the office who left at 5:00 p.m. every day. Literally, every day. So, naturally, the pranksters took an old clock, replaced every numeral with a 5, and hung it in the office, leaving zero uncertainly about whom the clock was intended to lampoon. To be blunt, this wasn't the world I imagined I would join when I set my heart on a career in design.

These were like the friends you had in high school, not the peers you chose in your profession. Yes, they had passion, but their passion wasn't only their job—a difference I wasn't used to. I was quiet, serious, but curious—and eager to make friends. I quickly joined the office softball team because I saw how seriously the other guys took it. But my real breakthrough came when some of the guys in the office asked me to lunch. They had heard about "the van," and they wanted to take it for a spin. (Man, that van—there are so many reasons I am thankful for it.) The lunch proved to be the moment when I finally was accepted by my new coworkers. I was able to open up and show them who I was, not who I thought I had to be as an intern. I learned that they wanted to meet the real me, the guy behind the designer brands I had admired; they wanted the guy who rolled into Beaverton in his parents' van; not just the designer, but Greg from Minnetonka. So that was the guy I showed them, and they became my friends.

This was a culture unlike anything I could've imagined, but it worked. Ron Dumas, the chief of the Image Design team, had instilled an ethos among his team that basically followed Nike's slogan: Just do it. If you had an idea, just do it. Some symphonies are highly orchestrated, where the conductor is an omnipresent force, willing the other musicians to follow their cue. But there are also symphonies where the conductor is less present but no less felt. Ron's influence was palpable, even if he ran a highly decentralized operation. His expectations guided the work ethic of the office, and his team delivered time and again. Only on those rare occasions when the pranks would go too far—and they often did—would Ron step out of his office to wrangle the teenagers.

There was one exception to the laid-back, THC-laced esprit de corps that summer, and his name was John Norman. John made my own anal-retentiveness look almost lazy. This guy obsessed about every single detail in his projects, down to the exact place-ment of a letter in a headline: "Not a quarter of a millimeter, Greg; one thirty-second of a millimeter!" John also scorned com-puters, a tool I had been using in my creative endeavors through-out college. But in John I found a kindred spirit, a man who took design as seriously as I did. John in turn saw the same in me, and took me under his wing. I learned through John the importance of exactness, a thing that wasn't necessarily highly touted in the school of design I had attended. But when you have one second to capture a consumer's attention, the difference between 1/4 of a millimeter and 1/32 of a millimeter matters.

. . . .

It proved to be an extraordinary summer for Nike and sports. Early in the season, Agassi won Wimbledon—his first Grand Slam—by defeating Goran Ivanišević. He didn't just win with superior performance, he did it with a unique style that bucked the stuffy, all-white dress codes, wearing colorful new Air Tech Challenge Huarache tennis shoes and bold apparel to match. Of course, in previous years, Agassi had worn Nike denim shorts on the court.

Michael Jordan and the Chicago Bulls were a dominant force, and the Bulls were playing the Portland Trail Blazers in the NBA Finals that June. MJ and the Bulls would win, of course, and go on to dominate basketball and the entire sports world for the fol-lowing decade. Once the NBA Finals were over, it was time for the Tournament of the Americas, and Portland was the host city. This was the first-ever assembled Dream Team of NBA players. Up until that point, the USA team had always been composed of college players. All these superstars in Portland were playing other teams in the Americas as a prelude to the Olympics in Barcelona.

My love of basketball and its superstars was fed all summer, hitting a peak at the Barcelona Summer Olympics, where the Dream Team would go on to win gold. Nike won too, considering they sponsored most of the players on the court. The brand, always with perfect timing, had a commercial ready featuring the Dream Team as dynamic animated characters. These Olympics would be historic for other reasons. This would be the first time South Africa would be competing since 1960 after having the ban lifted for ending apartheid.

We were also witness to what in my opinion was the greatest Just Do It moment in history to that point. Derek Redmond, a sprinter from Great Britain, was running in the 400 meters semi-final heat when he fell to the ground with a torn hamstring. As he got up and began limping, his father came out of the crowd, shoved past security and onto the track, and helped carry Derek across the finish line. Making the moment even more poignant— for Nike, at least—was the fact that Derek's father was wearing a hat with the Just Do It slogan across the front. At the time, it didn't feel like marketing, just fate.

Being a member of the team, I shared these moments of fulfillment and pride with everyone else in the office. While I didn't personally design any of the logos, events, or commercials that had such an effect on that summer of sports, I was able to feel something that I hadn't as a designer: this sense that our work had meaning, that we were part of the national conversation, not speaking to ourselves, as designers sometimes do, but moving with world events and even shaping them. This wasn't the sort of "popular" design I had dismissed as a student at MCAD, with my eyes set on the elite world of the Walker; this was different. In the same way that one gets an emotional response to an athlete's performance, others responded to Nike's marketing with joy and a sense of purpose. It was visceral.

The summer of my internship coincided with Nike getting its first Apple Macintosh computers. My relationship and appreciation for Apple had started in 1982, when my father brought home an Apple II. Unable to afford the monitor that came with it, we used our small black-and-white television as the screen. The channel dial was missing, so we had to use pliers to toggle back and forth from the TV channels to the Mac channel. It was the first fusion of analog and digital experiences for me, and it sparked my understanding for how technology could power creativity or hold it back. A flashy computer program was not a substitute for an idea; the idea had to always come first. So the timing of those Macs could not have been more perfect, and the moment presented an ideal opportunity to make a reputation. My office had no experience in how to use them, and I happened to be fluent in multiple Macintosh programs coming right out of college. I wasn't there to make copies and file documents, and this gave me a perfect platform to make myself useful and show the team what my design skills were.

The internship culminated with an extraordinary design opportunity. There would be no assisting other designers on this one. I was on my own and had to prove myself to the higher-ups. I, along with other seasoned designers, was tasked with designing a logo for the next two-sport superstar, Deion Sanders, that would be on the tongue of a new shoe, the Air Diamond Turf, the first cross-training shoe for both baseball and football players. The logo had to express Deion's skill, style, and attitude ("Primetime")

16

into a brand mark. It had to tell a story, yes, but it also had to generate a response, an emotion, in the same way as the Jordan Jumpman generates an emotion. And of course the logo also had to incorporate his two sports, baseball and football, and his playing number and initials.

It would be no small feat to get all that information into a symbol the size of a quarter. I was ill prepared as I couldn't rely on the type of design work I had been doing through college, which was more print oriented. In school, I was designing things like posters, wine labels, stamps, and catalogs, where the goal was to offer something fresh and unique, something no one has done before. I knew how to do the kind of design that one stands back and admires for several moments, seeing something new from each angle. That's a far cry from designing a logo for a superstar, where uniqueness isn't itself the goal; the goal is generating a reaction, an emotional attachment to the brand, achieved in the split second it takes one to see it. Just think of the Jordan Jumpman logo—simple, clean, a silhouette, but the feeling it generates, the sense of immediate identification, and the thrill of poetry in motion. *That* is what a logo can achieve.

This was new territory for me, but I didn't dare tell anyone that. As I looked around at the other designers who were participating, it was clear that they were following old-school techniques: hand drawings on paper. I instead used Adobe Illustrator on an Apple computer. I thought it would be to my advantage, but it proved stifling, and my attempts, while original, lacked that visceral edge; in a word, they lacked Deion. The computer is great for print communication but less useful for logo design, where the goal is to unleash your imagination on the paper, letting your mind guide your hand. What I saw as old-school, and therefore a bit primitive, was in fact how Nike's designers were able to tap into that visceral emotion a logo must generate. But I was young and arrogant, and I pressed on, unwilling to let go of the digital tools I had mastered. I knew deep down that this was a struggle, but I pushed forward with my process. I got so desperate that I called my college professor to express the difficulties I was having and ask for some advice. He said, "Logo design is an old person's game." Well, that didn't help, as I was young, and that wasn't doing me any favors.

My logo wasn't chosen. It hurt, as I hadn't experienced a rejection like that in my young career. My first instinct was to say that maybe this wasn't the place for me, but my manager that summer cleared my head of those thoughts pretty quickly. He explained that in the process of innovation, you don't lose. You win by playing the long game and using moments like this to learn and come back stronger next time. He was right, of course, but I couldn't shake the feeling that a lot of the lessons I had learned about design had very little meaning in this dynamic landscape of split-second emotion. I was a marathon runner in a sprinter's world.

Perhaps sensing the sting of defeat—or maybe because he wanted to reward me for a summer of good work—Ron Dumas took me along to the meeting where the winning logo was presented to Tinker Hatfield, who is regarded as the greatest sneaker designer of all time. Yeah, that helped ease the pain.

......

The summer was over, and I spent the last weekend watching Buddy Guy and B. B. King mesmerize the audience at the Mount Hood Blues Festival. I thought it would be the last time I would be in Beaverton. Of course I wasn't allowed to leave before being on the receiving end of a good prank. On my last day, I walked into my cube to find a wall-sized poster of the van hanging there, with the words "Don't Design and Drive" etched across the front. The prank wasn't nearly as mean as it could've been, but then I assume they took it easy on me hoping I would come back one day. In any case, I said my good-byes, and got ready to drive the van back to Minnesota and start my internship at the Walker. It would prove to be the van's last drive. I had managed to save $500 from my three-month intern salary, which was still $200 more than when I had arrived. But on the drive back, the brakes went out, and the repairs cost me the $500 I had saved. So I rolled home much the same as I had left it: dead-ass broke.

My internship at the Walker started soon after, and suddenly I was thrust back in the world I had once loved and admired. If the Nike internship was intended to be a fun three-month pit stop, the Walker was serious business. No shorts or T-shirts here. No softball teams or practical jokes in the office. This was a place that defined artistic excellence, and there was instant pressure that came with living up to that legacy. Your design work needed to respect the past and, at the same time, define the future. With the pressure came an equal amount of freedom to experiment and create new ways to visually communicate the Walker programs, often to very niche audiences.

While there, I had incredible opportunities to expand the museum's reach and open up art exhibitions to new and under-served audiences. I was chosen as the design lead for the first national exhibition of its kind on the art of Malcolm X: a gallery of artistic expressions of the civil rights icon from a variety of artists, completed during and after his life. The programming culminated with a special early screening of Spike Lee's historic *Malcolm X* film, starring Denzel Washington. The film spoke to me, as it did to most young Black Americans at the time and has done since. It's too much to say that I identified with Malcolm, but I certainly understood his search for identity. With his feet set in two different worlds, Malcolm broke with African-American civil rights leaders of the past and forged a new path toward Black empowerment.

I remembered the sports stars of my youth, and how they too forged their own path of empowerment, not just by what they did on the field, but also by how the public saw them through the lens of Nike. I found my identity in them; I found strength, and hope, and a sense that they spoke to me. As a child, I was the audience, but as an intern at Nike, I had been one of those helping create those moments. The summer of '92 provided several such moments—from Jordan capturing his second title to the historic Dream Team to Jackie Joyner-Kersee winning gold in the heptathlon—I felt the same pride that everyone in the office felt. Why? Because Nike was tied to that moment. I got a taste of that as an intern, and I wanted more. At Nike, designers moved with the cultural currents, responded to momentous events, and shaped how people saw the world of sports. I wanted to be part of that work. Above all, there was power in what Nike did from its irreverent, countercultural (and much less diverse) outpost on the West Coast. The letters I received from my new friends in Beaverton, asking when I was coming back and joking about the summer we had together, also didn't hurt.

It was late April, eight months into the Walker internship, and I was thriving when Nike called to tell me they had an open design position with my name on it. There was only one condition: If I couldn't make a start date of May 15, it was off the table. There was no flexibility as Nike was experiencing tremendous business growth at the time and needed help immediately to continue to drive and deliver on the demand for the brand. I thought about my time at Nike often, and the moment I got that call, my heart, mind, and soul all pulled me back to the Swoosh. There was work to be done back in Oregon. There was potential for meaning and fulfillment in a way that I couldn't see if I remained on my current path. There was no question that I would go.

There was only one problem: I'd have to tell Laurie. By then, Laurie had become my mentor, and I learned many lessons in my time under her. One day I was working on a design layout, meticulously placing elements, when she grabbed the mouse and messed up my design, moving things around randomly on the screen. I was horrified but it was exactly what I needed. The point, Laurie said, was to stop trying to be perfect. Loosen up, and you'll begin to discover new creative territory, and in turn so will your audience. She was right. I had a tendency to play it too safe, and to this day, I use that lesson and her voice to keep pushing beyond the expected.

I revered Laurie and in a way I feared her, too. Imagine telling Anna Wintour that you're leaving a *Vogue* internship early. Who leaves the rarefied air of a global creative mecca to work in... sports? How could this be done respectfully? But when I finally told her I needed to trust my instincts and take what I had learned under her leadership and apply it in an arena with a massive global reach, she gave me her blessing.

I needed that closure. I needed that reassurance that what I was about to do was OK in the eyes of one of the people I admired most.

Of all the lessons I had learned from my summer at Nike, none affected my decision more than this: *Emotion was the point.* It also helped that my internship had coincided with that incredible summer of sport in 1992. There was the Bulls, the Olympics, the

Dream Team. There was Andre Agassi winning Wimbledon wearing all-white Nike apparel, including a hat bearing the Swoosh that would lead to Nike changing its corporate logo. There was the sheer audacity of some of the commercials, like "Godzilla vs. Charles Barkley," where the Phoenix Suns star challenges the monster to a one-on-one in the streets of Tokyo. Underneath this incredible energy there was a true focus on trying to build a brand that extended the definition of sport beyond the fields, courts, and great athletes. The phrase "Stay in your lane" didn't apply, and we actively merged our lane with other cultural currents. It was an exhilarating time for Nike as well as for a young designer like me. Little did I know that it was only the beginning.

At Nike, we stirred visceral emotions in our audience, our consumers, not just to get them to buy our shoes, but to get them to feel like they were part of the story themselves. The Walker did and continued to do great work, both by attracting the most cutting-edge artists in the world and also by urging its design team to bring focus to that art in equally cutting-edge ways. I know I would've been very happy there—had I never had my Nike experience. An artist will say that art can change the world, and this is true. But at Nike I came to understand that art only moves people when they feel inspired or heard or driven to excellence. And I saw that Nike had only just begun to understand what it could do with emotion, that there was more to be uncovered and explored, that the confluence between sport and the passions that moved the world was just beginning. I wasn't about to miss that.

So once again it was time to make that twenty-seven-hour drive back to Portland. This time in my own car, a GMC Jimmy: a step up from my parents' van but without the charm and mystique. The new job would be in Nike's Image Design department within the newly opened Nolan Ryan Building, which was named for another childhood idol, the Hall of Famer and career leader in strikeouts, with the fastest pitch in baseball at one time. Another opportunity to live up to a standard of greatness.

The last drive to Nike felt temporary, but this one had a feeling of finality to it. I knew in my heart that I would not be coming back to Minneapolis. There would be no more choices between art and sport. They would be forever intertwined.

CHAPTER 2

CREATIVITY IS A TEAM SPORT

We sat in our weekly brand-marketing staff meeting, getting ready to go around the table to share updates and plans. There was always a bit of strategy as to where you sat within this meeting because you didn't want to be called on first to share your update. Not because you weren't responsible, but because it was an incredibly busy moment in time for the brand team and you needed the extra time to come up with your update, as others gave theirs. Sometimes you made the right choice of chairs, and other times, well, you were first up.

Then, just as we got started, the door opened, and in walked Coach K, unannounced. The great Mike Krzyzewski, head coach of the Duke Blue Devils basketball team and five-time NCAA National Champion. I think everyone in that moment suddenly heard their inner child start to cheer. And then Coach K launched into a pep talk, just as if we were all sitting in a locker room five minutes before tip-off. Honestly, I'm not sure how everyone kept it together, but they did—acting as if we had been there before.

If that's all that happened, then this would be my Coach K story, a sports-obsessed kid's dream fulfilled as an adult. But Coach K had a deeper purpose for all of us that day, something that has stuck with me throughout the years. He could have been speaking to a basketball team, instead of a group of brand-marketing professionals. That didn't matter. His message was universal in that way, although it has particular relevance for this book.

"Your advantage is your eyes," Coach K said, staring at each of us around the table. "You see things that others don't see. As a marketing team, your vision is what separates you from everyone else." Incredible. Perfect metaphor, perfectly stated. What we see, how we see, what we choose to see, and how we show others what we have seen are all part of a brand marketer's job.

With that, the pep talk was over. Coach K wished us luck, thanked us for everything we'd done for his program, and left the room. Time to hit the court. Now I admit that I had passionately rooted against Duke with everything I had over the years. I was a fan of the Big East, particularly Georgetown, and I also hadn't recovered from Christian Laettner taking down the undefeated UNLV team in the 1991 Final Four. But, at that moment, after hearing Coach K's words and feeling his presence, I would have been their team mascot if they'd asked me.

As brand marketers, our job is to show the world to our audience in novel, insightful, and at times provocative ways. We do this with what Coach K called our "vision advantage," our ability to see the insights and the truths that others miss, and reveal those insights and truths to our audience through the means of images, films, campaigns, architecture, and products. It's a mistake to think that our role is simply to promote our brand or product in the most marketable way, whatever sells the most. No, we don't sell products; marketers tell stories. Whatever the medium, we share our brand's values and purpose through insightful stories that move our audience, that elicit a specific emotion, and that build lasting bonds between consumer and brand.

Throughout this book, we're going to be talking a lot about the process by which we do this: How do we tell the most effective story to connect with our consumers? Where do we start? What are we looking for? But before we get to those stories, we first need to lay the foundation. In the chapters that follow, there are elements that went into every successful bit of brand marketing that I was (or have ever been) a part of, one flowing from the other.

One essential element, the wellspring from which so many inspiring ideas originate, is empathy. Our ability to understand and share the feelings of someone else is what allows us to get to the deeper truths and begin fashioning a story around them. It's because of empathy that we can get outside ourselves and begin the search for what moves others. What are their concerns, their joys, their fears, their needs, and their dreams? Where does our brand intersect with those emotions? What does our product do to empower our consumers to satisfy or ease those emotions? Within that matrix we start to see the powerful insights that will inspire our storytelling and experiences.

There is more to this process than simply explaining it. And much of this book will take you into my process and the experience that I had at Nike for nearly thirty years. We didn't create some of the most memorable campaigns in the history of marketing because we had a big budget. We did so because we were able to reach our audience—speak to our consumers—on a level that moved them (and that few other brands have matched). And to know what moved them, we first had to understand them, as well as our subject, whether it was a product, an athlete, or an event.

Most of us understand and accept that not everyone sees the world in the same way. What's more difficult is to have the desire—the curiosity—to learn how others might view the world. But if we are to connect with our audiences, if we are to elicit that emotional bond through creative endeavors, then we must actively seek out new ways of looking at the world. Coach K might have said that we have a vision advantage, but he didn't tell us how to get it. I will tell you, though.

Unfortunately, it's not enough for *you* to understand this. Your organization must understand this, as well. Put another way, your organization—your brand—must be built with a deliberate intent to fuel empathy in your creative brainstorming: within your team, within your department or sector, and within your company. Only then can you hope to find those deep insights that will move your consumers and forge that bond that turns good brands into great ones.

Creative Chemistry

In 1997, the Brazil National Football team was at the top of its game, led by the twin threats of Ronaldo and Romario, when it entered a match against Mexico at the Orange Bowl in Miami. But this game in south Florida wasn't part of the World Cup. In fact, the outcome of the match had no bearing on any league or standings. It was an exhibition match, played on U.S. soil, for the pure joy of the game. It was also one of the first matches of Nike's Brasil World Tour, a multiyear campaign that would take the Brazilians around the globe in a series of matches that would be broadcast nationally over ESPN2, and internationally by stations in each team's home country as well as by other global carriers. For the late 1990s, and for an event that wasn't the Olympics, the World Cup, or the Super Bowl, this was about as big as it got.

The partnership was an audacious way for Nike to increase its presence in the international soccer market. At the end of 1996, soccer footwear sales accounted for only 1 percent of Nike's total footwear sales.[1] The multiyear extravaganza would put the most exciting team in the world in front of millions of viewers every year, and help establish Nike as a powerhouse in the field.

But there was another reason that also influenced Nike's decision. Brazilian football had always represented the ideal of "creativity is a team sport." In fact, the country had created its own way to play the beautiful game called Ginga, whose name literally means "sway." Ginga was the manifestation of Brazilian culture in sport that included infuences from Brazilian martial arts to samba dancing. It emphasized elegance and style versus just simply discipline and proper technique. As Pele once said, "We want to dance. We want to Ginga. Football is not about fighting to the death. You have to play beautifully."[2]

The Ginga style puts the focus on the individual players, allowing them the freedom to "play beautifully." And it was Brazil's player diversity—the radical individuality of each member—that was its advantage. Of course, each player was chosen specifically for what he could contribute to the team, but not in the way that used careful precision metrics, a la "Moneyball." The players were all colorful individuals, each with a unique story and style of play that they were encouraged to showcase on the pitch. Instead of a team that was designed for only efficiency and high performance, the Brazilian team used the creative eccentricities of its players to produce a playing style that was exciting, unpredictable, and dominant. They put on a show, and they won at the same time. The Brazilian ethos also contrasted sharply with the more controlling and methodical "German style" of play that many teams followed at the time, where uniformity left less room for spontaneity. Brazil relied on creative chemistry, not just precision, the mixing and matching of diverse elements to create something utterly unique. You had the rebels, the magicians, the stoic, and the playful. Under normal circumstances, this could result in disaster for a team, which requires that the players work together in a seamless way, especially in such a fluid sport like soccer. But Brazil made it work, and the result led to the most exciting soccer for a generation.

At Nike, we believed that we had found a team that represented our approach to innovation and creativity. We were a brand that reveled in defying convention, in bringing together a team of thoroughly unique individuals that nevertheless led the industry in creativity, storytelling, and forming a strong emotional bond with our consumers—just like the bond that Brazilians had for their team.

I was still a young designer at Nike during the Brasil World Tour, but I was responsible for creating the branding, art direction, and experience design for the Tour as well as Nike's other brand design efforts leading up to the World Cup in Paris a year later. As was the case over my first five years at Nike, no one ever asked if I was capable of doing any of these projects; they just gave them to me with the assumption that I would deliver. I wasn't an architect, but I had to design a store. I wasn't a writer, but I had to deliver the copy. I wasn't a film producer, but I had to develop stories through film. This was a time where you were often on your own, and had no choice but to get resourceful, ask for help as needed, and trust your gut and your talent.

Somehow, I had wrangled a trip to Goiania, Brazil, to shoot the National Team for the first time under the new partnership with Nike. We had nearly complete access to the team—a rarity back then—and would be able to follow the players both on and off the field. My team and I went down with a strategy already in mind; we left with something much better.

We were on hand during a scrimmage that was open to the public for free. It was a great gesture to the fans, if also one that wasn't exactly well-thought-out from a security perspective. The trouble started when one or two fans traversed the empty moat and climbed the fence surrounding the stadium. The security guards that *were* on hand could deal with one or two overly enthusiastic fans. But what started as a few swiftly became a flood, as hundreds began to swarm over the physical barriers and onto the field. The dam broke and the security guards were swallowed up by the mass.

I had only a few moments to recognize that my team and I were directly in the path of hundreds of excited fans. I quickly instructed the film crew to make a ring around Ronaldo, then the preeminent footballer on the planet. The flood of humanity that hit us was intense and many of the crew were pushed back, reducing the size of the circle and getting closer to Ronaldo. That was when I noticed that Ronaldo himself was talking to me, in Portuguese, which I only superficially understood. I was able to decipher that he wanted my team to stand down and let the fans in…to let them be near him. I didn't know what to do. I didn't want to be the guy responsible for getting the most popular footballer in the world crushed and injured by his fans, but I also knew that that might happen anyway the longer my team held the tide at bay. I relented, and the fans rushed around us. And they didn't crush Ronaldo. They idolized him. They just wanted to be nearer to him, and suddenly their frenzied approach turned into a moment of human connection.

This experience influenced my approach to the shoot, and I

threw away the plan we had brought with us. In addition to presenting the team in black-and-white documentary-style photography, I also wanted to include imagery of the passionate Brazilian people, many of them from the economically depressed areas of the country. My idea was not met with enthusiasm from the leadership of the Council of Brazilian Football. They preferred to present the team through imagery that focused solely on the players in heroic fashion, but I didn't back down. Brazilian football, I argued, wasn't only about the players; it was about the people, those who loved the game, and all the passion, the soul, and the culture that surrounded the team. No country on earth showed this level of devotion like Brazil. If our goal with the Tour and the shoot was to present the "world's team" to the world, then we *had* to also present what the team meant to its own people. In the end, I received the approval and was able to shoot the team—and its fans—in a way that told the story of this amazing team of individuals and what it meant to those who loved them.

My experience with the Brasil World Tour, and especially how we handled the shoot down in Goiania, emphasized the power of empathy and the creative magic to be found in diverse teams. After overcoming my own fear in the moment, I was able to recognize the true meaning of this team, and that it represented the hopes and dreams of a country in a way few other sports teams can. That was the insight; that was the moment when our empathy turned a shoot of a sports team into a celebration of a people and a culture. At the same time, I was also taken in by the experience of witnessing a team like Brazil, with its unique combination of individuals all pulling in the same direction, and wondering how that might explain Nike's own success in the area of creative collaboration. Nike wasn't always perfect when it came to the composition of its teams and their interaction both within and between each other, but it certainly had discovered a process that championed risk-taking and results, and that got the most out of its diverse array of individual skills and talents. It would be some years before I could fully implement these ideas, and even longer before I could look back and understand, with the benefit of hindsight, why my approach worked, but it started in Brazil, and a style of beautiful play known as Ginga.

A New Role, a New Way to Work

When I became vice president of Global Brand Creative at Nike in 2010, I was tasked with leading and restructuring the brand-marketing functions responsible for storytelling and experiences. The title and the job were completely new. We combined advertising, digital marketing, brand media, brand design, and retail and event marketing all under one umbrella. I was the one holding the umbrella. The reason for the restructure was fairly simple in purpose, if not in practice: We wanted to bring together all the teams so that we had a more unified approach to our creative output. What we strove to do was have the teams work together from the beginning. By leveraging each other's perspectives and experiences, we could start a concept or campaign working from the same central idea—the deep insight—and branding. Our goal was to get that creative alignment up front, which would allow us to unleash greater creative energy across different platforms and channels through which the idea would come to life. At least in the long-term that was the plan. Our immediate aims were to pull each department out of the isolating silos they had been working in, and reduce the tendency among separate departments to engage in protectionism and legacy behaviors.

This new organization ushered in a modern marketing era at the company, an era defined by "digital first." It allowed us to integrate our brand identity and voice across our online web, social channels, and apps, through world-class art direction, branding, and storytelling. We had been moving to and were now officially in a reality where television, print media, and billboards were no longer the dominant media through which we engaged consumers. It was now the digital platforms, and, more specifically, the mobile phone, which had come to dominate the brand-marketing landscape even faster than television had in the 1950s and '60s. We needed a structure that could shift as quickly as consumers' eyeballs had, while also remaining nimble enough to account for the terrific rate of consumption these new channels encouraged. There was a day when you could control how quickly consumers viewed your content—a commercial ran at specific intervals at specific times on specific channels. A print ad ran in a specific outlet that had a specific number of subscribers. But an online film? It could go viral at the beginning of the day, and by the end of the day it was old news. The game had changed, and Nike Marketing needed to lead the change as well. Over the next eight years, Nike's revenue would double.

But the sheer number of tools the new digital era gave us was and remains vast. With this acceleration, we had a greater ability to invite new consumers into our brand and to connect them to one another across an array of platforms, thus creating shared passion on a global scale. While each department continued to focus on their specialties, there was a greater emphasis on the common cause while doing so. We could tell and deliver stories like never before, in more intimate and personal ways, and capture imaginations on a scale that could unite nations and cultures around sport.

A Creative Dream Team

When I retired from Nike at the beginning of 2020, I gave a speech to my longtime friends and colleagues that emphasized the incredible value of each individual member on a team. To me, this was the reason I had found success at Nike. If the team didn't work, then nothing else would have. Everything depended on maximizing the strengths of each individual member without any of them either dominating the process or being left behind. It's not an easy balance to achieve, not least because the ingredients that go into building the right creative team seem so counterintuitive. But like the Brazil National Football team, if you can get it right, then magic will happen. One cannot appreciate the stories in the pages that follow without first understanding that it all begins with the right team. My speech that evening set forth the three elements that I came to learn produces not only the best creative results, but also the most satisfying creative work cultures.

Embrace the Daydreamers: I kicked off my speech with a call to embrace the "daydreamers," by which I meant the right-brained creative thinkers on your team with a penchant for driving you and everyone else, well, a bit mad. Traditionally, right-brained people, those who ask the question "What if...?" or say "Why not...?" and eschew process and order, haven't always felt welcome in corporate America, which often has embraced the analytical mind over the creative one mostly because the former fits in well within a hierarchical structure. And, yes, the daydreamers aren't always easy, but a brand that wants to put a premium on innovation must include them. A creative culture, where risk-taking and disruption are put ahead of the status quo, can become a brand's competitive advantage.

34

Let the Quiet Voices Speak the Loudest: I then talked about the "quiet ones." There's an unfortunate belief in a lot of organizations that the loudest voices are also the smartest voices, when in a lot of cases, they're just loud. Introverts make up a third to half the population, according to Susan Cain, author of *Quiet: The Power of Introverts in a World That Can't Stop Talking*. If that sounds high, that's because most introverts, says Cain, hide this side of themselves—either by fading into the background where they go unnoticed or pushing themselves to say something, anything, just to get along with the loudest members. Often the quiet ones are the individuals that are spending less time in the moment, and instead, they are dreaming of a new and better future, which is an incredible ability to have within high-performing teams. Steven Spielberg, Larry Page, even Albert Einstein are all known introverts, whose contributions to cinema, technology, and science have changed the world. So give the introvert the time and space they need to do what they do best, which is think before they leap.

Diversity Is Oxygen: It goes without saying that diversity in the workplace remains a goal for our profession. A 2020 Marketing Week Career and Salary Survey found that 88 percent of the 3,883 respondents identified as white, with 4 percent identifying as mixed-race, 5 percent as Asian, and 2 percent as Black.[3] So it's little wonder that I urged my colleagues to continue fighting to bring in outside voices, those that are least represented in the office and boardrooms. Diversity is about fairness in the workforce, and giving the underrepresented opportunities historically denied them. But there's another side to diversity. What we're talking about is Coach K's vision advantage, the ability to see what others don't. A homogenous team likely doesn't have the life experiences or even the knowledge to uncover those insights that might lead to a deeper truth. And if you and your team can't "see" the insight, then you won't be able to fashion a story or an experience that connects emotionally with that audience. Diversity is the oxygen that breathes life into the creative process. If one is to create a marketing dream team where innovation flows freely, there must be an emphasis on filling the roster with diverse skill sets, life experiences, and perspectives that are often forged by one's race and gender.

Far too often brands start to foster a culture of sameness. They limit themselves, often without realizing they're doing it, by building a team around the personalities of the leaders and of more established members. They avoid the right-brained day-dreamers, who they believe don't play well with others. They ignore the quiet ones because they assume shyness is a sign of weakness or ignorance. And they seek out those who look like themselves out of comfort and familiarity. Without a conscious effort to build a team around those qualities I listed above, brands will slide into complacency and creative apathy.

Instead, you must *actively* build your team for the best results. You must challenge yourself to include those who don't think like you, talk like you, or look like you. The creative journey doesn't begin when the team sits down together and starts imagining; it begins when you put that team together.

62 Passes

In April 2021, in a match against Athletic Bilbao, the FC Barcelona team, already up 3–0, passed sixty-two times in a two-in-a-half-minute sequence, resulting in a spectacular goal from Lionel Messi. This type of play wasn't unusual for the squad, which had

had previous matches with passing sequences in the forties and higher. And that's because FC Barcelona has followed a style of play known as *tiki-taka*, which was developed in Spain and is characterized by short passes, maintaining possession, and building gaps in the defense. In short, FC Barcelona exhibits team chemistry at its very best, with every member of the team working together toward a specific end, reading each other's thoughts, anticipating their actions, and achieving ultimate success.

Passing the ball back and forth, sharing the energy on the field—even building the energy with the conscious manipulation of the defense—every kick leading to something greater, perhaps imperceptible at first, but over time more apparent, until the moment arrives, then goooaaalll!

Sometimes a competitive working environment can lead to a lack of sharing. Whether within a small team or a team that stretches across different cities and regions, there can be a "not invented here, not happening here" syndrome that creeps into your creative culture. In other words, innovations that occur elsewhere aren't welcomed in, but shunned. So rather than passing the ball, some teams stop the *tiki-taka* and take the ball home. No innovation momentum, nothing to build on, nothing to work together toward. Just little pockets of individual players, calling for the ball so that *they* can score.

It was this exact mentality that I wanted to avoid when, starting around 2014, we began looking to enhance the consumer experience with our live events using emerging digital technology. Early in the process, I emphasized to all the teams working on these future concepts to not get territorial about ideas. Sharing and building on the ideas of another team wasn't just OK, it was encouraged. After all, we were on the same team. If another teammate makes a miraculous play, you don't complain. You get in position to make the next play happen. What transpired over the next four years around the world was a continuous flow of "first-ever" immersive brand experiences, each one building on the other's previous idea. The ball being passed from one team to the next, using that momentum, but also building that innovative energy. The result was a perfect illustration of the power of sharing and radical creative collaboration across international time zones.

We started with the House of Mamba LED Basketball Court in Shanghai, which Nike built in 2014 in partnership with the digital design and communications agency AKQA. With motion-tracking and reactive LED visualization technology (essentially, the court itself functioned somewhat like a massive iPad), the court was both an amazing visual display as well as a revolutionary training innovation. The "Black Mamba" himself, Kobe Bryant, played an active role in programming the court so that it used the same training lessons and techniques that the Los Angeles Lakers used for its practice sessions. In fact, during the court's opening, Bryant was on hand to help train and motivate players from across China.

Next, in 2015, the ball was passed back to the United States with the "Last Shot," a fully immersive and interactive LED half court that let players reenact three great moments from Michael Jordan's career. Launched during the NBA All-Star Weekend in New York City, the "Last Shot" experience transformed Penn Pavilion into a time machine, complete with ten million LED lights and visual displays showing the actual crowds that were on hand during those iconic Jordan moments. Players could follow Jordan's movements on the court, as the clock counted down before seeing if they too could nail the game winner as Jordan had. Dubbed "the World's Coolest Basketball Court" by *Wired* magazine, the "Last Shot," again built in partnership with AKQA, improved upon the innovations first seen in Shanghai, leading to a more immersive experience for consumers.

From there the ball traveled across the world to Manila for the Nike Unlimited running track, unveiled in 2017. We created the first-ever LED running track in the capital of the Philippines through a creative partnership with BBH Singapore. Covering a distance of an entire city block, the layout of "Unlimited Stadium" track was derived from the footprint of the Nike LunarEpic running shoe. The 200-meter, figure-eight track was lined with LED screens, where up to thirty runners could race against themselves. After completing a lap and getting an initial time, a runner would have a sensor attached to their shoe. This allowed the runners to then compete against a digital avatar that represented their previous time. Their avatar ran along the screens beside them. Imagine, literally competing against yourself in real time. What motivation.

And finally, also in 2017, the ball bounced back around the world to where we began to Shanghai. In partnership with our creative agency Wieden & Kennedy, we took over Metro City, a globe-shaped building in Shanghai, and turned it into an interactive spinning globe, as part of the Nike React footwear launch. The illusion we created was simple but highly effective. From the outside, it appeared that a runner was jogging along on top of the world, the silhouette projected against the Shanghai skyline, the massive globe spinning under their feet, as if they were literally rotating the earth as they ran. In actuality, the runner was underneath the building on a treadmill, and their image was projected on top of the globe over a five-meter invisible screen. The campaign was appropriately named "Running Makes the World Go Round," with the building-sized globe spinning faster the faster that the runner jogged. This was a wonder to those on the ground who witnessed it, but also a global viral moment through social media.

To the outside world, these individual experiences appeared like singular innovations. There was no external campaign that tied one live consumer event with the other. But internally, they were all part of one evolutionary journey, with the event innovations building off each other, one more amazing than the last. The *tiki-taka* of the separate teams produced a beautiful sequence of growing momentum, as one team's ideas then fed into another's, creating a whole series of goooaallls! The timeline I just shared is but one part of a larger, and ongoing, sequence where each team passes the ball back and forth, building the innovative energy, standing upon the shoulders of the previous team, to the point that no one can claim to have originated the idea. And that, of course, is the point of radical creative collaboration: We are a team, and we play like a team.

But even the best-managed and coached teams, with superior chemistry between players, require a constant flow of inspiration to maintain their offense-first mindset and stay ahead of the competition.

The Curiosity Catalyst

It took a moment for all of us to realize that the guy was serious. He really believed in Bigfoot and he had been hunting the elusive creature for years. He was, in short, a Bigfoot Hunter. He even looked the part, with a khaki vest, a tool sash and belt, and a hat to match—a cross between Frank Lloyd Wright and Crocodile Dundee. The two hundred or so of us designers who sat there listening to him talk about his exploits in hunting Sasquatch were at first shocked that someone had put this guy on the schedule. But shock turned to laughter which quickly turned to fascination. Yup. The guy was dead serious, and we couldn't get enough.

It was Day Two of a design team retreat in the dense wilderness of Washington State along the Columbia River. This so-called Design Camp was a way to build a strong team identity and culture, while also educate those of us who were new to the team. (It was 1993, and I had been on the Nike staff for less than a year.) Between plenty of outdoor sport activities, we were there to learn more about the direction of the brand as well as find inspiration in nonconventional ways. Sprinkled throughout the agenda were guest speakers, innovators in their fields who were brought in to challenge and inspire us. "Bigfoot Hunter" was, if nothing else, definitely unconventional.

Later that evening, a company design veteran, known for practical jokes, thought it would be funny to rent a Bigfoot costume to capitalize on the moment. As we were all having dinner, this Bigfoot walked out of the forest covered in thick brown hair head-to-toe, crossed the road, narrowly missing being hit by a local pickup truck, and lumbered into the outdoor dining area, scaring everyone. Fortunately, Bigfoot Hunter was not around—he had moved on to his next research assignment, apparently—otherwise there might have been a confrontation.

At the time, I didn't fully grasp the importance of inspiration and the process of finding it. But over the years, and looking back on this particular episode early in my career, I can now understand why we sat around and listened to Bigfoot Hunter. The point wasn't to laugh (although we certainly did); the point was to open our eyes—in an entertaining way—to something we otherwise never would have encountered. I can't say that Bigfoot Hunter inspired anything specific in my own creative journey, but

I can say that over my career as a designer and then as a marketing leader, I often thought of him when I knew I had to look for creative inspiration in unusual places.

Curiosity is the catalyst for creativity. It's what allows you to see opportunities and harness the inspiration to seize them. Finding inspiration can be difficult, despite how infinite it is. So rather than waiting for it to find you, create a plan that allows it to flow naturally through you and into your work. So, bring the outside world into yours through habits and rituals and, in turn, empower yourself and your team to achieve greater creative results.

Leaving inspiration to chance, where it just hits you in a random moment, is not a recipe for sustained success in the creative world. You have to go out and find it. While some may be born with a seeker's mentality, others can learn to be more curious. Curiosity is a muscle, and muscles need to be trained. Knowing this allowed Nike to consistently fuel its imagination and build a culture of creative curiosity.

The Design Camp (and Bigfoot Hunter himself) was one such moment when we were asked to build those curiosity muscles. But there have been many others over the years that taught me and others how to build team chemistry, incentivize risk-taking, and, most of all, get inspired. The following examples are just a taste of the type of ways we tried to synergize the idea of team building with inspiration.

Cardboard Chairs

At one of the most memorable Design Days, we broke into teams and each team was given large sheets of cardboard. Our brief was simple: Build a chair from the cardboard that could support a person's weight. Points were also going to be awarded for style—how cool and innovative was your design? And the selection of judges for the "Great Cardboard Chair Contest" showed that this was serious business: the Welsh designer Ross Lovegrove and the late American industrial designer Niels Diffrient, both titans in the chair-design industry.

As with all Nike team-building projects, there was a catch: At the end of the allotted time, we would play musical chairs with our cardboard creations. In other words, someone was definitely going to find themselves on the ground. And with that, we all went to work, a bunch of designers who knew their way around a color wheel or a shoe but hadn't exactly mastered the art and physics of chair design. Several hours later, each team had their chair ready to go—although some appeared as if a sneeze could knock them over. But, surprisingly, others looked like they were ready for mass production. A few looked like instant design classics. It was an impressive display of resourcefulness under pressure, since these exercises always had a time limit that prevented overplanning and instead rewarded rapid ideation.

After breaking for happy hour, the game then commenced, and as the music played and stopped and played again, one by one, the chairs failed under the weight of rival team members. Now, I think there were legitimate complaints about the weight disparities between the teams, and had this been an official competition, I think the rules on that score could've been tighter. Alas, the game went on, until there was one chair left, and the winner was crowned. No, my team didn't win.

The question, of course, is why. Why was this a good exercise for a bunch of image and product designers? Two reasons. The first is that with chairs, as with footwear, form follows function.

Chairs and shoes have to support weight, but they also have to be flexible to support many different body and foot types. Lean too heavily on function, and you have an ugly chair; go too far on form, and you have an uncomfortable chair that looks great. So it is with shoes. The second reason is that the contest stretched our imaginations, as well as the right and left sides of our brains. And to apply these techniques to a product that wasn't footwear or apparel simply challenged our skills. Yes, sometimes the chair will fold by a stiff breeze; but the practice itself is useful to expand your creative muscles and apply them to something entirely different.

Work With What You Have

Along the same lines, often our team-building activities took us out on wild adventures where the point of the contest or game wasn't as important as the fact that we were doing it as a team. For instance, we would find ourselves on scavenger hunts across major cities, finding hidden-away locations that only the locals knew about—and sometimes they didn't. We would be tasked with writing and illustrating a children's book. What did we know about children's books? Not much, but we were supposed to find inspiration by having dinner at the San Diego Zoo right beside the rhinos and zebras. The next challenge would be to design a city, which proved to be the ultimate team sport as urban planning requires the greatest collaboration. Another time we were writing and directing commercials with a Las Vegas theme, which inevitably leads to work that should have stayed in Vegas. What made all of these exercises stand out was the compressed time frame. Not weeks or months, but hours and at most days. The rapid ideation process forced participation and ingenuity. We had to work with what we had, rather than complain that we hadn't been given enough.

As we progress throughout this book, some readers may wonder how their small organization, with a staff of perhaps a dozen or less, can hope to match the campaigns I was a part of while at Nike. I'm very much sensitive to this question, which is why I'm mentioning these team-building exercises now, early on. Big budgets, the latest technology, multiple divisions all working on the same campaign—these are wonderful things to have when going through the creative journey, but they also aren't necessary. I didn't learn this after I left Nike; I learned it while I was at Nike, through these sometimes ridiculous exercises that found us designing a chair out of cardboard or writing children's books. The other important element of these exercises was that we were always working in small teams, with members often needing to wear two, three, or four hats at once. There weren't any of the typical "well, that's not my job" complaints that sometimes stifle collaboration. It was *all our job*. Not only did this reinforce the chemistry between the members of these small teams, but it also reminded us that even a small team focused on the same task can achieve remarkable results.

Which is also why you can never underestimate the power of inspiration and the sense of curiosity that compels us to look for it in unusual places.

Japanese Craftsmanship

In 2015, when I was vice president of Global Brand Creative, and had had the opportunity to design a variety of these team-building and inspiration-seeking events of my own over the years, I took my leadership team to Japan, a country and a culture that I had come to love over the years, in which craftsmanship is held to the highest standard. My team represented a range of leaders who were responsible for the brand's storytelling and experiences worldwide. Few places on earth are as beautiful as Kyoto in October, when the colors of the gardens at that time of year are beyond description.

I set up four experiences, each with a specific theme and desired outcome. The first was taking the group to see the oldest working sword-making family in Japan. Watching the swordsmith Yoshindo Yoshihara was to witness craftsmanship at the highest level. Every sword was a unique creation; no two were alike. We also watched the radical creative collaboration that existed between members of Yoshindo's own team, each one with a definite role to perform, but all working seamlessly together to ensure that each sword met a standard of excellence. Next up was a trip to Tsuen Tea, the oldest tea house in the world, which was built in 1160. Art isn't just found in static or moving images; as Japanese culture exemplifies, art is also found in ritual, where each movement, each moment, of the tea ceremony has been meticulously cultivated over the centuries to produce something that is sublimely beautiful. This is "design thinking" at its best—the art and science of considering every moment of a journey. From there, we got a tour from one of the most prominent Japanese Garden architects, from which we bore witness to the way nature, through design and organization, has the ability to stir emotions and tell a story. The final experience was inviting Marie Kondo, author of the massive best-seller *The Life-Changing Magic of Tidying Up* to come and speak to us. Marie's clear messaging, and her formula for ridding your life of unnecessary clutter—"Does it spark joy?"—had ample relevance for a team that often has to find ways to simplify its message and hone in on the deepest, most powerful insight.

Mad Men

One time, we invited the creator of AMC's *Mad Men*, Matthew Weiner, to talk about the art of "world building." At Nike, we often looked to create immersive worlds within our retail spaces. Weiner talked about how important the authenticity of the details within the imaginary environments was to the actors and the show's narrative. "Every object is another opportunity to tell the story," he said. I was struck by the fact that even the closed desk drawers in Don Draper's office were filled with the real, vintage pieces of that era; pens, paper, and folders. It didn't matter that the viewer would never see these amazing details; what mattered was that the actor did, and by seeing them, by touching them, by experiencing them, they were also transported back to that particular age. It helped them immerse themselves into that world and their character.

When it came to the process of achieving these results, Weiner made two profound points. "Less money equals more creativity." *Mad Men* had a much lower episodic budget than, say, AMC's other breadwinner, *The Walking Dead*. Far from being a disadvantage, this budget crunch forced the creative team to go the extra mile in building a world through authentic locations and environments, squeezing every ounce of creative energy to maximize believability. Quite naturally, the process wasn't easy on the team. "We are run ragged, but creatively satisfied," said Weiner. But when the result matches the vision, one accepts that sometimes exhaustion is the price for artistic fulfillment. Every detail in the production, no matter how small or unnoticed, contributed to a deeper story.

On the Field

Our team once had a marketing offsite in Chicago, and I was intrigued to see a "Soldier Field Experience" on the agenda. As a lifelong Minnesota Vikings fan, that field was definitely enemy territory. We took a bus out to Soldier Field and were led into the players' locker room. Then the organizers sprung the surprise. Everyone had their own locker, complete with pads, helmet, and a Bears jersey with their name on the back. After suiting up, it was time to take the field.

Once there, surrounded by the grandeur and history of the stadium, the Bears training staff took us through a series of drills in the eighty-degree heat. You'd think that they would have taken it easy on us, but no mercy was given. Finally, as the day was finishing up, we had a field goal contest. Thankfully, I could still put my fading soccer skills to work and launched one through the uprights.

One time we took archery lessons in Champagne, France, from instructors who were descended from an ancient line of archers. Another moment found us in a soccer scrimmage against a third-division Argentine football team in Buenos Aires. But whether it was Soldier Field, Argentina, or France, these moments were designed to teach us about growing together as a team and sharing unique experiences. We were all forced to step outside our comfort zones and try to put ourselves in the position of those who did these activities regularly, expanding our field of vision and providing us with that bit of empathy so necessary to our work.

Breaking Bread

One of the more regular team-building exercises was simply having meals together. Of course, there was always a larger point beyond simply spending time with your team, which is why we often set meals with restaurants and chefs who were willing to take us behind the scenes of their own craft. Cooking, as many appreciate, is an artistic form in its own way, and the best chefs use their food to take diners on a journey. In other words, they tell a story just as we do with our brand campaigns. Understanding how other creative people use their craft to fashion their own stories, to provide their own insights, is invaluable. We would look for inspiration in these chefs and not just what they made for us, but how they presented it. How did they talk about it when it was brought to the table? What ingredients stood out? Just as athletes and products are the means by which Nike tells its stories, these food experts used their own focal points to craft fascinating moments with their meals.

By these methods and moments, we as a team were able to get outside ourselves. We were able to explore the world around us, mining it for inspiration as well as learning how other experts did their work. In some cases, we found inspiration that would inform our own storytelling; in others, we simply got closer as a team. Regardless of the result, you cannot hope to build the level of chemistry we need in our work, nor the inspiration that is required, by remaining inside the virtual or physical office. A creative dream team functions like a dream team only when it is tested, when it explores together, when it steps outside in the broad light of day and shares moments together as a team. Only then can you bring what you learn back into the office.

Bring the Outside In

What do NASA-designed astronaut helmets have in common with Nike Air technology? Well, without those NASA helmets there wouldn't have been Nike Air technology. Although this was before my time at the brand, the story goes that a former NASA engineer pitched a technique known as "blow rubber molding," which was used in the design of NASA helmets, to Nike as a way to create hollow shoe soles that could be filled with air, thus improving the sneaker's shock absorption. Nike loved the idea, and used the engineer's ideas to create the first Nike Air sole.[4]

When you look at many iconic sneakers from Nike's history, you can see very direct points of inspiration. In addition, the aerodynamic lines of car designs have long been a source of sneaker inspiration. To shine a spotlight on this, we invited Jay Mays, who at the time was head of design for the Ford Motor Company, to talk to us. Mays first made his mark in automobile history by redesigning the VW Beetle, a car whose source of inspiration is in its very name. He came to Ford with a mission to reset the brand's trajectory, which had been trending downward for decades, and instituted a design philosophy known as Retro Futurism—essentially, imagining the future with design cues from the past. There was the new VW Beetle, which called back to the original design, but Mays also looked to the past to refashion the 2002 Ford Thunderbird, which drew heavily from the 1955 model, as well as to redesign the iconic Mustang. The 2005 model looked more like the classic 1967 version viewers saw Steve McQueen drive in *Bullitt*, than its most recent predecessors. Mays talked about designing emotion, creating cars with a story, and a promise to fulfill a dream. We connected to his message because car design has been an inspiration for Nike sneakers, with a focus on speed, aerodynamic shaping, and the elegance of form.

But perhaps product design's biggest source of inspiration is Nature itself, through the practice of biomimicry, which is the art of drawing inspiration from nature and applying it to design solutions for people. Sometimes this calls for taking design cues found in plants, animals, even insects. Other times it's drawing directly from the human body and the surrounding landscape, as Nike did with the Air Rift running sneaker. The split-toe rift was designed with input from the barefoot runners of Kenya, by far the best long-distance runners in the world. The "rift's" name and split-toe design comes from Kenya's Great Rift Valley, created to allow for better articulation between the first and second toes, thus encouraging a more natural motion when running.

We even tapped other artistic sources, such as the Japanese art of origami, for inspiration. The Nike City Knife 2 has an exterior of triangular shapes that are meant to recall the folded origami creations of Japanese artists. But the kicker is that the shoe itself folds flat when not being worn.

These product examples are the result of what can happen after you get outside yourself. You take the inspiration you discovered beyond the confines of your limited vision and apply it to your work. But the process of "bringing the outside in" isn't quite as simple as just applying origami or using the contours of car design for sneakers. Your approach must be much more deliberate, with the recognition that most of the inspiration you bring back in won't go anywhere. Or, in many cases, it might go somewhere you never imagined, after years of staying locked in an ideas folder somewhere.

What follows are some examples and ideas to help readers bring the outside inspiration back to their work.

Keep a Visual Journal

The last time I checked, I had seventy-nine thousand photos in my iCloud Photo Library. OK, I know, it's a bit obsessive, but, within this number, there were more than five thousand screenshots.

These are freeze frames of images from my phone and computer that I found inspiring enough to save. Most of them will never lead to anything, but some have certainly sparked my imagination and led to ideas. It is easier than ever to use the camera on your phone to act as a visual journal, capturing the world around you—or what you see scrolling around the internet—in a split second. The technology is there, so why not make the most of it? Your visual journal, whether physical or digital, can be as organized or as messy as you want, provided you can access the inspiration on demand. I'm a bit obsessive, so I organized folders for nature, architecture, branding and imagery, inspiring quotes, product design, and new technology.

Give Yourself Homework

Where can you go, what can you see, and who can you meet? These are all questions to ask before you go on a work or personal trip. Write it down and create a plan. It may feel like homework at first, but over time it becomes second nature. Whenever I traveled to a city, whether it was Tokyo or Tacoma, I created a plan for mind expansion and inspiration gathering—assuming I had any free time to do so. Even when we travel as a family for vacations, I make a point to find one historically significant example of modern architecture, and then drag the family to see it. They humor me, but I also feel they appreciate the innovative breakthroughs and the visionary architects behind them.

Share the Wealth

Any time a member of my team would travel for a work-related project, they would be asked to come back and share what they saw, who they interacted with, and what they experienced on the street. I called these "Outside In" sessions. I saw them as opportunities for the whole team to come together and get a dose of creative energy (and perhaps inspiration) by sharing in another's travels. While we hadn't been on the trip with the individual, their presentation served as a knowledge transfer, continually feeding our curiosity and expanding our horizons. If someone went to the TED Conference, we would get a download of the top five talks. If another leader went to the Consumer Electronics Show in Las Vegas, we would find out which business sectors had the most emerging breakthroughs in technology. We can't be everywhere, but through your team, you can experience a heck of a lot.

Kobe's Curiosity

If there is one person I worked with over the years who exemplified this constant search for inspiration, who lived an ethos of discovery and curiosity, and who shared what he had learned or uncovered with others, it is Kobe Bryant.

Kobe's curiosity was famous among other professional basketball players. When looking back at how he got the nerve to ask Michael Jordan for advice as a young player, Kobe said: "You can't learn if you don't ask." But there was also a story involving Hakeem Olajuwon, the Hall of Fame center for the Houston Rockets. Olajuwon was known to work with current players, helping them improve their skills, especially down in the paint. Later in his career, Kobe spent an entire day with Olajuwon to learn the former Rocket's patented post move. And after a game in 2016, which Olajuwon attended, the cameras caught Kobe shaking hands with his teacher. When asked about it in the postgame press conference, Kobe said: "I watched Hakeem so much growing up—so much of him. Then to be able to come out here and him being generous enough with his time and spend the entire day with him in his house working on footwork, going over every detail in the post...I just wanted to thank him." As for Olajuwon, when asked about his best students, he said simply, "I've worked with a lot of players, but the one who really capitalized on it the most is Kobe Bryant."[5]

You're never too old—or too great—to stop learning.

As for my own "curiosity" moment with Kobe, it was during our annual business and brand meeting where he couldn't stop talking about this new thing he had come across. His passion for this innovation was clear, but he wouldn't tell us what it was. He kept us waiting, until he invited one of the innovators behind the "special something" into the room so he could help give us all a presentation. The thing that had Kobe so excited was "augmented reality," which is an interactive experience where a real-world object is enhanced by looking at it through a device, such as a smartphone, which reveals beneficial and inspirational information and graphics. Today, AR is deployed all over the place, mostly on mobile phones, and Nike has long since included the technology as part of its marketing toolkit. But back then, most of the industry didn't have any idea what AR was, nor how we could possibly use it in our own work.

But here was a five-time NBA champion giving us all a lesson on this brand-new technology that was about to add an exciting new dimension to the consumer experience. And he even demonstrated the tech by holding up his phone to his shoe, which acted like a switch, releasing a world of information and imagery. This hadn't been on our agenda for the day, nor was it part of Kobe's work with Nike. This was just Kobe, a man whose capacity for curiosity and obsession with discovery acted as a source of inspiration (and awe) for all who worked with him.

Getting Outside Myself

Lead by example. Practice what you preach. Well, here it goes. I have been lucky in my career to have the opportunities to push brand-marketing innovation. From my earliest days on the Image Design team, when I would be free to come up with my own blue-sky ideas, to being CMO, and going all in on pushing brand storytelling and experiences into the future. Innovation is, you could say, one of my passions. I loved looking to the horizon and asking, alongside my team, "What if . . . ?"

But it was during my role as head of Global Brand Innovation that I really got to live a *lifestyle* of curiosity, one that led to invaluable insights that drove innovation. And I mean live it. What does that look like? Well, I had to become my own test subject, and perhaps I took it too far at times. I've always been fascinated by emerging innovations that strive to make you a fitter and healthier person. My goal in these self-experiments was to find the intersections between the world of sport and these products—how did they empower the athlete? Did they lessen the barriers between an athlete and their sport, or add to them? I wanted to find out. At one point, I was using four of these innovations a day until, well, I went over the handlebars. Let me explain.

It started simple enough. A couple years ago, the Whoop Strap came on the market and was getting some good consumer buzz as a powerful heart-rate monitor. I decided to give the earliest version a try. I was able to track my activity, sleep, and recovery with more data than I could ever dream of. Easy enough. What's more, this led to behavioral changes, where I would alter my daily ritual in pursuit of improving my scores and my overall well-being. I was hooked.

I decided to take it a step further. I was working on my body, why not my mind? I had heard about the Neuropeak Pro, a product that enhances brain function and performance through the use of mind training. It's marketed to athletes specifically, as a way of staying focused under intense pressure. I decided to invite the brand's founder, Dr. Tim Royer, to speak at my annual brand innovation offsite. He showed up early the morning of his presentation while everyone was grabbing coffee and food. Tim made a point to meet everyone in the room, most of whom were preoccupied with their breakfast, still wiping the sleep out of their eyes. When it was time for his talk, Tim kicked off his presentation by naming every single person in the room. All twenty of us. What sorcery was this? I wondered. For those like me, who are not great with names, this was an incredible feat. The audience was also stunned. It was probably the best ad Tim could have produced to get me to try a Neuropeak Pro of my own.

So, I started the program, hooking up a futuristic visor to my head with sensors a couple times a week and then playing games on my phone that were specifically designed to train my mind to stay in the moment during stressful situations. The device would produce your scores and give you a baseline, which you could try to improve through more sessions. Mind and body now covered, what's next?

I next turned to the Flow by Plume Labs, a device one straps to a backpack or handbag that connects to your phone and measures the air quality around you. The idea is that the Flow allows the user to plan their travel—walks, biking, car rides—that follows a path of least air pollution, leading to healthier lungs. The

Flow really opened my eyes to the way air "moves" through an urban environment, often collecting in specific locations. I started to obsess over my travel routes so as not to pass through these unclean air pockets.

Finally, I picked up the Skydio drone, a self-flying drone that video-records its route. The drone syncs with a user's phone, which then functions as a kind of homing beacon. Wherever you go, so goes the drone, filming all the way. Think of it as an aerial GoPro. I started using the drone to follow and film me while I ran, soon discovering that the faster I ran, the better the footage worked. Well, I decided I was too old for that. I then started using the Skydio drone to follow me mountain biking. Well, during one ride, I got a bit distracted, looking back at the drone and not on the path ahead of me. In a moment, my front tire hit an obstacle and over the handlebars I went, landing on my shoulder. Yes, all this was captured on camera. And yes, I posted it on Instagram. But that was the end of that. Nevertheless, despite my own user-error moment with the Skydio, I realized the tremendous potential the product had to create video content of athletes, be they runners, bikers, or skiers, in ways that hadn't been seen before.

I share these experiences with you as a way to illustrate the role that passion and curiosity play in innovation. The whole mantra of "Get Outside Yourself" sometimes means trying new products and experiences yourself. The idea is to see if in some way those innovations intersect with what you and your team are doing. Sometimes they will; sometimes they won't. But you don't know until you get outside yourself and try. For me, it was only by experiencing these innovations myself that I could appreciate the value to the consumer, and see how they empowered one to improve their own lives. That idea of positioning a product as a tool of empowerment—not as the latest gadget with the best technology—has always formed the core of how I looked at product and brand marketing. I also share these products because they were created with an art-and-science approach. They are physical experiences powered by digital platforms and capabilities. To use them, you must first live life. The future is human; it just happens to get an assist by technology powered by your personal data.

The Vision Advantage

When Coach K talked to us that day at Nike headquarters, he stressed two things: First, he said that brand marketers see things other don't. And, second, he said that this vision advantage is what separates us from the competition. Using Coach K's words as my own inspiration, I have come to believe that the reason we, as brand leaders, are able to see things others don't is because we value the twin characteristics of empathy and curiosity. Empathy allows us to see the world from someone else's perspective. We are able to step outside our own limiting experiences and embrace the view through someone else's eyes. This provides us insights that we might otherwise miss, and these insights are what power our solutions.

But empathy alone isn't sufficient to maintain this vision advantage. We must constantly put ourselves in positions to see something we never have before. This is the purpose of curiosity, the willingness to ask what's beyond the horizon of our own narrow view. Instead of imagining what's out there, we must actively go in search of it. We must place ourselves in new situations, sometimes uncomfortable situations, as a way of expanding our knowledge and finding inspiration in unlikely places. The breadth of exercises and activities that my team and I did was as important as what we actually did. I'm not saying you too must invite a Bigfoot Hunter to speak to your team. But I am saying that you should look for those eccentric, wild moments to spark a sense of wonder in your team.

Art and stories surround us. They are the lifeblood of our existence on this planet. They exist in every corner of this world, so long as we are curious enough to go looking for them. And maybe, once we find them, we too can use what we've found to inspire our own stories and our own art.

PRINCIPLES FOR CREATIVITY IS A
TEAM SPORT

1. BUILD A CREATIVE DREAM TEAM

Embrace the daydreamers. Empower the quiet voices to speak the loudest. Let diversity be the oxygen that breathes life into the creative pursuit.

2. GET OUTSIDE YOURSELF

Complacency is the enemy of creativity. Don't wait for inspiration to hit you. Make a plan to go out and find it. Where can you go, what can you see, and who can you meet? Spark your imagination by bringing the outside world inside yours.

3. SEE WHAT OTHERS SEE, FIND WHAT OTHERS DON'T

Empathy is what turns good brands into great ones. Use your broader vision to gain a greater understanding about the world and the people beyond your own experience. With this "Vision Advantage," you will uncover deeper insights beyond what you see directly in front of you.

4. ALLOW SPONTANEITY TO REVEAL OPPORTUNITY

You can't plan your way to every creative breakthrough. Rigidity can stifle creativity. Allow the structure of your team to unleash moments of self-expression.

5. TALENT STARTS THE GAME, CHEMISTRY WINS IT

Pass the ball. Create a culture where the left and right brains multiply each other. Drive radical creative collaboration between the minds, skills, and dreams of each other.

CHAPTER 3

NEVER PLAY IT SAFE, PLAY TO WIN

Footage of a bicycle kick by Swedish soccer player Zlatan Ibrahimović is paused in midstrike, as a man in a suit (with a turtleneck, no less) walks on the stage. He points to the suspended image of Zlatan in the air, and says in a tone that drips with condescension: "Seventy-six percent probability of missing the target. Reckless." The unseen audience laughs.

The man continues as if giving a TED Talk, the screen behind him flashing images of the greatest soccer players in the world, such as Cristiano Ronaldo, Zlatan, and Wayne Rooney: "Even the greatest players of our time make mistakes. They take too many risks! After all, they're only…human." He pauses briefly as the word "human" just hangs in the air, allowing the audience to appreciate all the fragility and potential for failure in such creatures. "But what if they weren't?"

Thus begins Nike's 2014 epic animated feature, "The Last Game," created in partnership with Wieden & Kennedy and Passion Pictures that took over a year to complete. Not only was the production the longest of any brand communication production in Nike history, but "The Last Game" also had the longest running time of any commercial at five minutes.

The films tells the story of the world's greatest footballers on a mission to save soccer from the hands of a villainous mastermind, the Scientist, and his Clones. "The future of football!" as the Scientist heralds them. "Flawless decision making. Guaranteed results. It's what the people want." The Clones have been programmed to remove all risk-taking from the game and replace it with ruthless efficiency. And at first the Clones win.

As the film progresses, showing quick scenes of the Clones dismantling team after team, the crowds slowly disappear, until the last fan gets up, disgusted, and walks out. The Scientist then is shown talking to a television reporter, laying out his plan to do to basketball what he's done to soccer, complete with a cloned "Perfect LeBron." The reporter asks what happened to the original players, to which the Scientist responds: "Who cares?"

Then we see Brazilian legend Ronaldo (O Fenómeno) gather up the "originals," such as Cristiano, Wayne Rooney, and Zlatan from their regular jobs, to "save football."

"Remember what makes you great," O Fenómeno says to them. "You are not afraid to take risks! You play like it's a game; [the Clones] play like it's a job. You risk everything…to win! There's no greater danger than playing it safe."

With a stirring score playing, the "originals" challenge the Clones to a sudden-death, winner-take-all match. Come game day, the stadium is packed once more—even an astronaut out on a spacewalk is watching with an iPad—and the match begins…

A Culture of Risk-Taking

"The Last Game" was the third of three films for Nike's Risk Everything campaign, launched to coincide with the 2014 World Cup. This was a critical moment for Nike, and an opportunity to become the number one brand in the global football business. The moment was ripe for a risky, all-out effort to seize the lead. To realize our goal of football brand dominance, we needed more than just a global campaign; we needed a global entertainment experience that would change how the consumer interacted with Nike via the World Cup. It was a highly ambitious plan but we knew the stakes. For Risk Everything, Nike had to live those words.

Not that this was new ground for Nike. I was fortunate to work for a brand that understood and cultivated risk-taking with everything it did. Especially as Nike grew and expanded into new markets—such as international soccer—the culture of risk-taking grew with it. This continuation of an ethos that had been part of the brand since the early days is probably one of the most remarkable things about Nike's success. A lot of established brands may start out bold and experimental, but once they reach a certain pinnacle, they turn from an offensive-minded strategy to defense. A fear can set in when a brand achieves a measure of dominance in a particular market, as the concern shifts from attainment to protection. Risk-taking suddenly becomes, well, too risky.

The challenge, whether a brand is old or new, is how do you first establish a culture of creative risk-taking, then protect it from those natural forces that try to crush it? There will always be those within an organization who are the voice of reason, those who try to keep the dreamers within the guardrails. Those voices are good to have, and I don't mean to suggest that to maintain a creative offensive strategy a brand must abandon all caution. But a brand can remain true to its purpose and voice while at the same time encouraging the dreamers to create new ways to reach consumers. A culture of risk-taking comes down to incentivization. Does an organization actively reward bold ideas? Does the leadership team make time to listen to those ideas? If an unconventional idea doesn't work, are the creators encouraged to try again? In short, how a brand handles and incorporates new ideas into its business process says a lot about whether that brand incentivizes risk-taking.

I also want to be clear about what I mean by "risk-taking," or even "playing to win." Too often the terms are used in a vague manner to represent some level of disruption. Whether it's product or marketing innovations, "disruption" is the catch-all term for what you're trying to achieve. And, sure, it is. But we can do better than that. Put simply, the purpose of taking risks in marketing is to create a new way to engage with consumers. You are trying to reach them on a level that has never been done before, but once done, changes the game forever (and often opens up new revenue opportunities). Some call that disruption; I call it innovation.

I was fortunate enough to be part of a culture that fostered risk-taking at every level, starting with very low-tech, nondigital innovations all the way through the digital revolution. I had the opportunity to be present at Nike during these transformational years, which included motion-capture animation, the launch of several apps, and a social media strategy that brought consumers closer to the brand. But regardless of the technology that Nike employed, each step along this creative journey began with a conversation among a small team of creatives that was allowed to dream big and ask the question: "What if…?"

Stay Mobile and Nimble

My creative collaborator, Jason Cohn, wasn't looking forward to the drive. He had to go from Beaverton, Oregon, to Sarasota, Florida, in an old 1981 Ford cargo van to make the Chicago White

Sox spring training. It was the mid-1990s, and the Sox had a new player on their roster: Michael Jordan. It was an exciting time for baseball, and Nike was going to be there. It was not, however, an exciting sixty-hour drive for Jason, journeying coast to coast with a coworker in a van nicknamed "Stinky," because it had previously been used to haul trash. No AC, a barely working AM/FM cassette radio, and a noxious odor pervading the interior of the vehicle, Stinky was hardly the type of wheels one would expect at a Nike event. But when Jason finally rolled up to the field, he popped open the doors and starting mingling with the fans who had swarmed the White Sox spring training in numbers never before seen—mostly because of Jordan.

Looking back on the trip almost twenty years later, Jason told me: "We sold thousands of dollars of product in thirty days, which also meant we created thousands of moments of direct interaction with people on the ground. And it's *that* kind of marketing that is invaluable to a brand. We even made it into *Sports Illustrated*!"

Stinky was the flagship vehicle of Nike's "SWAT," or Sports World Attack Team, one part of our event marketing efforts we launched in the early 1990s. Jason and I were part of the team that developed the idea for the 1994 World Cup. That was when the world's most popular sporting event would be on U.S. soil for the first time, played in nine different cities. I had volunteered (or was chosen) to head Nike's then under-the-radar soccer-image design efforts a couple years earlier. Nike hadn't yet made a full commitment to the international soccer market, and it showed. For the 1994 World Cup, we were given a budget of $10,000, which was low even for 1994 standards. Jason and I wondered how the brand could possibly hope to engage consumers around the country for an entire month on such a budget. But the lack of resources actually proved to be the creative juice we needed.

Our answer was a van, similar to the one my parents loaned me for the Nike internship. Rather than buying a used van, the head of the department said he had an old company Ford cargo van in the parking lot, collecting dust. That was how Stinky joined the team. The first order of business was to give Stinky an upgrade. So we painted it black and adorned the hood with a custom chrome Swoosh. We painted the van's sides with a new Nike Football logo and converted the interior so that, when opened, the van became a product showcase with banners of our roster of athletes as the backdrop. Since we blew through the initial $10,000 on Stinky's makeover, we had no extra money available to pay someone to drive it, so Jason drew the short straw and had the job of driving the van around the country that hot summer. While we may not have been an official sponsor at these events, we still rolled up to stadiums, under the radar, to evangelize Nike's soccer brand. While the sponsors had spent well more than $10,000 on signage, stages, billboards, catering, and what-not, we were the ones on the ground talking to fans. The whole premise was to serve as the anti–big event experience—the one for the people.

We wanted to get closer to the consumer, to remove the screen that so often separated the brand from those we had to reach. It was like we were showing a commercial but also collecting vital consumer feedback (and insights) at the same time. But—and here's the key—the consumer didn't feel like she was watching a commercial, nor did she think she was part of some stuffy focus group.

As the Great Stinky Tour rolled on, we quickly realized that by going mobile and being where the energy is, as a brand we could be almost omnipresent. So we expanded beyond the World Cup to include other sports, like baseball and basketball. We could work in multiple neighborhoods, visiting retailers and local sporting events. Every day could be different...one day, we could be visiting a local Boys & Girls Club; the next day, we could be delivering a Nike athlete to a clinic; and the next, we could be hanging out playing basketball at the local park. Beat us, and you win a pair of Nike Basketball shoes!

Jason and I would meet weekly for a dinner brainstorm session at Vista Springs Café in Portland. The rule was we would start with dessert and do our work, then move on to the actual dinner. Diving into sundaes, we'd scribble ideas on napkins, passing them back and forth. No matter where the session went, it would always start with a simple question: "What if?"

This is where and how we creatively brought to life the program that would eventually be formalized under the name SWAT. What an amazing time as a creative. Our almost nonexistent budget forced us to entertain the most off-the-wall ideas. Fortunately, we were given the green light at almost every creative intersection.

At some events we rolled up to, the consumers on the ground thought Nike was the official sponsor, just because we were the guys talking to them. While brands with an official partnership with the event would simply put their logo on everything from sideline boards to coffee cups, we spent our time and resources engaging directly with people.

Over the next two years, the fleet of SWAT vehicles grew from Stinky to a VW Bug—tricked out to look like a baseball with a giant baseball glove as a seat—a VW Bus for Outdoor Adventure Sports events, and, finally, a pair of black Humvees. I even rendered up a blimp and a train, but the team decided against that since that was really the opposite of stealth. Speed and agility were the real advantage of SWAT, as we looked to win the hearts and minds of consumers at sporting events through our mobile marketing efforts. This wasn't about creating revenue; it was a personal way to engage with the people who loved sports, just like us.

Given that our first efforts with Stinky were done with almost no budget, you could argue that the whole thing wasn't much of a risk. If Jason and I failed, oh well. At least Nike wasn't out millions of dollars. But there's another side to risk, and that's letting your team take chances. Not only that, but give them space and the freedom to improvise. Not everything needs to be carefully stage-managed and focus-grouped to achieve maximum message efficacy. A polished, thoroughly rehearsed production has its place, because you go in knowing you'll hit the targeted emotions. But some of my best memories at Nike came from our on-the-ground marketing efforts, where I was able to do my job face-to-face with the consumer. There's usually a wall between the people who make up the brand and the people the brand is trying to reach. We almost never shake hands. Our interactions are through a screen, or a billboard, or via a brand ambassador, such as an athlete. And yet, the moments I had with consumers were real human moments. We—Jason and I and all the others who came to SWAT—were the brand; we were Nike.

Nike's SWAT program wasn't the first grassroots-marketing effort that the brand did (Phil Knight was doing it in the early days), nor was it the only one. But the story of its creation, a story I was very much a part of, remains one of where taking a risk led to a marketing innovation. Even as the competition tried to outdo one another in putting on extravagant corporate showcases, we took a step back and did the opposite. In trying to get closer to the consumer, we innovated a new way for Nike to live its motto of "athletes serving athletes." We saw that mobility and agility were the keys in meeting consumers where they were, and bringing them closer to who we were.

Designing a Retail Revolution

The lights would dim and heads would turn. Retail shoppers would then see a screen descend from the ceiling of this five-story atrium, covering an entire wall like a movie-theater screen. Shopping ceased immediately as the screen lights up with a Nike brand film. Maybe it's a film about one of the greatest athletes on the planet. Maybe it's about all of us. Either way, the film speaks directly to the athlete, the person in the store. Why are they here? What brought them through those doors off of Fifth Avenue in New York City? Was it just to buy some shiny new shoes? No, the film reminds them, they're here because they're athletes. The short film ends, the lights come back on, and the screen ascends the five stories. There's a moment of silence as the shoppers—the athletes—digest what they've seen, applaud in unison, and the giant clock—similar to what you would see on an arena scoreboard—begins to count down to the next film. Now the shopping continues, and those shoes they're trying on or that jersey they're holding look different. They're not just products; they're the tools that will help them unlock their potential as athletes.

In 1996, Nike set out to change the retail shopping experience and I got to be a part of it. What would become Niketown NYC, on Fifty-Seventh Street just off Fifth Avenue, was the brainchild of two of my early mentors, Gordon Thompson and John Hoke. Gordon was the head of Nike Design at the time and the master-mind of Nike's first Niketown in Portland. John was his protégé and an incredibly gifted designer with a dynamic imagination and an ability to sketch anything. Together, they came up with a "ship-in-a-bottle" idea for the New York flagship: The exterior would look like an old gymnasium, while the interior would be an innovative vision of the future of sports. Old and new.

Niketown NYC was not going to be just a store; it was "retail theater" at its finest, a truly epic brand experience like no other. I was tasked with designing many of the old gym theme details on the building façade and interiors. But we weren't just going to build something that looked like an old gym; there's nothing particularly innovative about that. We wanted to make this old gym come to life; it was going to have a past, a place where the players' sneaker marks had stained the floor. We even gave it a designation proper for a New York City school from the 1930s: P.S. 6453 ("Nike" spelled out on your phone's keypad).

Of course anything this innovative is going to present new challenges. One of the first we ran into was finding the right design agency to push our vision into reality. There were plenty of companies that would create the look of an old gym. But we didn't just want the gym to look old; we wanted it to *feel* old. So instead we turned to the masters of visual storytelling, Broadway. We hired a theater set design team to help us craft the 1930s-style gym that would have the power to tell a story between old and new. By walking through the "old" brick façade, past the wood bleachers that were folded back into the wall, and into a vision of the future of sports, the consumer felt the immediate contrast but also the continuity, one era flowing into another.

More than that, I wanted to create an even deeper history for this gym, a visual backstory that included the actual team that had called this court home once upon a time. I settled upon the "Bowerman Knights," named after Nike's two cofounders: Phil Knight and Bill Bowerman, Phil's legendary track coach at the University of Oregon. I spent hours drawing and rendering the Knights helmets, based on the team's mascot, which adorned the outside of the building, along with the words "Honor," "Courage," "Victory," and "Teamwork," the values inherent in sports. The Broadway design team helped give that a necessary authenticity. Through extensive research into the period, an assortment of artisans—painters, sculptors, and designers—were able to re-create that bygone age with near-perfect realism. For example, they would treat leather that they used throughout the gym so that it looked as if it had decades of wear and tear. I even designed a commemorative Knights letterman jacket that a player would have worn in the '30s as a gift to Phil himself at the store launch celebration.

Inside the store, within the futuristic environment, I was also on the hook to design the team sports floor, including a set of trophy cases that also served as footwear walls on their exterior. This would allow consumers to shop as well as view and experience arguably the greatest collection of professional trophies in one place. During opening weekend, we had the Stanley Cup, the Vince Lombardi Trophy, and the World Series trophy all in one case—the first time that had ever happened. The Stanley Cup even came with its own armed guard, who always had to be in sight of the trophy. He stood near the trophy case for the duration of opening weekend, just in case anyone had the terrible idea of stealing the Cup.

To take things a step further, I had my sights on a trophy of a different kind: Lil' Penny, the Chris Rock–voiced puppet from the commercials made with Penny Hardaway, the point guard for the Orlando Magic, in the mid-1990s. Through some office back channels, I was able to get the Lil' Penny puppet to Niketown NYC and created a special display for him adjacent to the trophy cases. But Lil' Penny isn't Lil' Penny without that signature voice. Which means I also designed speakers into the case so that when shoppers walked by, they heard Chris Rock's voice talking all kinds of trash. I'm not sure if the insults were appreciated, but seeing Lil' Penny live and in person was a treat.

For every big idea that made it into the final store design, there were three others that didn't. This was a big learning experience for me when it came to the process of innovation. There is an "idea success rate" that sets in—kind of like a batting average—if you are really pushing for breakthroughs. Shoppers experienced the all-new infrared foot-sizing interactives; they saw the clear "shoe tubes" that shot sneakers up five floors from the storeroom to them; and they admired a special display for sprinting legend Michael Johnson's golden track spikes from his Olympic triumphs. Behind all these audacious concepts were literally hundreds of other ideas that never made it. If you were only comfortable working on projects that were assured of 100 percent completion, then this was not a place for you. You could not be afraid of failure. Because it wasn't failure. It was the price of innovation. And over the course of the next few years, I would learn that most ideas, even when discarded, show up and influence future concepts in small or large ways.

In the end, Niketown NYC was an inherent risk because buildings are permanent, but it paid off handsomely. We had set out to build a retail experience that transformed a store into a complete consumer experience that would engage every sense and elicit multiple emotional responses. From the old gym feel, to the innovations inside, to the five-story screen, the entire store was designed with enveloping the shopper with a flood of emotions. Even the way we showcased products was part of the immersive experience. Sneakers with Air technology in them were featured on a wall of "air." Nothing was simply put on a uniform rack or shelf. Instead, a conscious effort was made to design retail fixtures that took their inspiration directly from the product designs they displayed. Just by walking through the store, consumers would know which athlete wore which sneaker or piece of apparel; they would know how a bit of technology empowered *them* to be better athletes. The store wasn't a museum in which consumers read about the story; they were brought into the story and given the tools to become part of the story themselves.

And what we were able to show with this innovation is that a retail space can be an incredible opportunity to tell a brand story as vividly and as imaginatively as anything else. Looking at today's landscape, with a brick-and-mortar retail industry that often lacks differentiation, it's a challenge to give consumers a reason to move out of their digital environments and into their stores (made more so by the effects of COVID-19). A physical retail destination must have a point of distinction, a reason for being, beyond traditional shopping. Niketown NYC—and its many sister sites around the world—were destinations in themselves, places people wanted to visit even if they walked out sometimes without a single purchase.

Working with What You Have

A handheld camcorder—remember those?—catches FC Barcelona soccer star Ronaldinho going through some warm-ups before practice. A man then walks out with a briefcase, and Ronaldinho jogs over. In the case are a new pair of white-and-gold Nike soccer boots. Ronaldinho laces them up, then jogs back out on the field. The camera follows him as he starts to juggle a soccer ball, doing the sort of tricks that the great ones make look easy, but which require years of practice. Ronaldinho flicks the ball up in the air with his new boot, then rips a shot right toward the crossbar of the goal roughly thirty yards away. The ball strikes the crossbar then rockets back toward Ronaldinho, who fields the ball with his body, juggles it some more, before kicking it back against the crossbar, hitting it perfectly again. The ball bounces back to Ronaldinho, who once more fields it and plays with it a few more times before he jogs back over to the sideline and the camcorder stops recording. It takes the viewer a second to realize that, in addition to all the other impossible things they've just watched, the soccer ball never touched the ground once.

In the fall of 2005, with the new soccer season underway, Nike was planning to launch a quick-strike white-and-gold football boot for Ronaldinho. The marketing fell to Nike's then European content manager, Ean Lensch, based out of the Netherlands. Ean had a month to create and deliver a launch concept for the new boot, which didn't allow much room for error—or extravagance.

Ean's orders were to find a "disruptive" way to create some energy and awareness for the new Ronaldinho boot, and steal some of our competition's thunder. Keep in mind, this was well before "disruptive" was a dominant marketing term. The budget Ean and his team had to work with wasn't specified, but it was assumed that it wouldn't be much and that they would need to be resourceful. There simply wasn't enough time and enough money to put together a concept that matches the well-produced, visually stunning, and beautifully directed films Nike is most known for. But, as my manager used to say, quoting the AC/DC song, "Dirty deeds, done dirt cheap." Cheap, yes, but nothing dirty about it.

Locked away in their offices in the Netherlands, Ean's team eventually came up with the idea of using the game of "crossbar" as the central motif, where players take turns trying to hit the crossbar of the goal from a distance. The first to hit the bar wins. It's not an impossible feat, but even the world's best soccer players might take a few tries to do it. It would certainly look cool to use the crossbar game as a "wow moment" for the ad, but hardly ground-breaking. So *what if* Ronaldinho hit it twice? Closer. Still, since the ball would need to be brought back to Ronaldinho, there would be lots of edits, and that could kill the energy and excitement that Ean and the team wanted to generate. So *what if* there were no edits? *What if* it was just a single shot, where the ball *bounces back* to Ronaldinho after the first kick, letting him kick it again?

Now we're talking, but there was just one problem. The shot the team had in mind wasn't exactly *possible* in the physical world. In other words, Ronaldinho could probably hit the crossbar after a few tries, but to make the ball bounce back to him outside the goalie box was basically impossible. Then doing it all again was just making it impossible twice. But everyone loved the idea and knew that it would make for an amazing shot...so what to do? Well, the first thing Ean did was bring in Nike's digital agency partner, Framfab, who immediately saw the power of the idea and wanted to help. The team there brought in a great director and a really good visual-effects person, which were critical to the success of the shoot. Once the effects had been added, the film looked like a candid moment captured by a handheld camera.

"Crossbar" was a turning point in content sharing and social media. In February 2005, YouTube went live but had not yet become the dominant video-content platform. That was a few years off. The concept of a viral video wasn't really a thing, at least not as it related to marketing. At the time most content was spreading via email. Friends where sharing pictures, or even email threads that they found interesting. But when Nike put "Crossbar" on YouTube, the video exploded and became the first brand film to reach one million views in the young platform's history. Now, someone was going to reach the million-view mark sooner or later, but for an established brand like Nike, with the resources to buy any ad space it wants, to launch a film on YouTube, one whose "amateur" look was such a departure from its normal film-making, was a testament to the risk-taking culture embedded in the company. Not only did the film innovate the use of reality-bending CGI for advertisers, but it also saw tremendous value in an untried medium for content. After "Crossbar," the marketing world was never the same. (And YouTube eventually put a stop to unpaid advertorial content from brands.)

We took a very similar approach to the 2008 viral video featuring Kobe Bryant. The shot opens, looking as if Kobe has just set up his camera phone to capture a small moment: showing off his new basketball shoes. A friend is with him, laughing along, but also kind of telling Kobe not to attempt what he's about to do. The audience of course has no idea what's coming (which is the key to both videos). Then Kobe sets up facing to the left of the shot, then OH MY GOD IS THAT A CAR? In the fraction of a second, Kobe lifts off as the car, an Aston Martin, speeds right underneath him. Some celebrating afterward follows with Kobe looking at the camera: "That's how you do it!"

Both films triggered a flurry of "Is it real?" articles across the internet and I can think of no better way to gauge the films' technical success (or novelty). Of course the point isn't to fool people forever; the point is to create something so visually spectacular that for just a single moment (or two), the viewer thinks that what they just saw was real. They smack their heads, they laugh, then they watch it again. Then they share it, and thus is born a whole new way to distribute content.

To think that "Crossbar" came about because Ean was strapped for both money and time should tell readers that we are often at our most creative when our resources are limited. Here's what we got; so what can we do? This can lead to a level of innovation that might not outshine the big-budget projects in terms of style or flair, but gives one the incentive to take a chance. More, because neither of the films were to be released on traditional media, the creators were encouraged to discover and understand the promise of new channels. Think of it like digital grassroots marketing in the world of advertising; "Crossbar" reached consumers on a level (both in content and platform) that most brands hadn't even considered yet. And yet, afterward, no brand could afford to ignore it.

The Power of Passion

Do you remember your childhood bedroom? Do you remember the posters you put on the wall, the pictures that lined your desk, the books and objects that filled out the shelves? Walk into your bedroom now, in your mind, and think about what you see. Think about the feeling you got when you hung up a poster of your favorite athlete or team. Where did you put it in your room and why? Think about what these displays said about you and your passions. No one would have any doubt about what you loved. The images on the walls might have changed over the years, as one passion gave way to another, but designing the perfect bedroom isn't something a teenager necessarily thinks about. They don't usually consider color composition; they don't particularly care if one poster overlaps another, or if one picture doesn't match another. It's the eclectic nature of the presentation that drives you; the feeling you get when you were alone in your room and surrounded by images, mementos, and ideas, and that gave you joy.

In May 2007, Nike opened the first Foot Locker House of Hoops on 125th Street in Harlem. This was truly a basketball mecca where all the brands within the Nike portfolio came together—Nike

Basketball, Brand Jordan, and Converse—to showcase the past, present, and future of the game. The store window featured a basketball half court. Consumers would enter the front door and walk down the hall that featured images of New York basketball legends. They would then round the corner and come upon a presentation with life-size, realistic LeBron and Kobe mannequins, complete with their tattoos, which were airbrushed on by an artist. A massive mural of New York's own Patrick Ewing, composed of subway tiles, adorned the wall. The wallpaper, Victorian in style, depicted intricate patterns made up of elements of the game, and the sneakers were each lit and displayed on engraved wood platforms. One could then walk into the footwear boutique area, where the sneakers would be displayed as if they were trophies, set atop plinths made of leather. Dramatic lighting casts a reverent glow over the dark wood paneling, emphasizing the idea that these sneakers are sacred objects. The whole project was an exercise in passion and a representation of one of the most important creative principles: Hold the smallest detail to the highest standard. The first House of Hoops was just the first of what would eventually become more than a hundred destinations over the next three years, including locations internationally.

The origin of this concept can be traced back to a conversation I had with Ray Butts, Nike's basketball creative director, about a year earlier.

Our conversation was simple enough on the surface. We were discussing how young people express their love of basketball in the environments they live in. You go into a teenager's bedroom, and the walls and shelves are curated with images, posters, trophies, and memorabilia that showcase their passion and tell their favorite stories about the game. A teenager usually isn't planning for perfection; they go by a gut feeling. They revel in the exercise of self-expression. While the idea didn't need to be solely about basketball, both Ray and I were drawing on our own childhoods, remembering how we used our rooms as showcases for our favorite players and sports.

But if this is how teens choose to celebrate the game and the products and players they love, then why don't stores represent that same love of the game? Most sporting goods stores were missing the rich culture that surrounded basketball—oftentimes they had just rows of shoes sitting on tables or shelves with very little in the way of storytelling. Thus, the insight. What if the basketball-obsessed teen's room, with that depth of storytelling, could serve as inspiration for an actual store? What if you took that same passion and care and created an immersive environment with layers of stories and characters? And what if the store was a traditional brownstone apartment in New York, where so much of the culture of basketball has been created and cultivated by generations of the city's players? The idea began to grow: The store would look like an apartment on the outside, but when you entered the space, you stepped into the ultimate destination for basketball passion.

From that initial idea, our intent now was to create an illustrated journey of what the consumer's experience would be and get it into the hands of the leaders focused on growing the basketball business. They would see a journey at that point in the creative process that was less about precision and more about imagination. We wanted to elicit a sense of wonder within them, as we virtually walked them through the front door and into the different spaces. We packaged our concept and ideas into a set of presentation books with covers wrapped with actual NBA jerseys. Our goal was to produce a book that was all but impossible not to pick up and start flipping through—soon, we accomplished that goal.

A month later, Ray and I are in front of Nike's president and the CEO of Foot Locker. We are given the floor and walk the team through the concept, using the books as visual guides. As we're presenting I notice with a smile that our small audience is sort of fighting over the books, since we hadn't created enough for everyone. That was always a good sign, and it foreshadowed the success that followed that meeting.

Visually stunning concept books aside, the speed at which Ray and I moved from idea to visualization was central in turning the concept from a conversation into something real. How often do you and your teams find yourself talking about an idea in a meeting, leaving the room, and then not addressing it again until a month or even a year later? "Hey, remember that idea we talked about? What ever happened to that?" It's usually because no one took the essence of the conversation and visualized it. I liken this to creating a "movie poster of the idea." How can you distill the story, the concept, into a singular image that immediately takes the viewer into the idea? My mantra was: Be quick and be visual. Don't waste time talking about an idea in countless meetings; use that time on making the idea a reality. An image of the idea will either get everyone excited and on board—or it won't. Perhaps the image reveals the hard questions, the flaws, that need to be addressed before moving forward. Either way, you create a clearer picture of the idea. Along with this, you're also adopting speed as a trait within your creative process. This is crucial. There is usually a bit of natural discomfort with showing an idea in its early forms. Unless the visual or prototype of the idea is flawless (so goes this thinking) then we don't dare present it. I say, don't let perfection be the enemy of progress.

House of Hoops worked both in concept and in practice because it's a case of passion on display. If Niketown provided retail theater on a grand scale, a feast for the senses as well as a journey through the world of sport from the lens of a single brand, then the House of Hoops is an intimate story of passion and basketball, perhaps small in scale, but no less grand. No ostentatious five-story screens here. Just as a kid's passion for their favorite sport comes alive in their bedroom, so too was the passion we put into the vibrancy of this retail mecca for basketball. Too often brands shy away from overt displays of passion because they are too hard to operationalize. Space that might be used for a more immersive experience is instead filled with more product. Thus, that initial passion that fuels a novel idea gets pushed out as more practical concerns move in. But in this case, that passion on display was infectious, and having less product, giving it space to breathe, allowed the consumer to connect to the stories better. That passion led to conversions, driving both the brand and business of Nike Basketball.

Passion is a risk-taking emotion because it demands that we reveal so much of ourselves to others. If you've ever found yourself in a conversation with someone about *their passion*, then you know what I mean. You can feel it; they get carried away. And when they finally stop talking, they can be a little embarrassed. But *that's* good. Show that to your audience. Imbue your brand, your stories, your spaces with passion unbridled. Start talking about what you love and don't ever stop.

House of Hoops is the story about how a simple conversation led to a highly successful retail innovation. A conversation led to a brainstorm, which led to a concept that led to a store, which, in no time at all, grew to more than one hundred stores all over the world. The initial concept that Ray and I came up with remained intact throughout the process, from the moment he and I first imagined a basketball-obsessed teenager's bedroom as the ultimate haven, to the presentation in front of those with the power to support or stop the idea, to the moment when those doors opened and consumers were allowed onto the court of basketball passion. Throughout this journey, the idea was allowed to thrive, because we kept moving forward—and we were allowed to move forward. *That's* a culture that incentivizes risk-taking. *That's* how you ignite a retail industry that has been stagnant at times and create something that becomes a global franchise. Let the idea live and build through the internal processes. Let the idea reinvigorate a marketplace and build a stronger relationship between a brand and the consumer, and between the consumer and the game they love.

The Last Game

"First goal wins. No second chance."

So the announcer says and so begins "The Last Game," with the perfectly efficient Clones going up against their flawed, risk-taking challengers, the original superstars. The match starts out badly for the human players, with the Clones easily outdribbling and overpowering them with flawless footwork. Zlatan's shot into the upper corner of the Clones' goal, a near-impossible shot to defend, is easily grabbed by the goalie. A dejected Zlatan holds up his hands, a look of disbelief on his face. The Clones quickly counter, moving the ball downfield to within striking range of the originals' goal. The Clone striker kicks, sending the ball through the air effortlessly toward an undefended goal... before Brazilian star David Luiz somehow stops the ball inches away from going in.

Now it's the originals' turn. With remarkable passes, footwork with flair, and a joy to their playing, the human players move the ball toward the Clones' net—even as an irate Scientist unleashes more Clones onto the field (a likely illegal move that somehow wasn't flagged...). Ronaldo finds himself with the ball at the top of the goalie box. He looks at the number of defenders between him and the goal. "No, that's too easy," he says. More defenders rush in. "That's better." Then it's the Ronaldo Show, as he moves through the maze of defenders, the Portuguese star embarrassing the Clones with imaginative moves until he's all alone with the ball, on the goal line. He smiles back at the Clones, then taps the ball in. The crowd erupts. Human imagination and risk-taking wins.

"The Last Game" is daring filmmaking on a number of levels—that is also deceptively simple. The film is so well made, and tells the story so well, that it's easy to miss just how innovative the entire production truly was. After Wieden & Kennedy's creative directors, Alberto Ponte and Ryan O'Rourke, came up with the general story line, they began a process unlike anything the creative team had done before. First, they created a writers room, with writers of every type present: dialogue writers, story writers, and joke writers. Their first pass at a script came out to forty-five minutes. That's forty-four minutes longer than a standard commercial. That could have been a sign that the story we wanted to tell was simply too long for the medium through which we wanted to tell it. Some teams might have killed the idea then and there as unworkable. Instead, we asked ourselves whether the story could still be told in five minutes. That led to our second decision: We couldn't release a film of that length for normal television commercial slots, so what to do? Once more, a lot of brands would've decided that the project wasn't worth the trouble. If you couldn't release it as a normal commercial, then why release it at all?

Answer: Because the story deserved to be told. Because we weren't going to be bound by traditional methods when the whole concept was untraditional. If you're trying to reach consumers in a new way, then you have to be willing to forgo how things normally work. That's the whole point, and it's damn scary when you're in the middle of it and you don't know how it's going to turn out. In any case, the writers room went back to work to edit the film down to five minutes without compromising the quality of the story. (Although I've always wondered how that original script would've done as a short film.)

From there, the team brought aboard Passion Pictures as the animation house, which developed the visual world and the personality of each player. We weren't sure how the animation should look, except that it couldn't look like what had come before. It had to be different but appealing at the same time. Moreover, the style had to strike the right balance between something that was fun but not too childish.

Compounding the animation challenge was athlete approval—a typical challenge for any piece of Nike creative. The athletes featured within a brand communication have the right to refuse their inclusion. But the problem with "The Last Game" was that this was the first time athletes like Cristiano Ronaldo and Zlatan—no strangers to giving approval—were seeing themselves in animated form. What I mean is that it took some selling. In the first few rounds of character design, I was concerned when I saw the first rough animations. With so much on the line, I started to really question whether this would work.

If you make animation look too realistic, then you start confining the artistic expression of the medium. So, we needed to find a balance. There would be no film if any one of the players were uncomfortable with how they showed up. Thankfully, the balance was found and the animators showed the players as true to form, if a bit "larger than life."

These animations didn't just serve us well in the film itself.

Our idea was to provide real-time (or as real as the technology and human endurance allowed) content responding to events from the World Cup itself. The problem was that, because of copyright agreements, we couldn't just pull a great moment on the pitch and use it as our own. Nor were the players available for more traditional photo shoots that would have given us proprietary material to use. Which was why we focused our innovative efforts on animation. Animation freed us from all these challenges—even if it generated a bunch of new ones. This had never been done before, and not simply because the technology to do it was so new. There's simply the lack of proximity between teams spread throughout the country necessary to make it happen.

The solution was to build a two-hundred-person Nike Football Command Center in downtown Portland, which housed writers, art directors, and agency partners in one location, working side by side to deliver pieces of content with speed and agility. The Command Center was operational twenty-four hours a day for thirty straight days, serving twenty-two languages. If Cristiano Ronaldo did something amazing on the football pitch, the team could quickly create a social media post with an animated Ronaldo and a headline that reinforced the Risk Everything mantra. In all, we created more than two hundred pieces of unique content in real time, distributed across global digital platforms. Once again, never been done before.

Part of the magic and the success of the Command Center was the space itself. Rather than just go through the normal channels of the corporate-facilities team, where you pull from the inventory of furniture and repurpose an existing space, this space was designed for a purpose: to cultivate the most creative and collaborative process possible. The art, the quotes on the wall, the photography and lighting, everything was intentionally staged and curated to immerse the team in the mission and inspire and motivate their imaginations. When you are proud of the space you are in—and we were proud—you live up to it. The space itself was a living representation of the pursuit.

There was a sense of family about the Command Center. A rare feat considering these agencies were often in competition with one another for both business and recognition. As Nike's head of social media at the time, Musa Tariq, said: "We would eat together, watch the World Cup together, and build a community together." Given the lack of hierarchy and separation between agencies; everyone was on the same level. In the end, Risk Everything was bigger than Nike. The purpose went beyond the brand. Everyone had bought into the idea to deliver the first real-time global-marketing offense on the world's biggest stage. "Nike gave you the permission to dream," said Musa. "And we had the best people in the world to do the dreaming, all under one roof."

One of the featured players in the film, Zlatan Ibrahimović, part of the Swedish National Team, did not qualify for the World Cup. Yet Zlatan's, let's say, *unique* personality was central to both "The Last Game" and our other marketing efforts. We had to figure out how to bring Zlatan into the campaign experience, even if his team was out of the event.

Fortunately, the very thing that made Zlatan a fan favorite— he's basically a walking one-liner—provided our answer. With his propensity to speak in the third person, and his unlimited confidence, Zlatan would become the unofficial spokesman of the tournament. I mean, this was a player who once said, "I can't help but laugh at how perfect I am." You get the picture.

To do this we created the beating heart of the Command Center, which was a revolutionary digital puppeteering and animation studio. An actor in a motion-capture suit, as well as a digital puppeteer who created facial gestures, would bring Zlatan's reading to life, with the final touch being the animation on top of it. This breakthrough process allowed the Swedish forward to answer fans' questions in Google hangout, which had been submitted via social media through the #AskZlatan hashtag, with a short, animated video.

To give a sense of how these chats went, when the moderator asks animated Zlatan if he could hear him, the soccer star replies: "Zlatan could hear you even before you started talking."

Moderator: "Zlatan, we got people around the world who are ready to ask you a few questions."

Zlatan: "Good, because Zlatan has all the answers."

In addition, the real-time animated Zlatan would appear each night on ESPN's *Sport Center* in a segment called "Zlatan Imbrahimović's 'Risk Taking Take on the Day.'" We were able to go from an initial script to completed animation in under six hours.

When all these elements came together—almost miraculously given the sheer number of moving parts—the campaign exceeded expectations. The film itself was a tremendous hit; the real-time animated videos responding to World Cup events gave consumers something they'd never experienced before; and Zlatan proved once again why he was so loved. The success of the campaign created a new standard on how a brand can deliver an experience on a global level, while staying locally relevant. Such are the power of revolutions.

Nike was not only the most-viewed brand of the World Cup, but the campaign represented the most viewed Nike campaign in its history. We can appreciate the campaign's impact with just a few numbers: Over 400 million views of the three Risk Everything campaign films on digital platforms, 23 million people engaged with the content by liking, retweeting, or commenting on the campaign. And the "Last Game" film was Facebook's most-shared video ever.

Never Play It Safe, Play to Win

Innovation breakthroughs are rarely created with caution. Whether in the realm of science or in brand marketing, these new concepts require bold, almost fearless risk-taking. We do not take risks simply because we want to try something new. We take risks because we want to create new modes of thought, of communication, of engagement. We take risks because the world never stops turning and the consumer's expectations never stop expanding.

But the pursuit of brand innovation should not be at the expense of the well-managed strategies and processes that bring you closer to your consumer. Brands today have an extraordinary ability to interact with their consumer in real time, making them part of the story. This takes time—and resources. The trick is to find the balance between serving the needs of consumers across social media and other digital channels while also igniting their imaginations, and expanding their understanding of what your brand can achieve. If we truly believe in an approach that values relationships over transactions, that means we need to be there for the consumers when they need us most, while at the same time opening up their minds to new aspirations. A balance of art and science is needed to achieve this. When in harmony, art and science—data and imagination—drives the bottom line and creates success.

It's easy to get swallowed up in the pace of work and believe that keeping up is good enough. But as brands, we must never forget that one of our principle tasks is to move consumers emotionally in ways that bring them closer to us, and us closer to them. Allow your imaginations to set the pace for consumer engagement, along with the technology that drives it. Do so in a way that tests your limits and demands that risks be taken. As the legendary advertising art director George Lois once said, "You can be cautious or you can be creative. (But there's no such thing as a cautious creative.)"

PRINCIPLES FOR "NEVER PLAY IT SAFE, PLAY TO WIN"

1. DON'T ASK FOR PERMISSION

The fastest way to suck imagination out of your brand culture is to require the team to ask for permission to use theirs. Build daydreaming into a daily habit with time that is protected.

2. TAKE BIG SWINGS

The average major league player in the Baseball Hall of Fame has a .301 career batting average, meaning they get out more than they get on base, but they are still considered all-time greats. Take the big, innovative swings. Even the misses will lead to success down the road.

3. MAKE THE MOVIE POSTER

What's the movie poster of your idea? How can you tell your story within an image in an instant? Talking about an idea can only go so far. Get visual, sooner, to bring the team into your idea, and the idea to the consumer.

4. EMBRACE THE LIMITATIONS

Sometimes it's better to have less time, and even less money. The pressure of time and budget restraints can be an imagination boon. Let the urgency generate ingenuity.

5. BUILD THE ARENA

It's hard to create emotion if your space is void of it. Whether it's physical or digital, expecting to spark brilliance within a rigid white cube is fleeting. Make the environment as innovative as the solutions you seek to create.

CHAPTER 4

GAME FACE FOR GREATNESS

"No bird soars too high if he soars with his own wings."

—William Blake

There's a significant percentage of the population for whom William Blake is just a name on a Michael Jordan poster, called "Wings." The nineteenth-century British poet and painter hardly conjures up images of athletic greatness, but he did have the great fortune of having one of his lines of verse chosen for what would become arguably the most popular poster of all time, dethroning Farrah Fawcett with a skateboard for the number one spot back in the early '90s. Of course, Jordan himself, arms outstretched, one hand palming a basketball, probably helped elevate Blake into the national consciousness and forever tie him—or at least his words—with sports and Nike.

The designer of the black-and-white "Wings" poster, Ron Dumas, said that he found Blake's words "aspirational and timeless," and lent a degree of "fine art" to a medium that mostly featured sports stars in full-color glory, usually in the process of doing something exceptional. The unusual artistic elements also probably explain why I, then a design student at the Minneapolis

College of Art and Design, had the poster hanging prominently on my apartment wall. Like thousands of other kids of the 1990s, I loved this poster, and still consider it the greatest sports poster of all time. And the reason I love it is because "Wings" isn't a normal sports poster, and was never meant to be.

I went to work for Dumas, who was then the creative director at Nike Image Design, not long after he designed "Wings." Dumas had already had the opportunity to work on a few Jordan posters in the 1980s and early '90s, most notably the classic image of MJ's winning free-throw-line dunk at the 1988 Slam Dunk Contest. The other famous Jordan poster from a few years earlier, created by Nike Design legend Peter Moore, was taken from a staged shoot and showed the star in his iconic "jump man" dunk pose. In fact, that poster influenced what would become the Jordan Jumpman logo, also creatively directed by Moore.

Given this history, you can see why Dumas's idea for a new Jordan poster raised some eyebrows. It was just such a huge departure from previous (and popular) Jordan posters—and it wouldn't even show the man doing anything more with a basketball than palming it! "The good news was that Jordan and sports marketing loved it and so we went forward with it," Dumas later told me.

From the very beginning, Dumas wanted to do something "upscale," as he said to me. The images of Jordan in amazing athletic feats were by then well-trodden ground. Nike had already led on that front, with both the "Jump Man" poster and the "Slam Dunk Contest" poster. While those images have their amazing artistic merit—and certainly sold well—repeating past successes simply isn't what Dumas does. Could a poster achieve a deeper purpose, a layering of meaning and insight that one finds in, well, fine art? One could argue that the technical skill players like Jordan exhibit on the court or field rises to artistic levels, the ancient

Greek idea of beauty in motion. What's more, Nike's championing of sports as a field that is as much a part of the humanistic tradition as art or literature means that showcasing the most famous athlete in the world at that time as artwork fits absolutely within the Nike brand—even expands that brand into new territories.

Indeed, "Wings" stands out because it is more an expression of artistry than athletics. "When I sketched out the idea it was immediate that it would be a black-and-white image like fine art photography," said Dumas. Much like the best of photography, the image functions like a painting, with its subject clear and prominent, but whose meaning remains open to interpretation. The very purpose of Jordan's outstretched arms can convey different meanings to different audiences. In other words, I see something different from what you might see. And I was surprised to hear what the creator, Ron himself, saw when he came up with the pose: It reminded him of "how kids love to run with their arms outstretched, pretending to fly," he said. The Blake quote seems to fit this idea of childhood innocence, a call to the young to dream big, to smash through barriers, and throw off the weights of doubt and fear, and soar. At the same time, Jordan's expression, as well as the almost ritualistic extension of his arms, recalls a person in a meditative state. He isn't soaring; he's imagining. The stillness of the image reflects the way in which the human *mind* governs the body.

"Wings," then, isn't so much a celebration of Jordan the athlete as it is of the human spirit, with Jordan serving as the symbol of the greatness inside the young. Viewed in this way, the poster does far more than showcase another great athlete; it distills the very purpose of Nike—the core of its brand—into an image: You too are an athlete capable of greatness. This poster's appeal goes beyond the basketball fan. Perhaps this is the reason that it sold so well, adorning the bedroom walls of those who otherwise had never held a basketball. Which also explains the "Wings" poster's timelessness. It is an image that conveys a set of values and strength of purpose that stir in the viewer the highest of emotions. Nothing is limiting you except yourself. Spread those wings and there's no telling how far you can fly.

Well, Blake said it better.

The Picture and the Frame

Some may think that "Wings" is just a very popular poster—unique in style, maybe, but not very significant in a larger discussion around Nike's brand identity. When they think of Nike, they think of the Swoosh. They think of a logo. When they think about Michael Jordan, or any one of the athletes whose brand is tied with Nike's, they too may think of a logo—the "Jump Man," for instance. We will be discussing logos in this chapter, and I don't want to diminish their overall importance in a discussion about brand identity. But logos are just one element in a brand's toolbox used to convey identity. "Wings"—and other designs we will be discussing—also are created with a very firm, and deliberate, identity in mind.

Brand identity itself is often an overlooked part of marketing. When I'm speaking with start-ups and entrepreneurs they can sometimes underestimate the importance of presenting their company or organization through a look that represents a set of values and signifies a purpose. This neglects the emotional bond that the strongest brands have established with their consumers, which makes them proud of using your product or services. Of course a brand must first build equity with a consumer base before that brand loyalty can occur, but it begins with a strong *visual language* that conveys the brand's ethos and image.

Think about someone's signature. There is a reason why the signature is (and has been) a mark of distinct individuality. No two signatures are alike, and each one possesses a distinct style and look that represents the person. Your brand identity should be as distinctive as a signature. Your customers must immediately recognize that this identity signals your brand's values and purpose as well as the unique qualities that set it apart from competitors. Does your identity tell your brand story as well as any mission statement or written communication? Does your brand have a personality that is mirrored in this identity, a set of characteristics that powerfully come through in every identifier that crosses the consumer's field of vision?

Most clearly, a brand's identity comes through with its logo, but we must move beyond this constrained definition and embrace a much broader view. When I speak about brand identity to my audiences, I often use the metaphor of a picture frame. Your brand identity is how you frame every image, every product, every bit of output from your brand. The frame shouldn't overshadow the picture—or the thing you're trying to showcase—but it should contain recognizable elements that would tell anyone this picture belongs to your brand. Nor does each frame need to be identical. Playing with your identifiers is part of the fun (and challenge) of building a strong and consistent brand identity. But those frames should be alike enough in shape, color, and style to immediately tell a viewer that they belong to your brand. "Wings" is a poster of Michael Jordan. The GOAT is the picture; but the way Jordan is framed, the use of black-and-white, the starkness of the image, the word "Wings" across the top, the elongated shape, and the message the poster is trying to convey—these are all part of Nike's brand frame. They identify the poster as clearly coming from Nike, because the frame represents the values and purpose of the Nike brand: to inspire others to achieve greatness. Sports is a state of mind, and excellence requires a mental state that achieves a sense of stillness within a maelstrom of emotions. And it starts with a willingness to dream.

The frame, noticeably, doesn't overpower the picture. In the end, "Wings" is a poster of Jordan and couldn't have been accomplished with anyone else. The Nike brand isn't taking over that specific purpose; but it's still there, part of the background, providing the necessary emotional tie to the consumer that elevates the poster into something more than just another image of Michael Jordan. I'm not saying this is easy to achieve—and I'm well aware that using the most popular sports poster of all time may seem a bit unfair. But as long as you now see "Wings" as more than a poster, if you now see it as fulfilling a multitude of purposes and generating a variety of emotions, then you can start to see how brand identity can be used in the smallest and largest ways. Most brands, I'll admit, don't bother with this level of detail, but the best ones do, because they understand and deeply value the importance of creating a brand identity across multiple platforms that says one thing: *This* is who we are.

The Frame: A Brand's Visual Language

Now think of some of your favorite brands. I bet you can describe a few elements of their visual language without much difficulty. A distinct color. A type of font. A logo. Don't make the mistake of thinking that some of these elements are happy accidents, that the brand itself just sort of stumbled into a look that everyone now knows. The companies that have built strong identities for their brands have done so with uncompromising commitment. For over 170 years, Tiffany's brand identifier has been the signature blue color. When it was first introduced, it was just the color blue. But over a century of building equity with consumers has turned that simple blue into "Tiffany's blue." The color and the brand are inseparable. Another luxury brand, Burberry, has used an iconic checkered pattern—a tartan—on its most coveted garments. When you see the pattern, you know it's Burberry. Or recall the way a tech brand such as Google consistently plays with the versions of its logo to represent what's happening in the world on a given day. Or the way a media company such as Netflix uses the color red as a recognizable frame for its brand experiences. Whether in luxury, tech, the auto industry, or sportswear, a commitment and investment into a brand's visual identity has a direct impact on the bottom line. These visual cues are never arbitrary; they're always intentional.

Over the years, I often collaborated with Apple's Brand Design team, especially with Apple's then creative director of marketing communications, Hiroki Asai. Under Hiroki's creative leadership, the company embodied the Emotion by Design ethos through its obsession with details and its complete understanding of the power of a strong visual identity. What does most Apple packaging, product imagery, in-store signage, and web presence have—I mean, aside from the brand's logo? The use of white space and the absence of clutter. Its brand identity is built on the power of simplicity, the whiteness serving as a sort of blank sheet to showcase the heroes of the story, the products themselves, putting them center stage. In other words, what isn't there is as important as what is.

For decades, Apple's use of white space has been an identifier for its brand. The color, or absence of color, can be seen across its whole branded ecosystem. One cannot trademark a color, but Apple owns white as surely as it owns its logo. It frames the product or output in a way that makes it clear to anyone that this is Apple. The "frame"—Apple's brand identifier—doesn't over-power the picture within, the product, but its presence is felt by the consumer, so much so that the consumer's first impression is that this is Apple. While simplicity should be the hallmark of any frame, Apple's use of clean, minimalist designs has become as tied to the brand as the Apple logo itself. It not only defines Apple; it also generates an emotional response in the consumer, who asso-ciates the simplicity with their attachment to the company, much as a smell can trigger memories.

But whether we're talking about Apple's distinctive packag-ing or, say, the way the retailer giant, Target, creatively uses its iconic logo as a visual punctuation within its communication, these brands strive relentlessly to convey their unique identities from the moment a consumer steps into the store (or online shop) to the moment they open the product. This thoughtfulness and understanding of the brand's purpose have allowed these iconic brands to build and grow their identities over time, earning their customers' loyalty. In other words, this isn't a one-and-done thing; a brand is constantly building out and developing that identity, giving careful consideration to ensure that its identity is repre-sented in every aspect of the brand. What this says is that these brands have an internal culture that has developed a deep respect for brand standards. Their teams understand acutely that every visual detail is an opportunity to tell the brand story.

Meanwhile, start-ups and entrepreneurs might miss the opportunity to rigorously obsess over their brand identity from the beginning. They hear me mention the most iconic brands in the world, and they think that this can't possibly apply to them. Besides, they are busy launching companies, getting products to market. They don't have the time to define their brand beyond a logo. I sympathize with this mindset. In today's world of start-up culture, we move at breakneck speed to bring an idea to market. There are only so many hours in a day, so the thinking goes, and one can't spare any of them to work on creating a visual stage for their product that doesn't provide an immediate tangible result. "We'll get to it later" can be the refrain. But brand identity is more than a set of colors, templates, and images that one uses to distinguish their company. To put it simply, your brand identity is the foundation upon which you will build a company for the long-term. It will evolve and it will grow, but rarely can a brand remake its image. Once the public has an impression of your brand, good or bad, it is very hard to alter that impression. So start out being deliberate in the impression you want it to have. Don't leave it to chance, and don't think that you can "get to it later." Start now, and you will grow your identity into the shape, style, and form that best represents your brand. The payoff may not be discernible in the beginning, but the benefits over the long run are undeniable.

A Swoosh Comeback

In the summer of 2000, I got word that the head of Nike Image Design, my manager, would be leaving the company. Now was the time to step up and declare that I was ready to take the stage. I was ready to move from a designer to a leader. I went into my manager's office and declared myself ready to succeed him. He was taken aback at first, as he had not left yet, but said he would put my name into the hat for consideration. By the end of the summer, while the world watched the Olympic Games in Sydney, I became the new leader of Nike Image Design, responsible for creating and managing Nike's brand identity and experiences around the world.

One challenge I faced immediately was that only eight years earlier I had been interning for some of the very individuals I was now directly managing. That was tough for some of the veterans to stomach. Working through that dynamic would take some time. As with everything, respect is earned, not given. But I came to the new job with a purpose and a plan. My first order of business was to change the name of the department. The word Image seemed to be limiting in terms of the responsibility for the brand that the team carried. So, I pitched Brand Design as a new name. (This is long before that was an actual moniker within the design industry.) It stuck. Out with Image, in with Brand.

My new leadership role brought with it what would become a twenty-year responsibility—overseeing the logos of Nike's innovations, athletes, and most of all, the Swoosh.

Yes, I was responsible for the integrity and application of one of the most iconic brand logos in the world.

No pressure.

As it happened, one of my first tasks was helping bring back the Swoosh. Since the mid-1990s, Nike had used only the Swoosh as its primary icon, having moved on from the NIKE wordmark, set in the typeface Futura, which used to rest just on top of the Swoosh itself. For a brief period in 2000, we had decided to go even further back into our branding heritage, and bring back the Nike Script logo which had been featured on Nike's packaging in the early '70s, for a variety of reasons. The Swoosh had become overused, sometimes showing up twelve times on a single pair of shoes, and needed to be scaled back. By using this retro handwritten Nike Script logo, we believed we could curtail our reliance on the Swoosh and bring in other identifiers for the brand. But, we quickly realized, the Script logo lacked the emotive power and brand equity of its predecessor. It went from a brand mark that was clear, simple, and, most of all, iconic and complicated it. The Swoosh is Nike; Nike is the Swoosh. The actual word is redundant.

Nevertheless, the Swoosh time-out did its job; we had given it a breather, but now it was being called up again. As we returned the Swoosh to its essential role as our brand signature, we instituted a new set of brand standards. I pulled the creative team together to discuss the most optimal way to signal the shift to the rest of the organization. This came in the form of a small, metallic silver brand book with an embossed Swoosh on the cover. This "branding bible" wasn't just for marketers and designers; it went out to everyone in the company to signal just how important our brand mark was. Within it, we set forth the rules for the Swoosh, setting boundaries around it, the dos and the don'ts, the whens and the wheres. The whole idea was to elevate the Swoosh into the realm of the sacred, and these rules were how we protected it. Call it a Swoosh Revival. We wanted to create excitement for returning to the simplicity of the iconic logo (without the script) within the headquarters at Beaverton, before rolling out the new (old) logo to the world. Once again, signaling to the entire company that no detail was too small to consider. The importance of branding was engrained in Nike's culture as much as advertising.

All this may seem like much ado about nothing. I mean, with the vintage Nike Script logo or not, hadn't the Swoosh been the company's brand mark for nearly thirty years? Few brands are fortunate in possessing an icon as beautifully simple and effective as Carolyn Davidson's design. (Phil's legendary reply when seeing it: "Well, I don't love it, but maybe it'll grow on me.") That sort of luck can't be taken for granted, and I always stressed to my teams how grateful we should be to have the Swoosh, which was and remains the envy of the brand marketers everywhere.

What difference really did the Script logo make in the end? Hadn't the standalone swoosh appeared on the side of Nike shoes for decades? Well, to understand the importance of the decision we first have to understand when the Swoosh became the company's brand mark. One may think—given its place as one of the most recognizable brand marks in the world, one which has adorned the profiles of its sneakers since the beginnings of the company—that the Swoosh was always the brand sign-off for everything. But, before 1994, the Nike Futura logo was actually how we signed off all marketing communications, from television and print ads to billboards and shoeboxes. So what happened?

The Agassi Effect

In 1994 Ron Dumas and a group of brand leaders had an idea. They watched the Wimbledon Championships in June, as Andre Agassi competed in all-white Nike Tennis apparel. More important, Agassi's Nike hat was all white with a simple black Swoosh across the front. No Nike Futura typeface. The public response to the Agassi hat was immediate. Inside Beaverton headquarters, the simple, elegant logo was a hit.

"The buzz around the purity of the symbol on a piece of apparel worn on the world stage—and the general enthusiasm internally—eventually led to the question of how Nike could translate the simple design to all areas of communication and brand identity," Dumas told me.

But it wasn't as simple as moving on from the Nike Script logo years later. One must appreciate how much Nike's brand mark was used on every bit of corporate branding and communication, not to mention the equity the mark had built with consumers. Dumas and the team had to work on identifying all the applications that the new Swoosh identity would apply to, including, but of course not limited to, advertising, packaging, retail, and printed materials. In short, it was a massive undertaking.

There were other considerations as well that Dumas had to keep in mind. What did the new Swoosh-only design *say* about Nike's brand? What had changed? Why had it changed? You don't take a beloved brand mark and erase half of it without expecting some response, positive or negative. Few people would defend the decision by saying, "What difference does it make?" Small changes, but transformational differences.

From there, Dumas prepared a pitch to the executive team and presented it in the John McEnroe Building on campus. He set up large poster boards that stretched across the entire conference room, showing all the proposed applications of a Swoosh-only identity. By Dumas's reckoning the presentation took about an hour, and the top brass seemed pleased, if noncommittal, with the proposed changes.

"Although I loved what we had created and thought it was very fresh, I was still a bit nervous, since we were proposing to change the entire brand identity of a global company to just a symbol," Dumas recalled. "At the time, I don't think there were any Fortune 500 companies in the world that had made such a move. I thought, 'Great, I'll be the creative director who craters a great brand!'"

The very next day, Ron got the call that said the changes were approved. No focus groups. No consumer surveys. The leadership team felt that the new simple design was the way to go. But for Ron, his work was just beginning.

"At the time, this was probably the largest-scale project of my career," he said. "We spent probably the next six months working the details out."

What was needed was a comprehensive program to implement the new design across all Nike packaging and products. It wasn't until the spring of 1996 that the new Swoosh-only brand identity was officially executed across the globe.

The overall reaction from our consumers and the industry

was very positive. "Something very fresh and iconic had just happened, and I believe it contributed to Nike's continued growth and brand strength for years to come," concluded Ron.

So, yeah, changing your logo is kind of a big deal...

But what's important to understand is not that we changed the Nike logo (and back, then back again), but why we changed it. For Ron and others, seeing the simple Swoosh across Agassi's hat—a design decision no one at the time thought would lead to a corporate makeover—had provided the inspiration to look anew at something we and the world had imbued with incredible meaning. There's a journey that takes place when a brand first designs its logo—its signature—to when that very same logo becomes sacred, and the mere mention of ever changing it seems like heresy. You go from Phil shrugging and saying that the Swoosh will "grow on him," to Ron embarking on the biggest project of his career (one that was very full of big projects). The intervening years—from 1971 to 1994—were years when Nike was able to build equity into its identity, and, by extension, its logo. What starts as a cool symbol that you hope helps your brand stand out from the rest will become something that will fill you and your team with immense pride. If you do it right, then it will also fill your customers with pride and a sense of belonging to and belief in the brand itself. A logo without those values and purpose is just a picture. It means nothing unless it stands for something.

First Instincts

The Swoosh comeback wasn't the only memorable moment from my first year as head of Brand Design. We we re getting ready to launch the all-new Nike Shox footwear platfor n, a n ajor innova- tion in midsole design. The Shox circula colur ns ur derneatl the shoe worked like springs, first absorbing the impact of the heel as it pressed down, then releasing the stored energy as the spring activated. It was a shoe for the future. Perfect for the new century.

Mark Parker, head of all product creation at the time, asked me to lead the brand identity work for the all-new Nike Shox innovation, which essentially meant designing a logo as innovative as the new line of shoes. Logos were my bread and butter at the time, although I understood that my new role would have me doing less of them. I was leading a creative team now, and I needed to empower them. Nevertheless, as he spoke, I couldn't help but jot down some notes and draw a quick sketch of a Shox logo based on Mark's words. It was a scribble, just my brain conceptualizing the purpose and identity of the shoe into a simple design. Again, bread-and-butter stuff. The sketch had an S that looked like a backward letter *Z* with a dash on the top and bottom, basically a spring. I closed my notebook and forgot about it. On with the real design work.

It wasn't unusual during this period for my team to spend significant resources on logo development for innovations. It was a small price to pay for branding that would be seen on the feet of millions of athletes around the world. I hired two different design firms who came back with a combined eighty potential Shox logos. That sounds like a lot, but we left no stone unturned when it came to branding. As we reviewed and edited the logos, none of them seemed like a clear winner. I remembered my old quick sketch and pulled it out. I still wasn't looking at it as anything more than a guidepost by which to judge the other designs. But as we worked through the entries, I kept going back to the simplicity of that initial sketch I did. Finally, I admitted to myself that my sketch was more than a sketch. It was a contender, and I added it to the mix. Mark and I then reviewed all the logos and we both kept coming back to mine. Perhaps I had disregarded it at first because it was a bit too literal. Surely, two different design firms can come up with something better than a backward Z? At the same time, I remembered why the best logos are considered the best: They're simple, they're visually distinct, and they tell a story. Mark looked at me and said that it was the one.

Sometimes you take a long, circular route back to where you started, a place where your first instincts are the right instincts. And so my backward Z became the logo for the new Nike Shox. The logo worked because it checked all three of the boxes that define a successful symbol: It looked like the innovation (a spring), it had a kinetic quality that brought attention to the innovation itself (almost like the spring was bouncing off the page), and it included a phonetic element (the backward Z was really an S for "Shox"). It's rare to get all three of these boxes checked in one logo. Not a bad way to end my logo-design days at Nike.

But we weren't quite finished. Next up was creating a tagline for Nike Shox that expressed its innovation in a fun, memorable way. Thus, "Boing." Perfect. Playful, simple, and descriptive. Of course, it sprung from the minds of Wieden & Kennedy. Nothing more was needed. Our campaign was no doubt helped during the Olympics that summer in Sydney, where Vince Carter, who played on the USA Men's Basketball Team, would be wearing Nike Shox. Already known as one of the best dunkers in the game, Carter intercepted a pass during a game with the French National team. He took two dribbles, then launched himself ("boing!") into the air, impossibly over the head of the French center, the seven-foot-two Frederic Weis, slamming the ball home in spectacular Carter-esque fashion. It was a good logo; it was a good tagline. But all the marketing in the world cannot compete with a moment like that.

Albert Einstein once said: "Make it as simple as possible. But not simpler." I'm reminded of that adage when thinking about logo design. The simplicity of my Nike Shox logo came from a brief jolt of inspiration. But even that is giving the moment more credit than it deserves. I simply listened to what Mark was saying and jotted down the first thing that came (sprung?) to mind. It was instinct more than inspiration. What's more, I wasn't *trying* to create something exceptional. I put my thoughts down and walked away. I didn't have time to complicate it, to agonize over it, to screw it all up by making it far more involved than it needed to be. It was simple because it was instinct.

Over the years we would unleash our talents to create logos for basketball sneakers that would give you "Force" or give you "Flight." We made logos for running shoes that provided "Max Air" or "Zoom Air" cushioning. We even moved into city branding rooted in the culture of "Nike LA" versus "Nike NYC," and designed brand logos that distilled the essence of transcendent athletes like Tiger Woods or Serena Williams. The point is, whether you get it on the first try or spend a year obsessing over various logo directions, a brand must commit fully to its visual center, the anchor that grounds every other element in its visual language.

The Picture Within the Frame

At Nike, every product launch was an opportunity to take the consumer someplace new. A fully realized and visceral world that was both accessible and aspirational. For innovation to become more than just a utility or commodity, and for the elite athletes who validated them to motivate and inspire us, we had to surround and infuse these innovations with emotion. Figuratively speaking, creating the brand picture within the frame is about building an emotive world of images that are full of imagination and metaphors, that build desire in the products, and that communicate their benefits in extraordinary ways. These are not just images; these are stories, and each story embodies a moment in time, while also contributing to the overall reflection of the Nike's brand.

So much can be communicated through an image. As Heather Amuny-Dey, an incredibly gifted former Nike design vice president, says, "A great image can have the power of the most elaborate movie set, all brought together in a moment. We as humans respond in a unique way when we see visuals of people doing extraordinary things."

Toward this end, we believed in the power of art direction and photography to shape the persona of a brand and to tell the stories of our athletes and products. Whether it was working with photographers such as Annie Leibovitz to capture the heroic nature of the competitive athlete, or Carlos Serrao's ability to capture athleticism and movement, or John Huet being able to draw out the soul that exists in sports. Each collaboration brought a different dimension to the brand through the lenses of these talented collaborators. They were able to add their own signatures to the picture, the image Nike was using to convey its brand to the world.

Photographers have the challenging task of not only technically capturing an image that reveals something deep about the subject, but also motivating the subject to get to that place. By which I mean a place of authenticity and a moment of magic that will allow the viewer to connect emotionally to the picture. This was more apparent than ever when I had the opportunity to help brand the championship run of the 1999 USA Women's National Soccer team, on their way to the World Cup trophy in Pasadena. A tall order, given the momentum they were riding going into the tournament. I needed to create a national photo-driven campaign to promote the partnership between Nike and the team, at events, in store, and on the walls of the bedrooms of kids who aspired to be them. I chose the Australian photographer Ben Watts to collaborate with me. Ben not only had a distinct documentary style to his work, but he also possessed a nearly superhuman reserve of energy that he brought to every shoot. It was infectious, and it was just what we needed to bring these amazing athletes to life.

Our job—and Ben's responsibility—was to draw out the individual personalities of the players while also building on the overall team identity. We spent multiple days and locations around five extraordinary athletes—Brandi Chastain, Mia Hamm, Tisha Venturini, Tiffeny Milbrett, and Briana Scurry. Each player had a unique persona and a specific role on the team. We needed to showcase both qualities. Given that we were filming around training sessions, you couldn't guarantee high energy from the players, so Ben would need to bring it. And he did. We got the soulful determination of Mia, the energetic leadership of Brandi, and the quiet confidence of Briana. All through singular photographs.

We also complemented the individual portraits by documenting the moments within the moments: training together, eating meals together, interacting with the fans, lounging and laughing, and so on. While perhaps less dramatic than a shot of a player scoring, these images gave viewers a window into the lives of these amazing athletes off the pitch, how they lived and played together. The audience was supposed to take this "Road to Pasadena" with the team, to be there for the mundane moments as well as the dramatic ones. And considering this specific team is remembered as one of the greatest in U.S. history, I say it was a journey worth taking.

But there was something more to that project with these incredible women. There was an authenticity that we were able to capture, which is the rarest of things in this industry. The ability to see the real person requires that that person decides to reveal themselves to you. Previously, the women's team over the years had been expressed only through in-game action photography, where the players are in moments of tremendous athleticism or heroism. Our intention was to showcase these players as individuals, to reveal each person who wore the uniform and present them all as amazing *people*, not just players. By committing the necessary time, resources, and talent, we were able to celebrate the human and relatable side of these extraordinary athletes.

A Nike writer who worked on the shoot, Dennie Wendt, told me later: "One of the reasons those shoots and so much of what the soccer team did worked is because it was based in relationships and authenticity. It never actually felt like a marketing exercise. It just felt like we were the fortunate conduits between those players and the kids who wanted to get to know them better."

Which, in the end, was our purpose. To bring the fans, especially the kids who looked up to these phenomenal athletes, closer to their heroes. That's the power of portraits and photography, to bring a captured moment to the consumer and connect them emotionally to the athlete.

The Art of the Metaphor

Yes, it was goofy. I mean, who shaves their entire head, except for an oval spot right above the forehead? I'm asking as someone who's been shaving my head for decades. There is a right way and a wrong way to do it, and during the 2002 World Cup, the Brazilian Ronaldo, at the time the most well-known footballer on the planet, did it *the wrong way*. But, as bizarre as it may have first looked, Ronaldo's haircut wasn't the result of an unfortunate accident with clippers. He knew how to get people to take notice and, more important, knew he could back it up through his play—which he did by winning the Golden Boot award for the top goal scorer of the tournament. For athletes, style without performance can be fleeting and empty. In the world of brands, a beautiful product without usefulness will simply gather dust. In my eighteen years of leading the image of the brand, and its athletes and products, I preached the important role that image played in multiplying athletic performance and the benefits of our innovations. Years after Ronaldo's follicle statement at the World Cup, Enrico Balleri, a creative force in Nike's legacy of great brand communication, used the mantra "Haircuts Matter" as a way to emphasize the point.

In the end, Ronaldo's haircut isn't the point; the point is that Ronaldo understood, as Balleri also understood, that playing with one's image to create a sensation was just another way to fill out the "picture" in the frame. To continue on the theme of imaging soccer, coming out of the 2006 World Cup in Berlin, one of the ways we began to grow the Nike soccer business was by treating our top footballers and their signature footwear like brands in their own right. The creative team would conduct these (sometimes eccentric) exercises to get to the core of who they were as players and persons. This would directly lead to what their brand identities should be, and the characteristics they should convey: what they feel like, sound like, and look like.

To spark the process, the creative team would fashion "mood boards" featuring metaphors to get them to react too, associating them to certain entities. For instance: On the football pitch are you a sports car or a motorbike? Do you play with linear speed or side to side? What type of animal are you? A snake, a hawk, or a tiger? All are predators, but all have different methods of attack. What's yours? Are you sharp like a diamond, or expressive like graffiti, in terms of attitude?

We would put this exercise in front of them and get their reaction. Mostly positive, sometimes funny, sometimes complete disagreement, but always useful. Generally, they were decisive, and knew exactly what we meant and who they were. But provoking reaction was key. An athlete like Cristiano Ronaldo was clear: He was a diamond. This meant keeping Cristiano's visual persona simple, polished, and refined. This helped us build edges for the overall football brand, while being true to the attributes of the players. The creative team turned these insights and conversations into visual personas for the athletes and their shoes, so they would become more than athletes and more than a football boot. They became visceral extensions of their personalities and brands. The elements of a diamond, space travel, and a supercar were smashed together to create an identity for the explosive speed of Cristiano. In other words, this wasn't just one metaphor; it was several metaphorical images that were combined to create a provocative world that defined the athlete's style of play and the brand of football.

The Mamba Mentality

Then there's Kobe Bryant, a man who needed no mood boards to figure out his metaphor. In working with Kobe to design not only his own brand identity, but one for his signature shoe as well, the Kobe VII, we quickly learned that he needed zero encouragement to seek outside inspiration. In particular, Kobe drew a lot of inspiration from art. One artist he found captivating was the Mexican surrealist painter Octavio Ocampo. Octavio is known for creating art with optical illusions through a metamorphic painting style, where smaller intricate images are integrated to create a larger image. The deeper you look at the painting, the more is revealed.

As Kobe relayed to our creative team, he was fascinated with Ocampo's "picture within a picture" style. He said that the art related to how he saw his own game and mentality and how people perceived them. Like Octavio's art, his play could look one way to one opponent and entirely different to another. This insight led directly to the creation of the "Different Animal, Same Beast" campaign. David Creech, a former Nike and Brand Jordan design vice president, led the team in creating three dynamic images. At first glance, each one looks like pairs of shoes, but upon further viewing, they reveal themselves to be the heads of a snake, a leopard, and a great white shark. Thus, the images are a metaphor for Kobe's on-court mentality and style of play. What started with the Black Mamba now included other animals that have that same killer instinct, the inner beasts that take over in game situations, giving the consumer a look into the Mamba persona through "a picture within a picture."

Of course, we still had to make sure the consumer knew what the benefit of Kobe's shoe was on the court. I was always reminding the creative team that we ultimately had to serve the needs of the athletes who were buying the products, in this case, the Kobe VII. That was and continues to be the Nike brand's purpose. How could the storytelling convey the inner beast that Kobe's alter egos represented while at the same time showcasing the advantage that the athletes would get by wearing the product? For the player, wearing this shoe gave you the advantage of two angles of attack on the court. Attack fast or attack strong. Just like the Mamba.

Kobe pushed us further than any other athlete to use our imagination and go beyond conventional marketing. We partnered with the artist Christophe Roberts on a gallery display that transformed used Kobe shoeboxes into a life-size great white shark. We displayed his shoes in terrariums as if the shoe itself were a Black Mamba. Going back to Ocampo's "picture within a picture" approach, in each of these examples, we looked to create expressions of his brand that could be read in multiple ways depending on how you experienced it, just like Kobe's opponents.

Kobe's obsession with infusing every part of his brand identity with deeper meaning also extended to his logo. At first glance, it's a symbol composed of six shapes, using design inspiration from Japanese samurai warriors. But with Kobe, the elements within his brand identity were never just to be taken at face value, much like an Ocampo painting. As Kobe told *Esquire* magazine, the logo represented a sword in a sheath. "The sword is the raw talent," explained Kobe. "The sheath is the package it's kept in—everything you go through, your calluses and your baggage, what you learn."[6]

That's the Mamba Mentality.

Kobe's commitment to communicating his inner beast made it easy for us to create concepts because he was always consistent with what he was trying to do. Creatively, Kobe made us better. He was a teacher who taught us to be more curious and didn't mind being a student himself to elevate his craft further.

Designing Dreams

We've moved from the role of branding to imagery, but we must also consider the environment, whether physical or digital, when talking about the importance of brand identity. There is no better way to immerse your audience in your brand values than through a space. A place where they can engage all the senses and literally see, hear, and touch your brand.

Let's consider an example. You're walking down a busy street and pass a storefront with windows that reveal a richly curated display featuring flags, framed paintings, and vintage trophies. With the dark wood-paneled backdrop, it looks like the scene out of a movie. You move inside and see walls adorned with what look like collegiate pennants, black-and-white team photos, and furniture that matches the wood of the window displays. All these elements contrast with and spotlight the layered colors of apparel on the mannequins. Elegant, but not too refined, it is a look that defines a style but is not of a specific time. It's not something that defines a certain era; it is timeless. As you continue to move through the space, you find scene after scene with environments that feel classic, and traditional, and most likely looked good fifty years ago and will look good fifty years from now.

The story of the Ralph Lauren brand is one that I've been interested in since my childhood. Lauren himself once said: "I don't design products; I design dreams." And that is what one feels when walking into a Ralph Lauren store; one is drawn to the promise of a lifestyle, one based on classic American tropes of elegant leisure, because what's being sold aren't clothes but aspirations. The basic Ralph Lauren polo shirt hasn't changed in decades (since 1975, in fact), and there's a reason for that. Lauren also once said: "I am not a fashion person. I am anti-fashion. I am interested in longevity, timelessness, style." From the polo-player logo to the storefront to the interior to the clothes themselves, Ralph Lauren is a brand that is obsessed with a specific identity. Or put another way, it's creating a scene, as if out of a movie, another very deliberate strategy.

"Every time I design clothes, I'm making a movie."

In fact, its identity is what it is selling. The attention paid to the smallest detail within each scene is why Ralph Lauren has grown a brand from being just a tie shop in a department store to one of the most recognizable luxury brands in the world.

Designing Obama

In 2010 we had a global marketing meeting in Seattle. I was now in the newly created position of vice president of Global Brand Creative, responsible for driving Nike's brand storytelling and the creative for its identity, voice, and experiences. The CMO at the time, Davide Grasso, asked me to present the Nike Brand Creative Ethos, a presentation I had created with my leadership team that brought to life the different characteristics of the brand that we needed to convey to the consumer. I would be following a guest speaker, but Davide didn't want to give me the name. I could tell by his excitement that the mystery guest was going to be someone special.

Well, come game time, Magic Johnson walks out, surprising everyone. He then goes on to break down his historic forty-two-point Game 6 NBA Championship Finals game in 1980. In that game against Philadelphia, when Johnson stepped in for the injured Kareem Abdul-Jabbar, the Magic legend was born. He played every position that night and invented his own version of the sky hook, known as the baby sky hook. Magic's message was clear. Everyone thought they were done when Kareem got hurt, but he didn't. When the stakes are at the highest and the odds are most against you, that's when you need to deliver your very best.

How the hell do you follow that? But I also knew I had my own ace up the sleeve. To emphasize the important role that branding would play to grow both the Nike brand and business, I had invited Scott Thomas, the design director of the 2008 Obama presidential campaign and the author of the book *Designing Obama*, a portfolio of the art, design, and the stories behind the historic run. It was a bit risky, considering that some might look at it as bringing politics into the workplace, but I felt I could set it up in a way that kept everyone focused on the story and the lesson.

Never before had branding and visual communication design played such a vital role in a presidential campaign. The anchor for the whole campaign was the Obama logo: an iconic blue letter *O* with a red-and-white flag filling the bottom of the leterform, inspired by a rising sun. Not before or since has there been such an iconic candidate logo. It wasn't just the emotional power and simplicity of the logo that made it successful, it was its ability to be customized for each audience. Scott and the team created versions of the logo for twelve different identity groups and another fifty versions for each state in America.

Scott talked about using design to create a visual language to not only match the voice of the candidate but to accentuate and amplify it. By using a combination of colors, typography, and graphic forms, they were able to give people a sense of hope, optimism, and belief. The icon was designed to be a representation of the candidate himself, rather than a nifty-looking logo with his name beside " '08." Scott and his team understood why their candidate resonated with people from all walks of life, and their work was to create an icon that embodied this universal feeling. They knew that if they did their work right—and if the candidate himself could provide the necessary meaning to the visuals—then they would be creating an icon that captured the feeling surging through his supporters.

In the end, it wasn't about matching Magic's thrilling Game 6 story (admittedly, one of the greatest sports stories in history); it was about showing the level of craft and commitment necessary to create something legendary, whether it's on the court or the campaign trail.

A Game Face for Greatness

Athletes speak about wearing their game face as they enter the field of competition. The focus, the determination, the drive. The singularity of purpose. The image on their face reflects the feeling in their heart. They are ready, and nothing will deter them from their course. Your brand identity—the image you show to the world—is your game face. It's what your consumers see when they see you. Behind the scenes, you may work and prepare with all the effort and focus the competition demands, but if you don't show that side of you to your consumers, then all they will see is an unfocused, disinterested player. How we present ourselves to the world matters. How the world sees our brand determines their attachment to our brand. The strength of that attachment must grow over time—you can't create it from scratch—but there needs to be a visual representation, a symbol, that serves as your standard. Wherever and however your consumers interact with your brand, they must feel that standard in the moment. They must know that everything your brand touches—every output, every communication, every product—bears your signature mark. So develop your game face and rise to that level of greatness.

PRINCIPLES FOR "GAME FACE FOR GREATNESS"

1. MORE THAN A LOGO

Your logo may feel like just a visual signature in the beginning, but treat it like the most important part of your brand
future. Commit to getting it right, and it will be able to carry
the weight of your consumer's lifelong aspirations.

2. THE PICTURE AND THE FRAME

Create a strong and identifiable brand frame, but don't let
that frame outshine the picture within it. Your brand foundation is a stage for the stories you want to tell. The stronger
the frame, the more powerful the stories.

3. HAIRCUTS MATTER

Style without performance is fleeting and forgotten. Performance without style can be respected but doesn't transcend. When performance and style multiply each other, you
get brand distinction.

4. THE PICTURE WITHIN THE PICTURE

Provide depth and discovery within the image of your brand.
Let there be layers of meaning. The closer the consumer gets
to seeing who you are, the deeper their connection to your
brand will be.

5. SET THE SCENE

What movie has the consumer just walked into and what are
the scenes they are a part of? Build an immersive world for

your brand and its products to play a movie that engages all senses and—more important—tell a story where the consumer is one of the characters.

6. SIMPLIFY WITHOUT COMPROMISE

Sometimes what you don't say is as important as what you do. Your brand identity is an exercise of addition and subtraction. Reveal what matters most and let the rest fade away.

7. OBSESS OVER THE LAST 10 PERCENT

Make even the smallest details meet the highest standard. Each of those details, no matter how small, is an opportunity to reveal more about your brand story and say, "*This* is who we are." Over time, your respect for quality will be returned by the consumer's respect for you.

CHAPTER 5

DARE TO BE REMEMBERED

Moments before I was scheduled to go onstage with Nike founder Phil Knight, he turned to me and said that he had looked over the questions I had prepared for him and the other panelists and felt that we would have to do a lot of dancing. What he meant was that my questions wouldn't quite fill all the time we had.

With that, we walked out onto the makeshift stage to the applause of hundreds of Nike employees who were waiting in the atrium of the Jerry Rice Building, not to mention the thousands who would be watching virtually around the world. I had given plenty of presentations before on the power of Nike's brand voice, but nothing like this. And with no one as large—professionally speaking—as Phil Knight, Dan Wieden of Wieden & Kennedy, and Tom Clarke, a Nike veteran since 1980 and president of Nike Innovation.

So, yeah, I was feeling the pressure before Phil's pep talk. Now, I was sweating.

In 2013, Nike celebrated the twenty-fifth anniversary of the Just Do It slogan, coined by Dan himself all those decades ago. As the VP of Global Brand Creative, my role in the festivities was to moderate a forty-minute panel discussion among these three titans behind Nike's history and brand success. Given the incredible

121

importance of Just Do It in Nike's advertising over the previous two and a half decades, I knew how important this moment would be in honoring the past to help shape the future. While feeling the weight of the moment, I was excited to be on that stage, and came prepared to deliver an inspiring panel.

And then Phil tells me, seconds before we start, that he's not exactly impressed with my proposed questions. So much for preparation.

We kicked off the event with the official launch of the new "Just Do It: Possibilities" commercial. In it, viewers are inspired to push their limits through a variety of scenarios featuring an all-star cast of athletes and celebrities. The film encapsulated Just Do It (and the Nike brand) perfectly. What, after all, is the point behind "just do it" if not to challenge yourself beyond what you think is possible (for you)? Of course, the film had to tell the decades-old Just Do It story in a way that was both utterly unique and relevant for the newer generation of viewers. A lot of brands retire older slogans or mottos as a way to stay fresh and relevant, but Just Do It has formed the foundation of Nike's brand for more than thirty years. At this point, it's as synonymous with Nike as the Swoosh. Rather than replacing it, Nike has doubled down on it again and again, reinventing the way in which the Just Do It story is told, but not the fundamental story itself. There's a reason those words are as iconic as the Swoosh, and not—as so many brand mottos have become over the years—a phrase that ignites the nostalgia of audiences over a certain age. Your child knows Just Do It as much as your grandparents—and that is the point.

The new film was met with thunderous applause, and I followed it up with a series of initial questions for the panel. With the depth and expansiveness of their answers and stories, we ended up covering all the questions I had but still had half a panel to go.

Fortunately, I had also prepped a bit of a film montage of some iconic Just Do It ads to finish up the program. I might have had to start this portion of the panel sooner than I expected, but they at least gave me some breathing room to think of my closing questions. The first commercial was the legendary "Bo Knows," which introduced the sport of cross-training to the world and was the first Nike ad to sign off with "Just Do It." After I showed the commercial, Phil mentioned that it was on his short list of the best Nike ads of all time. It's on mine as well. The ad dropped when I was eighteen years old, and obsessed with strength and conditioning. More than any other Nike ad from my youth, "Bo Knows" formed a strong (and, as it would turn out, an unbreakable) emotional attachment to the brand.

Next up was "Instant Karma" from 1992, featuring the famous John Lennon song over footage of both regular and professional athletes (notably Olympian Michael Johnson) going about their training routine. The ad works because the song, with its powerful drumbeat and chorus—"We all shine on"—syncs so well with the imagery. Dan talked about what it took to get approval for the song from Lennon's wife, Yoko Ono.

This was actually the second time Dan's team had used Lennon in a Nike ad. The first—featuring the Beatles' "Revolution"—had been the music behind the Nike ad of the same name in 1987. Readers today may not remember that the first ad caused a minor stir (and a legal battle), which, more than thirty years later, seems a little ridiculous. The point is that before "Revolution," brands would use only covers for famous tracks, not the original tracks themselves. Nike broke this tradition (and started a trend that continues to this very day), which was why "Instant Karma" was a little like poking the bear. Of course, the culture had changed in those intervening five years, and "Instant Karma" was an instant classic.

I recall these moments in Nike history now because each ad, eight years after I chose them to celebrate Just Do It, showcases how Nike's voice, in the way it communicates the story of its brand to the world through film, reflects the values and personality of the brand itself. These stories are remembered decades after they first were seen because they stirred such intense emotions within the audience. "Bo Knows" promoted a new way for all athletes, not just professional ones, to train. It also launched a slogan that continues to this very day. Just Do It has reinvented itself many times, but the heart of the campaign has always been what viewers first saw in the (admittedly funny) way Bo Jackson just went out and played every sport that he could. In "Instant Karma" we see the convergence of past (the song) and present (the footage of athletes), a combination of music and sport. Today, these genres are combined regularly, but at the time it was unconventional. Music and sport are essential companions for athletes, professional or amateur. Nike's insight was to put them together.

These, however, are just a sample of the films that propelled Nike's brand and introduced different angles of a familiar picture to newer audiences. In the end, the ads I chose to celebrate Just Do It were ads that have stood the test of time. History has decided their worth, but I wanted to explain their importance in Nike's brand story, particularly in a slogan that has been a part of the brand for more than thirty years.

Finishing up the panel, I asked one final question of the group: "What advice do you have for the next generation of Nike storytellers?" Phil's answer struck the deepest chord. Using a golf analogy, he said that, as storytellers for a brand, you have a set of clubs and you need to choose the right club based on the shot you need to hit at that moment. "Different moments require different shots," he said. It's the sum of those shots that make up a brand's voice over time. The game doesn't change; the goal is the same, but how you reach that goal depends on what you choose to get there. I could search forever and not find a better way to explain how a brand employs its voice to connect with its audience. In the end, we might have had to do some dancing, as Phil said, but I got some great answers...

The Mosaic of a Brand's Personality

Your brand is your story. It's how you choose to express your product, your ideas, your services to the world. But there isn't one way to tell this story, because your brand isn't just one idea or characteristic. Like any good story, it's comprised of multiple elements and subplots, tangents, and twists. Unlike a good story, your brand's story never ends. You are always telling it. Every time you put something out into the world, you are telling your brand's story. An Instagram post tells a story; a brand website tells a story; a holistic campaign made up of retail windows, event experiences, television ads, and social media content fits them all together to tell a story.

A story without heart, passion, and purpose doesn't make a good brand any better than it makes a good person. And thinking about a person is quite apt here. We are all individuals—singular and unique, whole and complete. We are one thing. *You* are your brand. But dig a little deeper into any person and you find a mosaic of characteristics, beliefs, strengths, and even contradictions. To know someone is not to know one thing about them. It's to know the entirety—or at least a good chunk—of their story. Where they came from, what they do, what they love, what they don't, how they think and feel, and how they see the world. Look at the clos-est people in your life—your spouse, your children, your parents, your siblings, or your best friend—and ask yourself if you could tell their story.

For Nike, the story always begins with the athlete. It was and remains the foundational element in the Nike brand. But how Nike has chosen to tell this story of the athlete over the decades is also part of the brand, because it has revealed the brand's characteristics, its values, and its purpose. While I don't think these have changed dramatically over the years, they have certainly expanded. What has changed is the way in which Nike has told this story. Just like any good fiction book, there are multiple ways to tell a brand's story and multiple genres with which to tell it. A story of inspiration, a story of greatness, a story of humor, a story of defying the odds or of failure. Nike has explored many genres, or mediums, and it will continue to explore more. The point is that the art of storytelling is always in flux; it's a constantly shifting landscape upon which hundreds of mediums ply for consumers' attention. There is no right one for any brand; but there are the best ones for *your* brand.

There are many mediums through which a brand can build its personality. Still, the power of film, in particular, has always been an effective way to tell profound stories, create a relatable and visceral voice, and stir the deepest of emotions within your brand audience. Nike's longtime creative partner, Wieden & Kennedy, has been a leader in the ability to translate insights within the world of sports into immersive narratives through film. Sometimes the best way you can show the benefits of innovation is through movement, especially as it relates to athletic performance. Film moves us by engaging all our senses, even within a thirty- to sixty-second format. Today, as we look at all the streaming services we have at our fingertips, it's clear we are in the golden age of short- and long-form storytelling through film. This could and should relate to brand communication, too. While the importance and role of television advertising for brands has evolved, and the platforms and channels through which you can communicate your stories have grown, a lot of the core tenets of great brand storytelling through film have stayed the same.

Regardless of how you define your brand, what characteristics it entails, and the way in which you choose to share it with the world, all the best stories have one thing in common: They touch on the human imagination and elicit an emotional response. I don't care what industry or product or service your brand represents, if your creative output doesn't try to ignite imagination and spark a feeling, then you're missing the opportunity. In the examples to follow, we'll be looking at the ways we creatively achieved both goals through storytelling, not just by what the story says, but how it says it, where it says it, and why it says it.

A New Position and New Offense

When I took on the role of vice president of Global Brand Creative at Nike in 2010, the marketing world was experiencing profound changes. The position I held was brand new and had been created to solve several emerging opportunities at once. In Chapter 2, I mentioned that I became responsible for several departments that previously had operated more or less independently. The goal was to integrate them and develop chemistry and creative alignment among these diverse teams from the start.

But the other major reason pushing the restructure was the profound change occurring in the media landscape. My new role—and how we were organizing—coincided with the disruptive rise of social media, particularly the way these new platforms could engage the consumer directly. To truly reach the consumer on all these new platforms, we had to get our separate teams on the same page creatively, which would then allow the subsequent brand stories to be more distinct and meaningful, with a far more consistent look and feel. This evolving multimedia environment demanded cooperation from the very beginning.

Now thrust into this new position, I had to figure out how to do it. On day one (literally), I was in the room with the new team evaluating a new ad concept for Tiger Woods that would be aired just before the Masters in 2010. The concept was simple in design: Tiger looks directly at the camera, filmed in stark black-and-white, while a recording of his late father, Earl, provides the voice-over. Earl is talking to Tiger about responsibility and asks him: "Did you learn anything?" The film became the first communication from the brand for Tiger, after his yearlong hiatus from golf and launched just before the most important tournament of the year. The ad was polarizing within the media, and with the fans. It was an intense way to start a new role on day one, but at the time, for me and the team, it underscored the brand's support of athletes through the ups and the downs.

Listen Before You Lead

In 2010, LeBron James made his decision to leave the Cleveland Cavaliers and go to the Miami Heat to join Chris Bosh and Dwyane Wade. "The Decision," as it came to be called, was revealed in a first-of-its-kind televised event that was hailed as innovative by some and criticized by others. Shortly afterward, we came together with LeBron on the Nike campus in Beaverton to discuss how we would bring to life his brand story for the season. LeBron arrived with his trusted team of Maverick Carter, Rich Paul, and Randy Mims, who were as inseparable then as they are today. The heightened energy in the room that day gave extra weight to the importance of the moment. When it was time to share the creative direction for the season, I talked about resetting the national conversation back to basketball. Our concept would show LeBron's otherworldly talent and athleticism on the court and why we, those who had deep passion for the game, drew so much inspiration from him. My team and I thought that it was best to create a film concept that focused on LeBron's love of the game and his once-in-a-generation skills and less on the controversy and noise surrounding the Decision. By focusing on LeBron's performance on the court, we could turn the national conversation away from the Decision and back to basketball.

But LeBron came to the meeting with a different purpose. He firmly rejected our concept. Everyone was stone-faced. He then made it clear that he wanted to answer his critics (not avoid them) with something powerful. He looked at each of us around the room, and reminded us that playing basketball is what *he* does. It was time for us to do what *we* do. The clarity and force with which he said it made all of us pause. Phil Knight, who always made a point to attend LeBron's annual meeting, then spoke for everyone in the room when he said if that was what LeBron wanted, then that was what Nike would do. Phil's point was clear: We weren't going to avoid anything. We were going to take on LeBron's critics directly. We say we amplify the voice of the athlete—Phil was reminding us that this was at the core of Nike's brand, this was *what we do*.

I think LeBron knew this. He wasn't asking us to do anything we didn't preach to ourselves and everyone else. But rarely did an athlete say exactly what they wanted from myself and the creative team. Most rely on our professional experience. But LeBron is LeBron, and he was ready to punch back. Message received.

The challenge, as we were to learn, was to find the most effective way to tell LeBron's story that stayed true both to the man himself and to Nike. I wish I could say that we immediately rose to the occasion and nailed it on the first try. But as good as the creative teams are at Nike and Wieden & Kennedy, we often don't nail it on the first try. That's the creative process for you.

But we did have Ryan O'Rourke and Alberto Ponte, Wieden & Kennedy's creative directors for Nike, a prolific duo who played off each other's strengths but were not afraid to challenge each other (or anyone else) when necessary. This was their (and Nike's) competitive advantage: These two were always creatively pushing everyone around them, including themselves. Ryan loved sports and had a great ability to see the fun and humor in it. Then there was Alberto's extraordinary understanding of the human condition, which mixed well with his broader international perspective, that brought a depth of purpose to the work. This was a big task before them, but I knew that I wouldn't want anyone else on the job.

The initial concepts by the creative team played into the haters' worst caricatures of LeBron, and would show him doing everything they said he was doing behind the scenes. The tone and style was obviously playful and intended to expose the ridiculous nature of the attacks. However, the consensus was that these ideas failed as an "answer." Instead, they simply lampooned the charges, and the humor and sarcasm only trivialized the entire episode. One of the other concepts would have had him asking for more hate, implying that it fed his drive and competitive edge. I think this idea would have worked for some athletes—those who embrace a "villain" role—but that's not LeBron.

Discarded concepts often help focus your efforts, if only to discover what doesn't work. In this case, our breakthrough came when we finally realized that the thing we were consciously avoiding—the Decision itself—was the very thing we needed to address.

What Should I Do?

All the previous concepts had been dancing around the Decision, trying to avoid taking it on directly. And so maybe that was the key? Maybe the answer we had been looking for was to put LeBron back in that chair, and have him answer the critics himself. We made sure that LeBron himself was comfortable with this idea, and he confirmed he was. So off we went, batting around ideas that made the Decision the central focus of the ad.

Which is how Ryan, Alberto, and the creative team eventually came up with "What Should I Do?" When the spot opens, LeBron is shown sitting in the Decision chair, wearing the exact same shirt he wore on that day, immediately communicating to the viewer that this is a response to the event itself. But is it an answer to his critics? There's a brief moment where the viewer is unsure. LeBron's head is bowed. Is he going to apologize? Then LeBron speaks:

"What should I do?

"Should I admit that I've made mistakes?

"Should I remind you that I've done this before?"

And with that, the viewer understands. No, LeBron isn't apologizing. "Should I be who you want me to be?" he asks the camera. There it is. LeBron doesn't owe anyone anything.

Which isn't to say that "What Should I Do?" is without humor. Humor has always been part of LeBron and how he communicates. He has a very self-deprecating side that makes him relatable. And humor is always good during tough times. At one point LeBron asks, "Should I have my tattoo removed?" The next cut shows him in the chair, with the tattoo artist removing his "Chosen 1" (a reference to a *Sports Illustrated* cover story that called him that[7]). At another point, LeBron, dressed as a cowboy, asks "Should I accept my role as a villain?" These humorous moments, which include a *Miami Vice* scene with Don Johnson, are interlaced with more serious questions, such as: "Should I stop listening to my friends?" Pause. "They're my friends."

Whether absurd or deadly serious, the film presents the critics as petty and patronizing. Ironically, by not showing sports—or really LeBron's otherworldly athleticism—aside from a few quick clips, the ad makes the point that the critics' accusations have nothing to do with sports. One by one, the film dismantles the charges as irrelevant, repetitive, and entitled. They're also disingenuous, which LeBron makes clear when he asks: "Should I just disappear?" One could almost hear all of LeBron's critics, whose livelihoods depended on what this player said and did, crying out: "No, no, no!"

But in the end, "What Should I Do?" is the response LeBron asked us to help him make. It's direct, it's powerful, and it's pure LeBron. As O'Rourke said to me at the time: "In the end our group confusion became the core of the idea. 'What should we do?' became 'What should I do?'" The ad closes with slow-motion footage of LeBron flying through the air toward the basket, and repeats the refrain: "Should I be who you want me to be?"

As viral videos go, "What Should I Do?" was about as viral as it got back then. Every major sports outlet covered the film like a news event, and more than a few of the targets of the ad spoke out against it. (Even *South Park* re-created the commercial.) It didn't necessarily silence the critics, but then, it wasn't meant to. It was LeBron's answer, it was our answer to LeBron. Back me up. Help me *fight back*. Amplify my voice! And so we did.

Expand the Edges

I have met few individuals whose greatness extends into so many facets of life as Kobe Bryant. Kobe will be remembered in history as one of the greatest basketball players of all time, which would be enough for most people. But Kobe stands out *for me* and for the hundreds of people with whom he worked over the years away from the court as an exemplar of curiosity, imagination, and creativity. No one who entered Kobe's orbit could ignore the man's tireless pursuit of greatness.

On the court, Kobe's persona was known as the Black Mamba, a relentless competitor on the hardwood who dashed the dreams of opposing teams and fanbases with heartbreaking threes and overwhelming defense. I should know, since Kobe crushed my Trail Blazers in Game 7 of the 2000 Western Conference Finals. (Ugh, the pain never really goes away.) Indeed, Kobe was the consummate competitor, an athlete who reached sports' highest peaks because of his discipline and drive to win at all costs. I mean, it was Kobe who gave himself the nickname Black Mamba!

Not only that, but Kobe also created an entire personality and methodology based on this extremely deadly African snake. This was made apparent to the Nike and agency creative teams over the years by Kobe, who would often speak about the Black Mamba in the third person. He would illustrate the mindset of his alter ego with statements like, "The Black Mamba doesn't have friends; it has teammates" and "The Black Mamba doesn't listen to music because it's a distraction." He would further express his competitive drive by talking about how he didn't let anybody win in even in the smallest way because he didn't want to feel compassion for an opponent. That would be bad for business.

As the conversations with Kobe continued, this intensity of purpose became one of the defining themes that he would return to again and again, punctuated with his advice: "Do not have a Plan B. If you have a Plan B, you might cave out." Commit to putting everything you have into the moment, which was pretty much what NBA fans (whether they rooted for or against Kobe) had come to expect. The point is that the creative teams were getting invaluable insights from the athlete, and this creative fuel powered what became one of the most popular and iconic Nike campaigns from that era.

What most fans didn't know is that, despite his Black Mamba personality, Kobe had a great capacity to laugh at himself. He could wink at his own intensity, which partly explains why over the years he was one of the best creative collaborators I have ever worked with. His self-awareness allowed him to dive deeply into our creative efforts to shape stories around him. And so, a concept, which Kobe very much was a participant in, began to take shape: What if we used this intensity, took it to the extreme, and had some fun with it? What if we showed this whole other dimension that so few have ever seen?

With this in mind, and with more insights and truths than we could ever ask for, Nike launched the "Kobe System: Success for the Successful" campaign in January 2012, which coincided with the release of his revolutionary new signature shoe, the Nike Kobe IX. The central idea of the film series was that Kobe was a self-help guru whose intensity more often confounded than inspired his audience. The very name "Success for the Successful" riffs on the idea that all too often these speakers sounded impressive but said very little of substance. Nevertheless, Kobe's "seminars" were filled with very successful people—the very people who least needed to hear the mantras Kobe was saying. I'm talking about Serena Williams, Jerry Rice, comedian Aziz Ansari, and, of course, Tony Robbins. In one, Sir Richard Branson is talking to Kobe onstage about the incredible achievements he's accomplished:

Branson: "Gone to the bottom of the ocean."
Kobe: "Me too."

Branson: "Gone to outer space."
Kobe: "Ditto"
Branson: "I feel like I'm already living 'success at success.'"
Kobe: "You're welcome."
[Applause]

That last bit—"You're welcome"—became something of a cultural moment. Nike has a legacy of introducing catchphrases into popular culture through its brand communication. Starting with "There Is No Finish Line," there was "Just Do It" to Mars Blackmon's "Got to Be the Shoes." Now, thanks to Kobe, we can add "You're welcome" to the list.

"The Kobe System" brought a completely different dimension to Kobe, one that played off his competitive reputation and alter ego, the Black Mamba, but which was also self-deprecating. In some of the films, basketball isn't even mentioned, so one might wonder how the "Kobe System" campaign advanced Nike's brand. Even more directly, what did this have to do with the Nike brand's personality? For starters, the series expressed different characteristics of Kobe himself. Before the campaign, Kobe was mostly seen through his on-court persona, the Black Mamba, a fierce competitor whose competitive spirit rivaled Jordan's. But now the audience saw these other dimensions of Kobe, most obviously the humorous side. Yes, he'd crush you on the court, but he could also see the humor in his intensity, and had the comedic timing to show you. There were also films in the campaign that were genuinely helpful, where Kobe would teach valuable basketball skills. In other words, Kobe wanted to share his talent and his love of the game with others, especially the younger generations. While he was always the Black Mamba on the court, off it there was a profound capacity for curiosity and creative collaboration.

In these ways, the campaign pushed the edges of Kobe's brand personality, filling out his characteristics with a more complete picture. Likewise, Nike was able to push the edges of its own brand by showcasing one of its near-superhuman athletes in an approachable and more human light. The marketing of sports can too often verge on idolization, transforming athletes into untouchable marble figures. What gets lost in such displays is the person behind the idol and, by extension, the emotional connection consumers like you and me want to feel when we think about our favorite athletes. We don't want to worship them. We want to be inspired by them. Marble figures can't do that; but human beings can.

Master Class, Before Master Class

The "Kobe System" campaign also is in this section on brand voice because it featured a revolutionary approach to a media and content distribution strategy. Rather than just one main television commercial, Enrico Balleri, Nike's head of Brand Communication, and Dan Sheniak, Wieden & Kennedy's head of Communications Planning, developed a strategy that led to the creation of an entire world of short-form content. Each of the featured successful members of the audience within the main ad also got their own thirty-second short with Kobe. In addition, as entertaining as the Kobe System was, it was equally serious in the level of basketball knowledge and skills included within the campaign. The idea was to create a system of content, to mirror the system within Kobe's shoe design. We had a series of video lessons that dropped each day—just like a master class—and they were promoted on ESPN's *SportsCenter* each day of the week. Kobe was completely onboard to do all of that video content. Each video lesson drove you to a deeper experience online that had practical basketball tips and lessons that could actually make you a better player for real. We also had a team that did daily digital reactive content throughout the basketball season on Twitter, both validating and putting that system in action. When it was all over, kids continued the campaign by creating their own content and testimonials to say, "I'm on the Kobe System."

By using platforms like YouTube, we were able to stream branded content—and engage consumers at a level that television commercials at the time simply couldn't match—before the rest of the industry was able to catch up. (And by then, YouTube had evolved its terms of services with brands.) "The Kobe System" would likely have been successful as a television campaign, although its scope would have been greatly reduced. But what makes the campaign stand out (then and now) is that Nike was making use of the growing opportunities afforded by new content platforms. We were able to reach audiences (mostly younger) that we otherwise would have missed, expanding the reach of our voice through new digital realms.

Find Your Greatness

Nike often used its voice as a way to open up the world of sports to new audiences. The brand itself insisted time and again that sports are for everyone, not just for the exceptional few. There are dozens of examples from Nike's history that showcase its efforts to reach beyond the traditional definition of an athlete, but perhaps none did so as effectively and as purposefully as 2012's "Find Your Greatness" campaign.

The Olympics always presented Nike with a great vehicle to launch major campaigns that retold or redefined a part of its brand for new (and often younger) audiences. The 2012 London Olympics was just such a moment, and my team and I focused on a line in Nike's brand mission statement: "If you have a body, you're an athlete." What, after all, do the Olympics represent than a celebration of human athleticism? It's a moment when all humanity can join together and rejoice in our shared love of sport. Yet while the Olympics showcases humanity's best athletes, we wanted to use the occasion to shine a light on one of Nike's core tenets. What's more, we saw an opportunity to *redefine greatness* for the rest of us humans. Greatness, in the end, is a relative term, and what makes each of us great athletes is as varied as all the things that make us unique human beings. And so was born the "Find Your Greatness" campaign, which at the time was the most globally expansive campaign Nike had done.

London Everywhere

During our planning sessions, Alberto Ponte from Wieden & Kennedy referenced the fact that there are at least twenty-nine cities in the world named London. What would otherwise be just a banal piece of trivia was for us the key that unlocked the whole campaign. If the greatest athletes in the world were competing in London, England, what were the athletes doing in the other Londons all around the world? They were surely achieving greatness in their own way, and this insight gave us the perfect creative device to launch a campaign whose core idea was that greatness is everywhere and for everyone.

The ad opens with a water tower in the town of London, Ohio. With quick cuts, the viewer sees athletes of all ages, engaged in various sports or activities in London, Jamaica; London, India; and London, Nigeria, to name a few. The voice-over, provided by actor Tom Hardy, begins:

"There are no grand celebrations here. No speeches, no bright lights. But there are great athletes. Somehow we've come to believe that greatness is reserved for the chosen few, for the superstars. The truth is, greatness is for all of us. This is not about lowering expectations; it's about raising them for every last one of us. Because greatness is not in one special place and it is not in one special person. Greatness is wherever somebody is trying to find it."

The film ends with the campaign logotype "Find Your Greatness," over the footage of a small child standing atop an Olympic diving platform. The boy is scratching his head and swaying, clearly unsure if he should jump or not. It's a long way down. And then he jumps.

Think about the first time you jumped off a high dive. If you were like most kids, you probably wanted to climb back down the ladder the moment you peeked over the edge. No one could have forced you to jump if you didn't want to. The boy in the film wasn't forced; he was empowered. He took that leap, not entirely sure how it would end, because he felt a surge of inspiration; that leap meant something to him. And he took it knowing he would be different when he resurfaced. The leap is not the end. It is the beginning of something amazing.

The Jogger

A country road. Buzzing flies. Summer. Heat. Humidity. Early morning or early evening. A lone jogger in the distance. Then Hardy's voice-over, as the jogger approaches the camera:

"Greatness—it's just something we made up. Somehow we've come to believe that greatness is a gift, reserved for a chosen few. For prodigies. For superstars. And the rest of us can only stand by watching. You can forget that. Greatness is not some rare DNA strand. It's not some precious thing. Greatness is no more unique to us than breathing. We're all capable of it. All of us."

Then the call to action "Find Your Greatness" over the final shots of the jogger, who, the viewer realizes halfway through the ad, is an overweight twelve-year-old boy. Maybe I'm biased, but "The Jogger" is masterful storytelling, perfectly articulating the point of the "Find Your Greatness" campaign (redefining greatness), and expanding Nike's brand personality at the same time.

Nathan Sorrell, the jogger, was the key, of course. How we portrayed him was absolutely critical, because we were balanced on a knife's edge of either generating a profound emotional moment or being accused of insensitivity. Many subtle creative decisions went into the execution, from wardrobe and art direction to location and sound design. As we talked about in the previous chapter, on brand identity, the last 10 percent of the creative process oftentimes determines if you'll hit the right note.

As an aside, eight months after the film launched, Nathan was invited onto the *Today* show, where he spoke about how inspired *he* was by the film and had lost thirty-two pounds. Looking back, he told the hosts: "I still can't believe that was me then, and this is me now."

Greatness, indeed.

A Brand Invitation

"Find Your Greatness" is many things. But it is above all an invitation to perceived nonathletes and nonsports fans, not just the superstars. Elevating the great ones and turning them into icons of inspiration takes up a lot of what we did. But a viewer watches a Nike ad that takes them to Londons all over the world and doesn't see a single superstar. They see people just playing. They're riding bikes. They're on a field playing rugby or baseball. Do you remember when you just used to ... play?

Brands need to continually look at creative ways in which to invite more people into their worlds. This requires having a pulse on the culture, an awareness of the trends, the styles, the artists who are shaping it. Then, a much harder trick, finding those areas where those cultural markers intersect with sport, thus opening doors for people who don't necessarily have a passion for the specific arena you are representing as a brand. In some cases, of course, this technique can work backward, by bringing the past into the present and pulling generations together. Trying to stay ahead of the culture more often than not helps a brand invite younger consumers. Mining the past and playing on nostalgia helps invite older generations. When mashed together, however, you can pull the generations closer.

Music is one such way that Nike used both methods. From using classic songs in a modern context to remixing them with the hottest DJs to using musicians that are just about to break out, Nike commercials (created in partnership with Wieden & Kennedy) have always told stories through images *and* sound. The 2002 World Cup film that featured Elvis Presley's "Little Less Conversation" as remixed by Dutch DJ JXL showed a secret tournament between the best footballers in the world. There was the Michael Mann–directed 2007 Nike ad "Leave Nothing," that showed NFL players Shawne Merriman and Steven Jackson blowing through offenses and defenses while "Promontory," the theme from *The Last of the Mohicans*, played in the background. Last but not least, we had musician Andre 3000 covering the Beatles' "All Together Now" as a backdrop for the NBA Finals Playoff ad featuring Kobe Bryant's greatest hits in pursuit of the Lakers' next championship.

There's a reason these ads were able to hit those powerful emotional chords. Music, perhaps more than any other creative medium, has the power to inspire us, to make us remember, and to bring us together.

Timing Is Everything

In 2015, the Cubs were ahead of schedule. What I mean is that the club had its eyes set on the World Series, and Cubs president Theo Epstein—who had brought championships to the Boston Red Sox—was building his team to reach the October Classic in 2017 or 2018. But the Cubs finished the 2015 regular season with the third-best record in baseball and earned a wild card spot in the playoffs. They then beat the Pittsburgh Pirates in the wild card game and advanced to the Division Series against the St. Louis Cardinals, whom they also beat three games to one. Now the Cubs found themselves in the National League Championship series, their first since 2003, and which they hadn't won since 1945. The Cubs were four wins away from the World Series.

There was no way that we at Nike were going to miss out on this literally once-in-a-lifetime moment. The Cubs winning the World Series, which they hadn't done since 1908, would be one of the greatest events in the history of sports. So we leapt into action and put together a story to commemorate what was a very real possibility. (But only a possibility.) The ad was pretty simple, too. A teenage boy, wearing his Cubs uniform, is talking to himself as he steps to the pitcher's mound in some neighborhood diamond, the Chicago skyline visible behind the outfield. To the voice of Willie Nelson, singing "Funny How Time Slips Away," the kid is doing the impossible: He's playing baseball by himself. He's pitching to ghost batters. He's knocking dingers over the fence. He's

142

trying to steal third...before the ghost pitcher attempts a pickoff. As the kid knocks one deep into left, we hear Harry Carey with the call: "Way back! It might be outta here...Cubs win! Cubs win!" The boy is dancing on home plate as the words flash across the screen: "Goodbye someday."

But not that day...or that season. The New York Mets swept the Cubs in four games, and we had to shelve our ad. Maybe forever. I mean, nowhere was it written that the Cubs would eventually win the World Series. Fortunately, they did, the very next year. In one of the greatest Game 7s in Series history, the Cubs beat the Cleveland Indians and took home the championship for Chicago for the first time in 108 years. And we were ready with a story to tell (albeit a year later than planned).

Like the "Find Your Greatness" campaign, "Someday" doesn't celebrate the superstar. It's an homage to the long-suffering Cub fans. But more than that, it's a film that goes to the heart of what baseball means to us as Americans: Many of us have the kid still inside us, wearing the uniform of their favorite team, dreaming of a day when that team takes it all.

When a brand uses its voice is as important as what that voice says and how it says it. "Someday" is a pretty extreme example of hitting a moment just right, but I use it to emphasize the larger point. Good timing comes down to preparation. With "Someday," as with "What Should I Do?" we are responding to an event that is outside our control. This is a much different challenge than, say, "The Kobe System," which is in fact a pure creation, borne from conversations with Kobe and looking at what we want to accomplish as a brand. But when you respond to an event, your principle challenge is discovering how you want to respond to it. What does your response say about your brand, your values, your vision, your direction as an organization? Where does the event intersect with your brand characteristics? Lastly, what is the real significance of the event? We could have easily put out an ad that celebrated the Chicago Cubs as a team, perhaps using old footage of Cubs teams over the years with some Hall of Famers thrown in. Instead, we celebrated the child inside all of us who isn't weighed down by "curses" or years of disappointment. The child is the stand-in for all the inner children over the century and eight years that had hoped the Cubs would win it all.

There is another side to preparation, too, that isn't as reactive. I'm referring to the preparation that an organization needs to have internally. Do you, when the event or moment occurs, have the processes and structure in place to turn on a dime and deliver an emotional story that not only responds to the event, but does so in a way that expands your brand personality? When I spoke about the restructure Nike performed back in chapter 2, it was so that we could respond—or anticipate—events like a Cubs World Series. This is a far harder challenge than simply being able to turn around something quick. It's about an organization's internal structure, its ability to see a moment coming and elevate its importance above other preexisting priorities; and to always be asking, "What if?" That's how you *win before the moment*, rather than waiting for the result.

Dare to Be Remembered

What are we as brand storytellers really trying to do with our work? Are we hoping to create only for the moment? Are we trying to just sell our products or services? The reason I use "Dare to Be Remembered" as the title for this chapter is because no story worth telling should be forgotten. We are engaged in building a life for our brand, one story at a time. We want these stories to be thoughtful. We want them to be funny. We want them to reveal something deeper about us and the world in which we live. We want them to connect with our audience in a way that compels them to *feel something*. In short, we want them to be stories that are remembered. Our work shouldn't cease to exist when we do; instead, it should carry on, retelling our brand's story again and again, just as the younger generations might discover a classic novel. Those words will never die, as long as there are eyes to read them. So too should you strive to build a brand with stories that leave behind something that will connect with audiences long after you've left the scene.

PRINCIPLES FOR "DARE TO BE REMEMBERED"

1. REVEAL YOUR SOUL

Pull back the curtain to offer a clear view of your brand values. Allow the audience to see your personality, and in turn, they will respond to your humanity.

2. EXPAND YOUR EDGES

Your brand voice should never be static. It is a constantly shifting blend of characteristics, beliefs, and passions. By expressing different traits, your relatability becomes the ultimate invitation into your brand.

3. LISTEN BEFORE YOU LEAD

You'll have plenty of ways to express yourself. Before you do, listen to who you are serving, know their environment, understand their mission, and see their challenges to fulfill their dream.

4. MAKE PEOPLE FEEL

We are at our best when we worry less about how people feel about us and more about how we make them feel about themselves and their ability to achieve their definition of greatness.

5. EMBRACE THE GAUNTLET

Fight for your creativity, but invite diverse perspectives into the room along the way. To achieve a story that is indeed remembered, welcome the rigor and discourse when creating it.

6. WIN BEFORE THE MOMENT

Don't wait until the moment of truth happens. Plan for the best outcome, and create a story that is ready when it matters most.

CHAPTER 6

DON'T CHASE COOL

If it's classic it's gonna last forever then
I'm everywhere you never been and better than I ever been
—"Classic (Better Than I've Ever Been)"

The first and only time this song was performed live was at the Gotham Hall venue in New York City in December 2006. The artists Rakim, Kanye West, Nas, and KRS-One sang it together on an incredibly small stage for about five hundred people who had been invited to this special event put on by Nike. Any one of these rappers could've filled a venue many times the size of Gotham Hall by himself, and yet they all had come to celebrate with Nike the anniversary of an icon. Underneath the domed ceiling of this one-time bank, the oval room had been transformed into both a stage and a showcase.

The guests entered through a large white shoebox, then walked down a brightly lit corridor that ran around the elliptical interior of the venue. The walls of the corridor were lined with 1,700 versions of a single sneaker, leading the guests to the floor. While the event was exclusive, MTV was on hand to record the performances of those legendary artists, who all also sang their own solo sets, and would air it a few weeks later. Never before (and never again) would this collection of artists perform together—and the audience knew it. Never before (and likely never again) would this collection of sneakers be on display in one place—and the audience definitely knew that, too. That was the point of the event and why we called it "1NightOnly." For a single moment, we were going to come together, from Patrick Ewing to Rasheed Wallace to Spike Lee, to celebrate something we all loved; that we all respected; and that we all believed was the pinnacle of function and style.

Seems kind of crazy that all this was for a single shoe, but that was the power of the Air Force 1, the most important sneaker in history.

The Creation of an Icon

As the head of Nike Brand Design at the time, I was in the audience, both as a representative of the company as well as a long-time Air Force 1 devotee. Like many teens of the '80s, my relationship with the Swoosh came alongside my own hoop dreams. In 1984, I played on the freshman basketball team in high school. I had the athleticism but a below-average jump shot. Instead of honing the game's technical aspects, I just wanted to imitate the superstars I saw on TV, especially Moses Malone, who at the time played center for the Philadelphia 76ers. The year prior, in 1983, Malone had led the Sixers to an NBA Championship. The shoes he was wearing during the season? Red-and-white Air Force 1s.

Of course, I had to have a pair of my own. My parents bought me some used Air Force 1 Highs, and I was in love immediately. Every time I put them on, repeating the ritual of lacing and pulling the strap across the top, I had this confidence and a belief that

I could float on air. Thus, my hoop dreams, however delusional they might have been, would grow. But I soon realized that even my Air Force 1s weren't going to improve my jump shot. Still, I loved those shoes. It was the beginning of my emotional attachment with a brand.

And I wasn't the only one, not by a long shot.

Nike launched the first Air Force 1 in 1982. At the time, Nike was most known as a running-shoe company, the designs for which are very different from a basketball shoe. When Bruce Kilgore started to design what would become the first AF1, he didn't look at running shoes—he looked at Nike's hiking boots for inspiration. The reason, he said, was because the hiking boot was built for flexibility and support throughout a range of motions, whereas a running shoe is designed for a single motion—heel, then toe. The movements of a basketball player on the court, especially the pivot motion, demanded a shoe that could provide support, comfort, and versatility. Throughout the process, Bruce "designed for performance," meaning that the AF1 was made *for* basketball players and *only* basketball players. Whether the players agreed is another matter, but there was an authenticity to the shoe from the very beginning. Bruce created several innovative basketball-focused design features, including a new circular outsole pattern that allowed the player to freely pivot without sliding. The innovation I remember most as a kid, of course, was the air bag inside the heel. This was emphasized by the first tagline for the Air Force 1: "Starting this season, air will be sold by the box." The poster on which this tagline was displayed literally just showed a white Air Force 1 shoebox with a basketball resting on top, conveying a sense of wonder and mystery, but also defined purpose.

Of course, as they say, the proof is in the pudding. The Air Force 1 wasn't the first Nike basketball shoe (the company had released the Blazer in 1972). But Nike's presence in the basketball market wasn't large. At the start of the 1982 NBA season, Nike figured it would go big. Six NBA players were selected to represent the shoe—Malone and Bobby Jones of the Sixers; Michael Cooper and Jamaal Wilkes of the LA Lakers; and Calvin Natt and Mychal Thompson of the hometown Portland Trail Blazers. The "Original Six," as they would come to be called, were immortalized in one of the only marketing pieces Nike did for the AF1, a poster of the six players in all-white flight suits on the tarmac with a glowing sky and a jet in the background, the Air Force 1 type across the bottom. So iconic was this poster and the players within it that decades later, the Japanese toy company Medicom created a pack of posable action figures of each player.

The poster raised the AF1's profile for sure, but nothing beat the images of those six players on the court, especially Malone, who took the Sixers all the way to the championship a year later. The usual marketing strategy, at this stage, would be to develop a commercial with Malone, fresh from his championship victory, sporting his AF1s. But Nike didn't do that. In fact, Nike has never created a single commercial for the shoe in its forty-year history. It didn't need to. And that would have been that, just the story of Nike's latest entry into the basketball market with a highly successful shoe. By 1984, the shoe had been discontinued, as the company moved on to designing its next court sneaker, the Dunk. At the time, this was normal business procedure, even if demand for the AF1 remained high. The AF1 now belonged to history.

But history didn't work out like that. The demand for the AF1 was so high that even distributors were calling on Nike for another run. By this point, the shoe had already become a sensation, no doubt helped by its scarcity on the market. Especially among the young, the shoe had achieved a kind of status that can only be compared to the Converse Chuck Taylor. Except in this case, a lot of the youth sporting them were from the cities along the I-95 corridor, from Philadelphia to New York City. Having moved from the court to the streets, the AF1 was no longer just a shoe for performance; it was an icon, a symbol to convey authenticity and a shared culture. In 1986, Nike bowed to the still white-hot market demand, and announced the launch of the Air Force 2.

Today, there are 1,700 versions of the AF1 in existence, and the shoe, with basically zero changes except color and material variations, remains in production. Not bad for a product that to this day has never had a single commercial.

Respect the Legacy

The original team behind the creation of the shoe could never have imagined the iconic status and cultural impact the Air Force 1 would have on the future of sport and style culture. Generation after generation of athletes and sneaker enthusiasts have had a deep respect and love for this shoe. Why? What made the Air Force 1 so special to so many? Why, even forty years later, does the shoe continue to have an enduring cultural relevance that sets it apart?

Brands have the ability to create cultural icons, even if this happens only in rare instances. Yet so much of what makes an icon is decided by the consumers, not the brand. In many ways, a brand can't predict what the consumers will launch into iconic status. But we can design products and stories that start from an authentic insight and are clear in the role they serve and play; if an innovation is to rise above the clutter and connect with an audience more deeply, it has to start there. The Air Force 1 is an example of a product that was designed authentically for the athlete's needs as its guiding star. An important reason it stands above the other basketball shoes that came after it is because its unique form was born out of its function. From there, not everything was in Nike's power to create brand resonance around the AF1, but it was certainly within our power to protect the icon we had created. And we did that by respecting both the shoe and those who loved it.

When you dig a little deeper into the history of the AF1, you see how important it was from the beginning to position the shoe as a player's shoe built for performance. That positioning, accomplished through storytelling and athletes, landed in the marketplace, on the court, and in the minds of consumers. The Air Force 1 wasn't tied to any *specific* athlete, as later Nike basketball sneakers would be. In fact, one of the reasons Nike used six different athletes, who all had their own game and played different positions, was to emphasize that the AF1 was for *every* basketball player. Initially, the shoe itself had to work without the trappings of a big-name star supporting it. And it did, as early testers of the shoe often refused to return them. That authentic positioning was reinforced by the way the professional players like Malone and others adopted the shoe as their own. They didn't just wear AF1s; they won in them. Consumers picked up on this, drawn to an innovation that was now proving to be a force on the court, a new product that had been endorsed by the pros—not through an overt display of corporate sponsorship, but through sheer grit on the court.

Over the years, Nike let this authenticity speak for itself. There was no barrage of marketing materials attached to the shoe or the players who wore it. I think this allowed a natural emotional attachment to form between the shoe and customers. By holding back, Nike added to the AF1's authenticity, and thus its adoption by the street.

Which brings us to the twenty-fifth anniversary of the Air Force 1 and a big brand event known as "1NightOnly," which coincided with the release of a new edition of the shoe. The challenge for us—and in my role as head of Brand Design at the time— was pretty clear: How do we celebrate the Air Force 1's iconic status without diminishing its legacy? Michael Shea, who was then a creative director on my team, working on storytelling for the Air Force 1, looking back at this important moment, made an apt analogy: "From the beginning, we had to reckon with the fact that the Air Force 1 had become much like the classic Levi 501 jeans; an icon re-adopted by generations."

Yet the very idea of celebrating the AF1 meant that we would be infringing on Nike's historic restraint in marketing a shoe that meant so much to so many. Since the AF1 had debuted in 1982, the culture—especially youth culture—had changed, and consumers tuned out when they felt overly marketed to. Less was more, as far as young consumers were concerned, and slapping your logo on everything was a surefire way to reduce that emotional attachment. If we weren't absolutely deliberate and careful in how we went about the AF1 anniversary, then we might actually harm the very thing we wanted to celebrate. Nobody wanted to be on the team that didn't protect and respect the legacy of the Air Force 1.

The Product Is the Hero

Before there were hip-hop artists attached, before MTV was going to be on hand to record the event, before there was going to be a huge white Air Force 1 shoebox to serve as a gateway to the event, there were the shoes. Whatever we decided to do, the shoes had to be the focus—the classic all-white AF1. Our initial planning called for creating the largest collection of AF1s ever exhibited in one place, and everything else was going to orbit around this central showcase like the planets around the sun. The company's Department of Nike Archives (or DNA) was the place to start amassing as many different varieties of AF1s as we could, but even DNA didn't have all 1,700 versions. So we expanded our search to the dedicated sneaker collectors around the world, asking if they'd be willing to loan us their AF1 collections. You may as well ask a mother to loan you her baby. These collectors were wary of any corporate entity—even Nike!—traveling around with their precious possessions. Our solution was to limit the loan to *one night only*. Many agreed, and we had our collection, and the focal point of our anniversary event.

After that, the other major elements of the celebration started to fall into place, including the location. Gotham Hall is actually just one room in what had once been the old Greenwich Savings Bank, which had closed its doors in 1981. The exterior of the building has the classical architecture popular in the 1920s and 1930s, with Corinthian columns on three sides of the building and a Roman-inspired dome. The central banking room was in the shape of an ellipse, with the dome rising magnificently overhead, and teller windows protecting an old-style vault. Perfect. We couldn't think of a better symbol than a bank to represent the importance of protecting the image of Air Force 1 as something extremely valuable. Every inch of this space was put to work to tell the story of the value of the AF1, and why its legacy must be protected. It wasn't valuable because of the price; it was valuable because of the attachment so many had for it. Memories, moments, the future—these were the jewels that glittered on each pair of AF1s. And so it was around this central ellipse that we built the glowing white display cases that showed off the 1,700 AF1 varieties, the treasure in the heart of the venue and in each guest.

Of course, the display cases weren't the only place where guests could admire the shoe itself. They could also look at what everyone else was wearing. Indeed, many sported their own AF1s to the celebration, which we knew was one of the major draws of the event. AF1 enthusiasts admiring each other's prized pairs. We decided to create a moment at the front door, where a photographer with a Polaroid camera could capture everyone entering the event along a white—not red—carpet. From there the guests would ascend a six-foot round stage built to resemble the pivot point on the AF1 sole—the innovation that Bruce had spent so much time designing in 1982—providing necessary and appreciated product cues to the guests. The pictures would be snapped from the knees down—no faces—emphasizing that the AF1 on the feet were the stars, not just the guests. It was about the shoes. Guests could then sign their own Polaroids, which would then be pinned to a mural nearby. Now we had this growing gallery of autographed Polaroids of all the best Air Force 1s ever gathered in one place. After the event, we packaged them all up like a book and sent one to every guest. Today, we still see some of them as profile photos on social media.

Throughout the planning process, we had to constantly remind ourselves about the event's purpose. When you're planning something with artists, celebrities, and professional athletes, there's a tendency to make *them* the central focus. In some cases, this makes sense, but in the case of the Air Force 1, it would have taken away from the icon. I remember a conversation in a crucial meeting early on when the question came up of why we thought people would come to "1NightOnly." Why would anyone think this was cool? Which was another way of asking: Why should the consumer care? In response someone said, "Because you will never be able to see all four of these hip-hop icons onstage at once, ever, anywhere else." I admit, this was compelling even *for me*, as someone who had grown up listening to the artists who would now be performing in one of the most intimate venues imaginable. But, looking at it another way, why were the artists there? Just to give a show? No. The same person then said, "It's because of the shoe collection." There it was, the ah-ha moment. As Mars Blackmon once said, "It's gotta be the shoes."

The Second Coming

"1NightOnly" was just part of Nike's efforts to commemorate the Air Force 1. In 2007, we introduced the new Air Force 1 poster featuring a whole new cast of basketball superstars. As Ray Butts, who was driving art direction for the AF1 anniversary, told me, "Frankly, the 'Original Six' Air Force 1 poster was so iconic it would have been crazy to deviate from that aesthetic. Our goal was just to put a modern spin on the original poster and hope that it would live up to the original." The poster wasn't an ad for the Air Force 1—neither old nor new—but rather a callback to the poster and the shoe that had helped elevate Nike Basketball in the first place.

Instead of six players, Butts and his team had ten stars: Shawn Marion, Rasheed Wallace, Steve Nash, Amare Stoudamire, LeBron James, Kobe Bryant, Chris Paul, Paul Pierce, Jermaine O'Neal, and

Tony Parker. As with the original poster, the players were dressed in all white, standing on a tarmac, the brilliantly shining sun behind them, outlining the hills and the airport terminals. The aesthetic was similar enough to pay homage to the original but was also brighter, the contrasts between the horizon, the tarmac, and the players clearer. It was a callback but also a step forward, bringing Nike Basketball into the future.

The twenty-fifth anniversary of the Air Force 1 gave us an opportunity to celebrate a cultural icon. From "1NightOnly" to "Second Coming" to the new edition of the shoe itself, we could recognize the impact of the original while introducing the shoe to an entirely new generation of players and consumers. There were right and wrong ways to do this. Had we strayed from the core of what had made the shoe great, then we would have diminished that legacy, one that exemplified the idea of communal ownership. Because, in many ways, the Air Force 1 no longer belonged to only Nike. If we treated the shoe and its heritage as exclusively Nike's, then we would have alienated the consumers whose attachment to the product came from something other than marketing. As Butts said, "We likened the AF1 to a Porsche 911 as an iconic form that stayed true to its original expression over time, while allowing an authentic, relevant evolution to thoughtfully take place." Nike didn't set out to make the AF1 a "street" shoe; consumers did that. We should avoid taking credit for what consumers do with our products that are beyond our scope and reach. But we should get out of the way and let it happen.

As a brand team, we were able to recognize the elements of the AF1 that had made it popular—its authenticity and Nike's strategy of empowering customers to make the shoe their own—and nurture them through the decades. Above all, as Ray said, "we never lost sight of who we came to the dance with." Whatever we did, the focus *had to be* on the shoe and those who loved it.

The Confluence of Art and Culture

Once upon a time, circa 2006, the HBO series *Entourage* was one of the biggest hit shows in the country. The show followed an actor and his friends as they navigated the world of Hollywood, the perils of celebrity, and loudmouthed agents. In one of the episodes, Vince the actor presents his friend Turtle, the show's resident "sneaker head," with a pair of laser-engraved Air Force 1s. The low-top sneakers have gold trim and Turtle's name engraved on the toe vamp. They're gorgeous, an ostentatious display of art and style—and Turtle loves them. Viewers might have thought that the shoes were made specifically for the show. I mean, would Nike really spend time and resources creating these finely engraved sneakers that look more like art than shoes? Yes, Nike would and did. In fact, the laser engraving was the work of my friend Mark Smith, who was the creative director within Nike's Innovation Kitchen.

People had been drawing on their sneakers for years as a way to personalize a mass-market product, one which they nevertheless felt a deep emotional attachment toward. Much like graffiti artists do with urban landscapes, the personal touches put on shoes could be said to be a kind of artwork—taking something that isn't supposed to be art and transforming it into something meaningful, if not to others, then at least to the owners. In other words, creating a personalized icon. The "shoe as canvas" was the inspiration behind the laser-engraved sneakers, but the story is much deeper than that.

In the early 2000s, Mark happened to see another Nike team-mate in the Kitchen experimenting with laser cutting to slice materials. This gave him an idea to use the laser not to cut leather, but to engrave it. He started experimenting with some designs, just for himself, using motifs as inspiration from ancient war-rior masks found in Maori culture. Soon, he reached out to art-ist friends to show them his work, only to discover that they too wanted to experiment and see what the laser could do with their own inspirations. The result of this experimental lasering led to designs inspired by surf art, street graffiti, and Celtic symbolism, to name a few. It was as if Mark and his artist friends were redis-covering an age-old method of expressing stories on objects. And that might have been that. Just Mark experimenting with a cool new technique, indulging his creative passion with a new art form.

Enter the Energy Centers, and my role in this story. In 2003, we created "innovation galleries" as a new form of high-touch mar-keting that allowed us to connect with the creative communities in the most influential cities, exploring the intersection between art and sports like never before. It was a way to get under the surface of a city and engage with the networks of creators: art-ists, DJs, stylists, photographers, and designers. One "Energy Cen-ter" was the legendary Blue House on 523 Ocean Front Walk in Venice Beach. The house was built in 1901 and had been a gath-ering place for a variety of colorful figures, including Jim Mor-rison of the Doors. Another was in New York City on Elizabeth Street in Soho. These were small spaces, hardly on the scale of the big galleries of LA or New York City. But they were perfect for our purposes.

It's a mistake, however, to think of these locations as mere art galleries, although that's certainly where the idea came from. There weren't any white walls, roped-off paintings, and "Please

Don't Touch" signs. These environments were designed to be hands-on and immersive, spaces that engaged all of the senses. Nike stores displayed our products, where consumers could touch and discover them across multiple categories. But there was only so much we could convey about the stories behind the innovations and the athletes they propelled. The Energy Centers solved the problem: They gave us the space and freedom to have a much more singular and deeper approach to storytelling. We could use the Centers to focus on a particular theme, much like a gallery has an exhibition on one artist or style. But we could also expand this idea to include workshops, events, even small concerts—all focused on one aspect of Nike innovation through storytelling. It's amazing what you can accomplish within a thousand square feet.

Some of the exhibitions we put on at the Centers included:

Reconstruct: An exhibition about recycling and repurposing Nike products into all-new forms, from tents to furniture to dresses. We wanted to build a conversation on sustainable innovation long before it became a focus for many brands.

The Genealogy of Speed: A showcase on Nike footwear innovation over the years with the focus on speed. Grooves along one wall were shaped to look like the air intake of a jet, and featured the groundbreaking shoes that allowed a viewer to understand the timeline and evolution of Nike's pursuit of creating faster footwear. The tagline of the event programing stated: "Fifteen curated stories of speed as told through time, motion, metaphor, and sound."

Given my experience at the Walker Art Center, I felt I was well prepared to lead the team in the design and curation of the Energy Centers. I was inspired by the idea of sharing the characteristics of the Nike brand through new artistic expressions. To do that, our team of architects, writers, art directors, and film producers created immersive spaces filled with dynamic storytelling that provided visitors with the opportunity to get closer to the magic of Nike's innovations.

One of the best parts of the Energy Centers—from a creative standpoint—was that we weren't bound by commercial concerns. Our primary motive wasn't to sell product; it was to serve a segment of our audience that drew inspiration from how artistic expression could come from Nike innovations and how those innovations could benefit the world beyond sports.

This space was for them to explore the world of Nike away from the field or court. Yes, it was rarefied air—hardly something for mass consumption—but that was why the scale, ultimately, was small. Just two locations, one on each coast, serving an eclectic creative community.

Within these locations, the canvas for artistic expression would be shoes—or, more precisely, Mark's laser-engraving method applied to shoes. Initially, his idea was to use shoes as a medium—tattooing the leather canvases to tell stories. As a gallery invites an artist to showcase their work in a creative way, so we wanted to give Mark the space of one of the Energy Centers to tell his story. The idea was to present a collection of shoes that Mark had engraved, with each expressing a different cultural visual language.

On some of the tongues of the shoes on display, Mark had lasered a flame, to signify the power of the sun's fire focused on a single point. Mark also added a few other personal touches, such as a smile on the heels of a pair of Nike Cortez and Air Force 1s. As Mark said, "Me just grinning at the world through this fun new technology."

The response from the community was tremendous, as people became fascinated with the lasering process itself. In fact, the laser-engraved shoes hit such a chord with the public that we decided to offer limited-run editions. One of those editions showed up on *Entourage*. What we realized was that we could use the lasering process to tell stories for specific shoes and specific athletes. Mark would go on a tour across the globe to talk about his method and demonstrate it in front of a variety of audiences. Eventually, the technique landed on the Air Jordan XX, with the complete enthusiasm of MJ himself. Mark designed the midfoot strap that featured a laser collage of iconography representing important moments in Jordan's career. For instance, there was a lasered image of the sportscar Jordan had bought after he had earned enough money, as well as a toolbox with the word "Pops" lasered across it—a reference to Jordan's father, who was a master with tools. The iconography was what allowed the owner of the sneakers to get closer to what shaped Michael on and off the court, like never before.

For many, the Air Jordan XX would be the pinnacle of the "lasered" shoes, but not for me. While Mark gladly lasered up kicks for an assortment of athletes and celebrities outside of his day job, it was in 2015, when President Barack Obama visited the Nike campus, and Mark and the rest of the team were able to present the forty-fourth president with a custom pair of Air Force 1s, laser engraved with the number 44.

From a technique that started as a way for Mark to simply exercise his curiosity and imagination, the laser-engraving method struck a cultural chord, aided by the support Nike gave "the process outside the process," especially by showcasing it at the Energy Centers. The laser innovation landed on a hit TV show; it found its way into the artistic communities of New York City and Los

Angeles, landed on the game shoe for the GOAT, and finally, it was presented to the president of the United States. This is how a product becomes a cultural icon: by becoming the canvas for a much deeper, and personalized experience.

Democratized Design

When I took my team into one of the iconic tailor shops in London's Savile Row, I wanted them to experience the four elements that have made these destinations world-famous: service, craft, personalization, and style. Centuries of tradition, fine-tuned down to the tiniest detail, can be found in these shops. The service that one experiences as the tailor takes your measurements is designed to ensure that the cut, fit, material, thread, buttons, and every other element will be considered to represent your body and your personality perfectly, through a suit. When you buy a suit from Savile Row, you aren't just paying for the cloth; you're paying for a level of service once reserved for royalty. And while I didn't buy a suit that day—as much as I wanted to—it reaffirmed to me that a high level of service is as important as the product itself when it comes to creating something custom.

We didn't have centuries to build our own tradition—so we decided to go to the best and draw inspiration from them. As I mentioned in chapter 2, curiosity is a critical element in any creative endeavor. You must consistently look for ways to "get outside yourself" to find inspiration in ways you'd never imagine. The question my team and I were there to answer was: Could we re-create the London tailor experience—except instead of suits, we'd be customizing shoes?

Sneaker customization wasn't new at the time, either in the industry or with Nike. In 1999, Nike launched NikeiD on its website that provided customers the ability to choose from an array of different materials and colors to create their own style of sneaker. The popularity of the service led to more customization options, such as the ability to add your name, nickname, or a slogan of your choice on the back heel of your shoe. Over the years, we learned that the fewer design variables we gave the consumer to deal with, the better. Limit the number of decisions a consumer had to make and increase the level of happiness. Maybe for a small number of people, NikeiD could simply be a blank canvas to just design whatever you wanted, but for most, they wanted guidance and assurance through fewer choices.

When I led the NikeiD brand design team in these early efforts, our work focused on creating the branding, storytelling, and user experience. But as the service grew both in scope and in popularity, we realized that the creative opportunity was much, much bigger than just a digital platform. And so, we began to study what the best in-person customization experiences within physical environments looked and felt like. We visited the London tailor shops, but also researched the best restaurants—those that strike that incredibly difficult balance of quality, service, and—often overlooked—space. The best restaurants don't just have the best service and food; they have a *feel*. The building, the interior design, the ambiance, the music, the lighting—all of it goes into giving the diner the perfect setting in which they can enjoy the food, the service, and the company. We traveled to different cities and connected with leaders at Four Seasons and Ritz Carlton resorts to learn about how they approached service and certified their staff as experts. In addition we also looked at the best packaging design in the world (after all, unlike a restaurant, customers wouldn't be consuming the product on-site, but would be handed it in a box). Whether it's Apple, Tiffany, or some of the best boutique stores in Tokyo, there's a ceremonial element to both the boxing by the staff and the unboxing by the consumer. With these experiences under our belts, we adopted best practices and threw the rest away.

In 2005, it was time to take our digital NikeiD experience and what we had learned from our travels, and put them into practice. Our first studio would be in the space we had used for the Energy Center on Elizabeth Street in New York. Here, as we had with so many other brand innovations, we'd prototype and test out our concept, live. That concept being a first of its kind, personal, high-touch, appointment-only NikeiD experience. Just like the tailors in the London suit shops, design consultants worked with clients to customize their sneakers down to the last detail. But while the London model for suits had been replicated in every part of the world, no one had thought about doing it for shoes. We thought it would be popular but had no idea that it would grow from a six-week pop-up shop to customization studios all over the world. True to its origins as a prototype, we learned a lot from the Elizabeth Street experience, and we built these lessons into our next efforts. While we wanted each NikeiD store to have similar personalization features, we also wanted them to be unique in themselves.

For example, in 2007 we opened a two-story sneaker customization experience within the heart of Niketown London. Its all-glass, square "fishbowl" structure was intended to provide shoppers who had walked into the flagship store a view of the energy and excitement going on in the "customization lab." Built into the glass walls were display cases for hundreds of uniquely designed Nike sneakers, footwear as art.

In Soho, the Bespoke NikeiD Studio at 21 Mercer Street stands out as a pinnacle example of how far you can take customization and how much people are willing to pay for a great experience. The store opened in 2008 as a small, premium boutique for Nike's most exclusive offerings, with the Bespoke Studio in the back of the store to host private, one-on-one design sessions to create truly original shoes. At a price point that could reach $800, a consumer, working with a design consultant, could customize thirty-one parts of the shoe, including the base, overlays, accents, lining, stitching, outsole color, laces, deubrés, and others. They could also choose from eighty-two (the year the Air Force 1 was launched) premium, iconic materials, and colors. I mean, there was a thousand different kinds of leather. This wasn't the solo endeavor of what the digital website service offered; this was a complete customization experience in person with a design expert helping the individual along every path of the journey.

What started as a sketch and moved to a prototype became the heart of Nike retail flagships worldwide. In just a few years after the launch of the Elizabeth Street experience, every Nike-owned space you walked into in any major city featured a NikeiD studio. The price point of each pair of sneakers had never been low, so it might sound odd to call this process "democratization." But I'm not using the term to refer to the idea that anyone, everywhere, can afford to experience this unique design opportunity. Rather, I'm referring to the democratization of design itself—the way in which NikeiD studios presented consumers with the chance to act as their own sneaker designer. Every bit of customization one could choose for their own unique sneakers called back to a moment in Nike's storied history. By choosing one element over another, a consumer was showcasing what parts of that tradition connected emotionally for them. At the Soho Bespoke Studio in

EMOTION BY DESIGN

NYC, for example, a consumer could choose elephant or safari material prints for their customized Air Force 1s. Why those prints? Because in 1987, Tinker Hatfield used those two naturally occurring designs in his Nike Air Safari running shoe and Nike Air Assault basketball shoe. Now these prints, powered with tradition and perhaps a memory that a consumer brings with them, are available to anyone. That's the point of democratizing design; it brings you into the brand story and makes you part of a cultural heritage by letting you create a version of something never seen before.

The Godfather of Sneaker Books

"What lies ahead on these pages is not really about shoes, it's more about the life the shoes have led, the places they've been, the stories they've never shared, the feet they've been on, the superstars that have bared their names, the trends they've set, the hearts they've broken, the future they'll embrace."

So writes Scoop Jackson in the introduction to *Sole Provider: 30 Years of Nike Basketball*. When I became head of Nike Brand Design, one of our first major projects was the creation of this book. This was certainly defying convention. Instead of using a marketing budget to create a film or put on an event, we focused on creating a book. Why? Why did we hit on an idea to produce a book that tracked Nike's journey in basketball through the stories of individual shoes?

Let's answer that question by asking another question: Why do we document history at all? Because the story of our past, the stories of where we came from, the moments that make up an era, an event, a life *matter*. When we decided to write a book about Nike basketball, it was because we looked back on this particular history of Nike and knew that it mattered—not just to us, but for millions of people whose own lives had been so affected by these moments, these stories. And there's a reason that Ray Butts, who led the art direction for *Sole Provider*, chose Scoop, then a journalist, to be his writing collaborator—because Scoop understood deeply that the only way a book like this could work was if it wasn't simply a marketing piece filled with wonderful images of popular footwear. It had to be about the stories these sneakers could tell. It had to be about history.

When we started to think about the book, our initial purpose was to capture stories that showed the history of Nike's basketball marketing efforts through the products and campaigns that came out over those thirty years. While written for the "sneakerhead," we also wrote this book as a reminder of Nike's rich legacy (a legacy that carried with it enormous responsibility), and as a guide for how we should approach future marketing efforts. Instead of rifling through archives and trying to remember what we did on that one shoe twenty years ago, we had it all in one complete package. Thus, *Sole Provider* was a history book, a book on culture, a book on icons, and a guidebook all wrapped up into one beautifully visualized volume.

The story begins, rightfully so, at the beginning of Nike's entry into the world of basketball with the Blazer from 1972. George "Iceman" Gervin sits atop a white bench, wearing a light-blue track suit, palming two white basketballs, and sporting his all-white Blazers with the blue Swoosh. In the voluminous section on the impact and enduring legacy of the Air Force 1, we jump twenty-five years from 1982 to Rasheed Wallace and the influence he had on resurrecting the AF1, not as a street shoe (Wallace didn't need to do that) but as a court necessity. Above images of "Sheed" sporting his old-school AF1s, Scoop writes: "Even before this retro thing started to be a retro thang, Rasheed Wallace was rocking the vintage. Dirty, clean; old, original or patent leathered. He, to this day, pays it no mind, instead pays tribute."

And, of course, readers can track the history of the Air Jordan, learning, for example, in the section on the Jordan XI, that the shoe was inspired by a . . . sock. "This completely lace-less design was meant to provide a custom fit with maximum comfort. Custom, high-tech fasteners were created to provide stability and lock in the foot. This all changed when MJ provided the input to use patent leather. He thought it would be cool to introduce a sophisticated hoop shoe that could be worn with a tux."

Even Nike packaging got a shout-out. In a section titled "A Shoe's Humidor," *Sole Provider* tracks the history of Nike boxes from simple cases to deliver a pair of kicks from the factory to the store, the store to the consumer, into a sort of treasure chest for those sneakerheads who cherish and collect their Nikes as a passion. "But more than why these 'heads' do what they do, the biggest most FAQ is 'how': How do they keep so many kicks so fresh so clean for so long? Enter the shoebox."

Although *Sole Provider* looks at a total of 650 shoes, Ray wanted to highlight and focus on twelve shoes in particular, shoes that "helped define, shape, and guide the footwear industry." Shoes like the AF1, the Air Jordan, and others whose cultural impact and popularity stretch back decades, providing their own unique story thread in the quilt that comprises Nike's (and consumers') history.

"We felt without these products, the industry and sneaker culture wouldn't have been at the scale it is today," said Ray. While every shoe was given its place, these dozen were the guideposts that best revealed the evolution of both the industry and the culture—the intersection where one flowed into the other almost seamlessly.

Our guiding efforts throughout the book were to convey the sense of past *and* future. The cover of *Sole Provider*, for example, sets the stage right up front showing an old white Nike Blazer matched, like a pair of shoes in a shoebox, with the black Nike Shox that Vince Carter wore. Past and future. Throughout the book, readers are also treated to schematics of the shoe designs, like an architect's blueprints, as well as the contrast of new images side by side with old ones. We wanted to build this seamless link between past and present, the idea that the story continues, and that readers—Scoop's sneakerheads—are part of the story themselves. From great things to even greater things.

Sole Provider was a presentation of Nike's history of meeting people at the intersection of culture and sports. Within that realm, icons can emerge and change the culture. It was a celebration of this history that consumers shared and helped build with Nike. We wanted to produce a book that focused on that shared passion and shared story. Together, Nike and those who loved its products wrote this story together. We had the power to tell that story in one place, both for those who had been with Nike on this journey and for those we had picked up along the way. In one volume Ray and Scoop set down the genealogy of thirty years of storytelling that would be available for future generations, not only as a history book but also as a guide for the future generation of Nike creators, who would be able to look to the past as they designed the future. And it provided the consumers, from the most obsessive sneakerhead to the one who simply loved their old pair of Nike kicks, with a book that chronicled their own role in shaping this slice of culture. For all brands, the stories you choose to tell at some point stop belonging to you. If told well, they are assimilated—like folklore or fairy tales—into the undefinable cauldron of culture, where they are passed down and shared, transformed in the retelling, and assume a legacy even greater than what you set out to create. Tell those stories; share your history. Give it back to your audience.

Air Max Day

The box-shaped building shone like a beacon for miles around. Lit up, with every surface exploding in dynamic color, as if the very walls were vibrating with life, images flow across the sides of the building and slowly come into focus. This is a building yes, with a line of people waiting patiently to enter and experience the wonders inside; but it's also a *sneaker box*. Specifically, it's the Nike SNKRS Box, a building the size of a house that offers a unique interactive experience. On this day, the interior is an exhibition for the mysterious Air Max 0 shoe—a prototype created by the design legend Tinker Hatfield in the mid-1980s but deemed too advanced for production at the time. The sketch would be shelved until 1987, when Tinker returned to it and used it as inspiration for the Air Max 1. Inside, visitors enter a mecca to the Air Max franchise and get a look at a fully rendered, never-before-seen Air Max 0. They also have a chance to meet with Tinker himself, buy and customize their own Air Max shoes, and otherwise share with each other their passion for this iconic shoe. While the Nike SNKRS Box could be used to celebrate a variety of Nike footwear, for almost any occasion, today its exterior is made to look like a box for the Air Max 1—fitting, given that it's March 26, 2015, also known as Air Max Day.

Did Nike build an entire day around a single shoe? Yes, it did. Why? Well, let's talk about that...

On March 26, 1987, Nike released the Air Max 1, which sported some very innovative design features. The most notable of these innovations was the "air bag window," which emphasized the shoe's air and spring technology and was inspired, said Hatfield, by the Pompidou Center in Paris, a building that was built "inside out." You can guess what the team then at Nike was hoping to achieve with this innovation when they released the first commercial to feature the Air Max to the tune of the Beatles song "Revolution." Given that thirty-five years later the Air Max remains one of the most iconic sneakers in history, and remains a staple of Nike's product line, I'd say the creative team did fairly well with the song choice.

In 2014, Nike released a new version of the Air Max that paid homage to its originator, first released twenty-seven years earlier. On the tongue of the new shoe was printed "3.26," the day the Air Max was born. But our sights were set a bit higher than simply releasing a new version of the shoe that commemorated the day of its creation. As my colleague, Gino Fisanotti, recounts: "The challenge was to create a moment, a day for the sneaker community to rally around like fashion brands do for their fashion weeks."

Like the Air Force 1, we understood that the Air Max had grown beyond the ownership of Nike, and was embraced by the consumers as their own. And like we had done for the AF1's twenty-fifth anniversary, we wanted to build a moment around the shoe that served as an opportunity to say "thank you" to those who had made it a cultural icon. The idea to look at this moment like fashion brands look at Fashion Week in Paris started to take hold in the office. At this point, the idea of a single day hadn't yet been considered.

But then Gino went to see Rick Shannon, who was the director of Nike's DNA team. Rick showed Gino the original press release announcing the launch of the Air Max. The date: March 26, 1987. You know what's a more powerful "moment" than a week? A single day. We don't usually celebrate anything for an entire week, but we blow roofs off for a day. New Year's Eve. Valentine's Day. Birthdays. Mother's Day. Father's Day.

Ah, the importance and scale of Valentine's Day, Mother's Day, and Father's Day were created by the florist and greeting card industries. And what a brilliant idea it had been. As most great ideas do, Air Max Day began when we said "*What if* Nike created a globally recognized holiday?" The idea began to form that, like these other holidays, we energize the community that has made this shoe into such a cultural icon and give them a reason to celebrate it.

We realized that this concept provided a perfect vehicle to align new sneaker releases leading up to the day, and even on the day itself, as well as an incredible platform with which to engage consumers, especially through social media. This building of excitement, this ability to create momentum leading up to a specific moment, would involve consumers in a way we had never done before. The community around the Air Max already existed. We didn't need to create it. But what we needed to do was give them something to rally around. They were already enthusiastic. Air Max Day was just a way to harness that enthusiasm toward a specific end.

Best of all, the day wasn't tied to anywhere specific. While we could set up locations in chosen cities for events, the day itself would exist digitally, as consumers shared with one another images, videos, and memories of their love for the Air Max. Nike might have provided the platform, but in the end Air Max Day was a consumer-focused idea, powered by the community.

The original Air Max Day in 2014 looks quaint in comparison to what Nike did in later years. We launched the new version of the Air Max 1, which was almost an exact replica of the OG, except for a couple modifications and design features, such as the "3.26" on the tongue. Nike held events in New York, LA, and Shanghai and posted a photo on Instagram—a rather simple image of the back of a pair of Air Max 1s, surrounded by shoeboxes—that swiftly became the most liked photo in Nike history. Nike had asked the community to show up and celebrate this new holiday...and the community did.

Yup, Nike created a holiday.

There are far too many specific moments and events that Nike, its partners, and the community at large have created for Air Max Day to list them all here. But a brief summary of some of the most memorable gives a pretty good idea of how the holiday has grown from simply a day to commemorate the birth of a sneaker into a global phenomenon.

Tokyo's Landscape Garden: In 2017, the thirtieth anniversary of the Air Max, the acclaimed Japanese interior design firm Wonderwall built a "garden" in Tokyo's National Museum made entirely of Air Max sneakers, bathed in white. Titled "Air Max Genealogy," the garden replaced the usual rocks found in Japanese rock gardens, typically set in spiral patterns, with all the versions of the Air Max over the years.

Shoe Into Space: Also in 2017, a Nike digital agency partner, space150, attached one of the new Vapormax shoes to a weather balloon and sent it into space. Seriously. With GoPro cameras recording the ascent from the balloon, viewers were able to watch the Vapormax rise 117,550 feet above the earth, before the balloon itself exploded, and the shoe parachuted back down. As space150 creative director Ned Lampert, who concocted this out-of-this-world idea, explained:

"We're really inspired by *Nike*, inspired by their approach to technology, their approach to culture and trying to push the limit as much as possible, and we felt this was the perfect intersection of sports and culture to tell the story of the lightest shoe in the world."[8]

Masters of Air: In 2016, Nike produced a film, "Masters of Air," that showcased nine of the biggest Air Max collectors in the world. The film told the stories of these individuals, who hailed from all over the world; Amsterdam, Beijing, Paris, London, Prague, Tokyo, Las Vegas, Mexico City, and Berlin. The Berlin collector, who goes by the name Icebox, owns two thousand Air Max pairs, comprising half of his four-thousand-pair collection.

Nike SNKRS Box: As previously mentioned, there was the house-sized digital shoebox that was a focal point of events in LA on Air Max Day in 2015. With an exterior seamlessly covered with the latest LED screen technology, the box looked like it was living and breathing, with films and images playing across its walls. We also had the SNKRS Box at other Air Max Days as well, where guests were given prearranged appointment times to enter the box. Once inside, they could buy old and new versions of the shoe, as well as meet athletes and Air Max designers. In 2016, guests had the opportunity to talk to the collectors who had been featured in "Masters of Air."

Since it was first celebrated in 2014, Air Max Day has been going strong for eight years. It has become part of the culture in a way that few brand-based "moments" rarely do. The reason, I believe, is that Air Max Day rests on central tenets of aligning a brand with culture. The first, and perhaps most important, is that Air Max Day puts the community at the center of the festivities. Nike's role is to make it easy for anyone to share their passion with others, either in-person or through digital channels. Like Valentine's Day, Mother's Day, and Father's Day, the event gives consumers a reason to celebrate that which they already love.

But there's another element that plays into this community-centric approach. Air Max Day encourages fans to express their passion in their own way. Nike gives people the tools and the inspiration to showcase their appreciation, then steps back. Another tenet that has been at the heart of Air Max Day has been giving actual voting power to the people. Every year, enthusiasts become voters and are able to decide the direction of the next Air Max version, literally allowing the community to be part of the creative process at Nike. And finally, across cities around the world, from Melbourne to Los Angeles, interactive experiences are created to show appreciation for the consumer. This was and always has been about more than a shoe, as the first print ad declared: "Nike-Air is not a shoe"; it's about what the Air Max sneaker represents. The holiday is a celebration of community, creativity, and self-expression.

There were so many ways that Nike could have done Air Max Day wrong, so many ways it could have tarnished the very thing it was trying to celebrate. But by always keeping the product and the community in the center, Nike was able to empower the people to make Air Max Day their own. In the end, the reason Air Max Day became a successful holiday in its own right is because Nike connected people to something they already loved. It's a day that allows people in the community to celebrate one another through their mutual love of a product.

Taking a broader view, and looking at Nike marketing history overall, you can see all the best of what we had learned come together at one time, on one day. I always considered Air Max Day to be the very best of Nike's brand marketing efforts, the moment when the brand in its purest, most ideal form, is able to shine. We managed to put the best of Nike, its people, its designs, its stories, its sneakers, into a once-in-a-lifetime experience, as if Air Max Day itself was a sneaker box into which we poured all our passion.

Don't Chase Cool

Every brand wants to create its own cultural icon. Every brand wants its own Levi's 501, its own Ford Mustang, its own Air Force 1. It is one of the highest points a product can reach, yet if that is the goal from the beginning, we will probably fail. What is cool if not authenticity; individuality; a strong sense of self and purpose? Yes, there are "cool" trends, but no one's created an icon by following a trend. You create an icon by starting a trend. If you chase one, then you're probably trying to be something you're not—and consumers are experts on exposing inauthenticity. Because brands don't decide what becomes an icon; consumers do.

If a brand is lucky enough to find itself holding on to a cultural icon—a symbol of cool—it must respect and protect it. The Air Force 1 has had many editions over the years, but it's the same shoe, it fulfills the same purpose as the very first AF1 that took Moses Malone to the NBA Championships—and led me to believe that one day I would be a professional basketball player. Well, one of these things happened, anyway.

But more often than not, a brand doesn't have its own AF1. More often than not, a brand is finding it challenging to stay relevant and remain part of the cultural conversation. Because of this, some brands chase the latest trend, influencer, or social media platform. Too many brands latch on to what everyone else is doing, and the result can be something that is inauthentic and lacking in any emotional power. You're chasing cool and, most likely, you won't catch it.

Cultural icons begin to take form when a brand remains authentic to its identity and purpose. Do that, and cool will chase you.

PRINCIPLES FOR "DON'T CHASE COOL"

1. LET AUTHENTICITY BE YOUR CULTURAL CURRENCY

Leverage your legacy. Your original mission is what got you here, so remember why you were loved in the first place. You can't manufacture authenticity, so protect yours. It will be here long after the latest trend disappears.

2. PLAY IN THE INTERSECTIONS

Don't stay in your lane. Merge into other cultural currents that share your brand values. By crossing paths with the worlds of art, music, and beyond, you can invite new consumers into your brand and, in turn, have a greater impact on culture.

3. CREATE WITH THE COMMUNITY

Brands don't create icons on their own; your success is due as much to the consumer as it is to you, so reward them. Make the relationship personal by giving them the tools, the moments, and the canvas upon which to share their passion for you with the world.

CHAPTER 7

SPARK A MOVEMENT

The world is stuck! It's stuck in a rut. It's stuck in a routine. It's stuck watching *this*! Today, we're going to try to convince some Angelinos to stop sitting in traffic and to choose GO. Al; right, load it up!"

At which point the speaker, comedian Kevin Hart, laces up his Nikes and jumps in the back of a truck—except that the back of the truck looks like a glass box, and there's a treadmill in the middle of it. With Kevin starting to jog, the truck drives through Los Angeles and onto the freeway in the middle of rush hour traffic. Kevin, running along in the back of the truck, is miked up, and calling out to motorists and pedestrians (or is it more like heckling?).

"You guys are in traffic doing nothing," says Kevin to the drivers. "I'm in training doing something." Which might sound a bit harsh for people who, you know, have jobs, but it's Kevin Hart. It's Kevin Hart in a glass box running on a treadmill. "Do I look as cool from out there as I think I do?" he asks…no one in particular.

On the freeway, jam-packed as usual, the horns honk as the motorists pass. Kevin, waving at them while he runs, says: "You're either honking because you love me or you're honking because I'm stopping traffic." Probably a little bit from column A and little bit from column B, honestly.

If you don't already know what's going on, then you might think this was all just some crazy stunt. Maybe Kevin was promoting a new movie or a new comedy act. But, no, Kevin was doing just what he said he was doing: Trying to get people to move. Get up. Go for a run.

But...Kevin Hart? Yes, Kevin Hart, comedian, actor, and a man whose passion for fitness, especially running, is second to none. But we'll get to that. Kevin's "stunt," if you want to call it that, was to promote the Nike "Go LA 10K," which was held in April 2018, and coincided with the launch of the all-new Nike React footwear innovation.

As the truck continues down the freeway, Kevin running along, the looks from the motorists range from hilarity to confusion. Mostly, people have their phones out, trying to capture something they've never seen before and likely will never see again. On the side of the road, a man in street clothes watches the truck pass, with Kevin shouting, then takes off in a run. Someone got the message to "Choose Go."

"This definitely counts as my cardio today, though."

The Catalyst

Kevin's involvement with Nike wasn't limited to the LA race. He was also involved in the campaign to promote the Apple Watch Nike+, which launched in 2017. Nike had an illustrious history of teaming up with creative talent beyond the realm of sports to add that level of cross-cultural excitement that makes a campaign resonate beyond a traditional audience. One of the first was Spike Lee, in the role of Mars Blackmon, standing beside Michael Jordan, saying, "It's gotta be the shoes." There was also the 1993 campaign featuring Dennis Hopper as a wildly eccentric referee holding up and smelling one of Buffalo Bills linebacker Bruce Smith's enormous shoes. This wasn't about cameos for the sake of cameos. These cultural icons were chosen because of the unique way they added to the story Nike was trying to tell.

So it's good to know why Nike and Kevin Hart came together in the first place.

In 2015, we began our search for someone who could not only authentically talk about fitness, specifically running, but one who could literally start a movement about movement. That person was Kevin Hart. To those who only know Kevin from his stand-up and cinema work, the choice seems odd. He's not a professional athlete, nor was he ever a professional athlete. But that's also the point. Nike's vision wasn't just to reach those who might respond to a known athlete, but to someone who was relatable in a different way. The runners were already running; it was the people sitting on the couch that we needed to reach; people who would look at someone like Kevin and not immediately tune out. Kevin's infectious personality and hilarious delivery would get this audience to sit up, to laugh, and, we hoped, to start running. To bring this movement to life, we needed to partner with someone who was influential but who had an authentic and relatable connection to running.

How did we know Kevin was perfect for the part? Well, here's one (out of many) stories that prove the point. In June 2015, the night before Kevin was to perform in Boston, he tweeted: "Boston, I want u 2 get up & run with me n the AM! Meet by the water shed 367 chestnut hill ave Brighton MA...Next 2 Reilly recreation center." The next day, at the appointed place, three hundred Bostonians came out to run with Kevin Hart. It was the first of what became a regular thing for the comedian while on the road, for a total of thirteen cities in five months. In Philadelphia alone, 6,500 people ran with Kevin through the City of Brotherly Love as he retraced the iconic run first performed by Rocky Balboa, ending atop the steps in front of the city's Museum of Art. In Dallas, Kevin, who had already finished the course, saw an overweight man in the group who had joined his run and jogged back to finish with him.[9] I mean, wow.

Speaking about that very first Boston run, Kevin said: "It was honestly a spontaneous decision. I felt like it would be a cool way to get people motivated about fitness."

Digging a bit deeper, however, we learn that Kevin wasn't always a runner. A few years earlier, he finally decided to get serious about fitness and picked up running. But he wasn't exactly great at it. He struggled to find a routine that got him out regularly, until one day, it all just clicked. The routine had turned into an addiction, and, like the zeal of the converted, Kevin wanted to use his tremendous platform (more than 20 million Twitter followers at the time) to share his love of fitness and running with others, and hopefully get them to start a running routine of their own.

So, to the question, why did we decide that Kevin Hart was our perfect ambassador to launch a movement about movement? Because he had already started it.

The Meeting Before the Meeting

Kevin came out to the Nike campus to meet the team. Before the meeting, I walked through the security check-in at the lobby of the Innovation Building, with Kevin right behind me. While we waited for the rest of the team to finish the check-in process, I introduced myself to Kevin, this being the first time we had met, just the two of us standing in the stairwell. Without missing a beat, Kevin launched into his ambition to get the world moving. I quickly noticed that this wasn't any act. I mean, the man exudes comedy, but at that moment, Kevin's passion for fitness and running was just pouring out of him—to a guy he just met seconds earlier. Listening to his vision, I was struck immediately by the fact that Kevin had a concrete plan. He knew what he wanted to do—which isn't typical. Mind you, there was no official partnership yet. Usually, it's people like me, the brand marketers and the rest of the creative team, that pitch ideas to the talent. But not here. Kevin, on his own initiative, has been working on a plan to bring fitness and a healthier lifestyle to underserved communities.

I already respected Kevin both as a person and as an entertainer, but his vision took my respect to new heights. He was also so naturally funny that I was fighting not to bend over laughing—not the best thing when it's me, not Kevin, who has to give a presentation in a few minutes.

Eventually the rest of the Nike crew assembled in the conference room, and I managed to pull myself together well enough to start our pitch to Kevin. I kicked it off with a Nike Brand overview—our purpose, mission, and values. It's the usual stuff, but always gives us an opportunity to make it crystal clear that we ground every relationship in sport and innovation for athletes. Then came Janett Nichol, head of apparel innovation, followed by Darla Vaughn, senior marketing director. As each presenter continued to bring to life the magic of Nike Marketing and Innovation, I noticed that Kevin had a surprised look on his face. After the presentations were finished, he leaned over to Pam McConnell, the head of Nike's entertainment marketing, and remarked how he'd never been in a pitch meeting with a brand where everyone presenting was Black.

We all looked around and realized Kevin was right. Everyone in the room who presented that day was Black. This was unintentional on our part, as it was just the simple fact that Black leaders headed up the groups responsible for partnering with him. Nevertheless, that it was true and that Kevin noticed it immediately stands as one of the high points for me when it comes to walking the walk of diversity and representation. It was a small moment, and wasn't the point of the meeting, to be sure, but it's also one I'll never forget.

In any case, the meeting wrapped and we walked over to the Mia Hamm Building for lunch. We had a surprise guest for Kevin. After we finished our meal, in walked Phil Knight. Kevin was beaming. Phil was very complimentary of all the success that Kevin had had and Kevin was equally effusive toward Knight as an inspiration to him. Pleasantries over, Kevin then launched into a bit of improv, declaring that earlier that day, he had broken all the athlete performance records within the Nike Sports Research Lab. Given that this list includes world record holders and champions across the whole field of sport, this is an impossibility, but Kevin's delivery and earnestness had us in stitches. Another small moment, but also one that showed us that Kevin Hart was just as excited to be partnering with Nike as we were to have him.

Yes, we had chosen the perfect ambassador, and going forward we knew we were about to embark on a memorable (and hilarious) partnership with him. I think one more story will show what I mean.

In January 2016, Kevin is a guest on *The Tonight Show with Jimmy Fallon*. Kevin shows up kitted out in Nike gear: a red Nike performance T-shirt and Nike Hustle Hart cross-training shoes. Jimmy asks Kevin about his new kicks, and Kevin, being Kevin, just can't express enough how much he loves them. "I don't think you can see them good enough," he shouts to the audience, and then proceeds to jump on top of Jimmy's legendary *Tonight Show* desk. He then gushes about his inspirational quotes that Nike had stitched into the shoe material: "Health is Wealth" and "Don't Stop Grinding." These are more than shoes, Kevin says, they were designed to help "bridge the gap between the athlete and the person that doesn't understand that there's an athlete within them."

Do I even need to explain how that made those of us at Nike feel? Have I mentioned that we had chosen the perfect ally to start a movement about movement? Yes?

Kevin Hart was exactly the person we needed.

The Man Who Kept Running

Against a black screen, yellow text appears: "In October, Kevin Hart got the Apple Watch Nike+." The film then cuts to Kevin, sitting in his car and using his camera phone, holding up a black box: "I'm about to show you all the first Apple Watch Nike+. Oh, my goodness, running just became a lot easier."

As Kevin continues to gush over his new watch, the viewer doesn't hear anything much more about the new gadget. Kevin doesn't talk about the features; he doesn't mention all the digital innovations that were put in this; all he says is "Running just became a lot easier."

The screen cuts to black and the text appears: "The next day, he vanished. Months later, a film crew found him 700 miles from home."

When we see Kevin next, he's in the desert with a full beard, running. He's been running for months, sleeping out in the wild like a nomad. "You see, running used to be hard for me," we hear Kevin say. "But then things changed when I woke up and started to hear this little voice in my head. It was the same question: Are we running today?"

The viewer eventually figures out that Kevin's "little voice" is actually his Apple Watch Nike+, buzzing him awake every morning, like an alarm clock, with the same question across the tiny screen: "Are we running today?"

"So you know what I started to do?" asks Kevin. "I started to answer that question." Cut to Kevin emerging from his tent in the early hours of the morning, raising his hands to greet the rising sun, and shouting: "YES!"

"So now," says Kevin, who's running beside a wolf (because why not). "So now I run. I run."

Nike's film "The Man Who Kept Running" debuted in 2017 to coincide with the product launch of the Apple Nike Watch+. The watch was a huge leap forward in fitness and mobile innovation from the two experts of the topic: Apple and Nike. It wasn't the first collaboration between the two brands, though. In 2006, the two companies worked together to launch Nike+, a running tracker in Nike sneakers that connected to an iPod. Twelve years later, we were together again, although the state of digital hardware had changed significantly. At the same time, I was no longer just accountable for the brand identity and experience design for the launch. As CMO, I was responsible for leading the teams through all the disciplines within our marketing effort.

When introducing a new innovation to the world, the goal is always to make the benefit of that innovation both intuitive and meaningful. Nike had a legacy of creating emotional connections between the consumer and footwear innovations. Just consider the iconic status that Nike Air holds within popular culture—a status that transcends the original performance enhancement that the air bag provided. Now the challenge was to create a similar emotional attachment to digital product, not just footwear. While the benefits of visible innovations tend to be highly intuitive (a lighter running shoe makes for a faster runner), the benefits of digital innovations are often less obvious, especially if the design enables something truly new and different.

To make things even more complicated, digital innovations tend to involve multiple features, each with their own unique set of benefits. To help guide our efforts here, we looked at other masters of "digital-service storytelling," Apple and Google. What's ironic is that both of these digital brands had achieved storytelling mastery by borrowing from Nike's marketing playbook. Imitation being the sincerest form of flattery, it was time for Nike to return the compliment. What Google and Apple did very well with their own product launches was focus on the amazing things that the innovation enabled the consumer to do, not on the specific technical features.

When we set out to communicate the benefits of the new Apple Watch Nike+, we needed to resist the temptation to focus on all the exciting things that the watch could do and, instead, ground our storytelling in what truly made the experience special. Why would a consumer want to buy this? In a word: Motivation. That's it. All those complex technical features were there to provide runners who wore the Apple Watch Nike+'s with the motivation needed to make running a more enjoyable and habitual experience. And what does every reluctant runner need more than anything else? Motivation. Making sure *this* was what consumers understood about the tech was our creative challenge.

Running is a uniquely challenging activity. Unlike a sport, where competition is the motivating factor, running is most often an individual pursuit. Alone, on the road, with nothing pushing you forward except your own motivation. It's no wonder so many of us choose other activities or give up on making running a habit. In short, it's just hard to stay motivated. So, how could we raise the cool factor of running authentically? How could we showcase that the Apple Watch Nike+ gives runners and would-be runners the one thing they need to keep...running?

Our answer to that question became a series of short films called "Vanishing," which Nike created in partnership with Wieden & Kennedy. Directed by Stacy Wall, all the films, including "The Man Who Kept Running," were shot on location in Moab, Utah. Stacy had written and directed several Nike commercials over the years and had a strong understanding of the Nike brand and our storytelling voice and standard. One of Wall's greatest contributions was to let Kevin improvise so much of his performance. With a performer like Kevin, you don't write lines; you write a framework and then get out of the way. As masterful as our writing partners were, the success would come from giving Kevin space to freestyle and reveal the truths about running to the viewer as only he can. And I do mean "truths," given that Kevin was talking not just as a Nike ambassador, but as a one-time reluctant runner who had found his motivation. What's more, as someone who had used that motivation to motivate others.

In the series, Kevin Hart plays a version of himself who gets motivated to run after receiving his Apple Watch with Nike+, only to be found months later by a film crew in the desert wilderness, talking with animals and battling the heat and loneliness. As the shooting continued, Kevin transformed into the role of the obsessed runner with ease. Kevin would dial up his excitement level from take to take—he could easily go from full-blown lunatic to just slightly off. It was a treat for everyone on the set to see a pro at the top of his craft. Kevin, as would be expected, brought his unique ideas to the project as well. Viewers may think that Kevin's nomad-like beard is fake. Nope. He actually grew it out. The beard was all his idea.

Each film in the series highlights one of the Apple Watch Nike+ motivational features, such as tracking your pace, distance, progress, or a feature that allows you to compete against your friends. The trick was to communicate these things not as an engineer would (no offense to engineers), but as your friend who just got this new gadget would. Thus, as we see in "The Man Who Kept Running," viewers have no clue how the watch works; they just see what it does. Kevin's comment at the beginning of the film—"Running just became a lot easier"—is what *every* would-be runner wants to hear.

What does this thing do?

It makes running a lot easier.

Sold!

A Movement About Movement

Kevin's partnership with Nike extended beyond the Apple Watch Nike+. We also produced a series of audio-guided runs voiced by him designed to motivate listeners. Imagine Kevin in your ear as you are trying to wake up or set your personal best, all the while increasing your heart rate in between laughs. And then there was the campaign mentioned at the beginning of this chapter, "Choose Go," which ran in 2018 and was tied to the new Nike

React footwear innovation. "Choose Go" was the most extensive global product launch to date. As fun as it was to see Kevin jogging in the back of the truck, the production paled next to the nearly two-minute-long "Choose Go" commercial film that featured not only Kevin but also Simone Biles, Odell Beckham Jr., and even Bill Nye the Science Guy.

The conceit of the film is that the world has stopped rotating on its axis—a "Stopocalypse," as one of the newsreels coined it. To get the earth moving again (get it?), everyone needs to start running. Throughout the world, from America to China, people are running out of their homes to join others in this all-humanity run. At one point, as the enormous crowd surges by, it encounters Kevin, running the other way all alone. Kevin stops, "Why is everybody going this way?" then follows the pack.

"This incredible effort appears to be our planet's last chance to get moving," says an anchorman. The plan starts to work and the earth starts to rotate again…until the news anchor has breaking news: "Everyone is running the wrong way!" The crowd stops, turns 180 degrees, and starts up again.

The last shot shows Kevin, distraught as the crowd runs past him, saying: "I knew it! I knew I was right!"

Kevin's partnership with Nike was groundbreaking on several levels. First, it was based on a natural and shared passion each had to serve and inspire athletes of all types. Once Kevin started running, he wanted others to run with him. Kevin, as ambassador, was the catalyst that would make people sit up and listen. Second, the link between Kevin and Nike was the Apple Watch Nike+, the tool that would help both Nike and Kevin achieve their vision of helping others. Finally, Kevin's personal story, as well as his efforts through social media, meant that his voice was authentic. Kevin was a master motivator precisely because he knew what it meant to need motivation. He knew what others needed to hear to change their lives—not just motivation for a single run, but motivation for a running lifestyle. And *that* was the purpose behind Nike's partnership with this exceptionally talented and driven man: to help inspire others to do what he did. To use Kevin's voice to start a movement about movement, with the Apple Watch Nike+ powering that movement. When one puts all these pieces together, we see how brands can do more than use marketing tools to sell products; we see how brands can use products to unleash human potential on a massive scale.

For the remainder of this chapter I'll share other experiences I was a part of where an innovation sparked a movement.

The Human Race: A Run for All Humanity

The Apple Watch Nike+ campaign was about creating a movement. Nine years earlier, Nike+, without the Apple Watch attached, was used to create *movement* in the literal sense. Imagine, as we did at Beaverton in 2007, the whole world (or as many human beings as we could) racing together, at one time, on the same day, in the same race. An impossibility just a few years earlier. Nothing on that scale could be accomplished, not with the best technology available. Even if Nike had organized an event where people all over the world ran a "race" on the same day, none of the runners would've felt like they were in a single race; nothing would have connected a runner in, say Melbourne, with a runner in Madrid. But the technology was now available. Yes, it would still require an enormous effort in human endurance and planning, but *what if…?*

This was the beginning of what would become The Nike+ Human Race, a 10K event that would span multiple continents and cover twenty-five cities, including LA, New York, London, Madrid, Paris, Istanbul, Melbourne, Shanghai, São Paulo, and Vancouver, to name the largest. And it would all occur on the same day, August 31, 2008, just a week after the Beijing Olympics. In the participating cities, the races would be followed by a concert featuring a top artist of the day: Moby, Kanye West, Ben Harper, Fall Out Boy, Kelly Rowland, and so on.

The innovation that changed all that was Nike+. As its descendant, the Apple Watch Nike+, would be almost a decade later, Nike+ was the tool that would help Nike achieve its vision of holding the world's biggest race event ever.

The Beginnings of a Movement

In the early 2000s, Nike came out with its own MP3 player—which was the best MP3 player on the market, I might add—and we also had a very innovative online running site that allowed experienced runners to log their runs. The only problem is that neither were very popular, at least in the mass market. They catered more to the seasoned runner than the amateur and for that reason, they just never caught on. What we *did* notice was that regular runners usually had an iPod Nano strapped to their wrist or arm and a pair of Nike running shoes on their feet.

We also recognized that your average runner, or wannabe runner, doesn't care about the coolness of the tech. They're not going to buy the more expensive Nike MP3 player because it has all these awesome features; they're going to buy the Apple iPod because they have iTunes and it's just easier. As for running itself, the chief complaints were: Running can be boring, it is lonely, it is tough to get started, and it is really hard to keep going. If Nike was to design a product that connected with these consumers, then we needed to meet them where they were...not where we wanted them to be.

So Nike took its experience with the MP3 player and the online log and then someone called up Apple. Which was how, in 2006, the world of sports and music came together in a partnership between Apple and Nike. The original Nike+ was a sensor in your shoe that would track how far and fast you ran, using the iPod as an interface. A consumer then could integrate their playlist with their running route, playing a specific song at a specific distance. Of course, the real breakthrough is that Nike+ was aimed at the jogger, the one who didn't have time to log their runs afterward, but would love the motivating effect of their runs being logged automatically. They could see, in real time, their progress, all the while being pushed by their favorite "power" song.

An interesting side note to this development story is that, perhaps naturally, there was initial resistance in some quarters to this approach to the product. The notable thing is those who were uncertain about the product's marketability were lifelong runners, for whom motivation wasn't an issue: running with music prevents them from hearing their breath, and tracking runs in a journal was sacred. Nike+, they argued, wasn't for serious runners. To which the believers replied, exactly.

It's hard to remember in our digitally connected, social media world that there was a time, in the not-too-distant past, when these things were brand-new. That's the world in which we started to build Nike+, when "apps" were still what one ordered before the main course. There was very little to guide our efforts, and next to nothing on following best practices. We had to blaze our own way, using little more than very nascent behaviors and digital tools that were just appearing across the online world. Today, of course, we have regulations and consumer approvals, but none of that was available back then. And this doesn't even touch on the consumer response. For many people, the internet was still what they saw when they opened up their laptops. It wasn't this ever-present thing that was embedded in all devices. How would consumers respond to this level of personal data capture? With the exception of the most tech-savvy consumer, Nike+ would be their first experience with so many of these new digital tools. On the other hand, Nike+ Running would be the introduction to running for so many people in the tech-digital industry. It took behavior that existed in emerging social networks and early community sites and applied it to the world of sports and fitness. In short, you could say, we were able to launch the entire wearables movement.

In this high-stakes environment, I was responsible for leading the teams in creating the branding, packaging, art direction, and environments for the launch and the campaign. With Nike, the bar is always high, but now that we were paired with Apple (another brand known for its high bars), there was no room for error, given Steve Jobs's personal involvement in all aspects of his brand's expression. Hiroki Asai, Apple's head of visual communication for the brand, whom I had gotten to know through a series of design team brand-to-brand sharing sessions, had relayed to me stories of Jobs's incredible attention to design details: from the letter spacing on a headline, to the placement of a logo, to the composition of a product photo. There was no detail too small that Jobs didn't scrutinize—not surprising, given that he was a branding genius. I thought I had received my education in exactness from John Norman, my mentor during my internship days at Nike almost fifteen years earlier. This was altogether a different level of obsession.

My team and I had to start with building a brand identity

for this new concept. From the very beginning, we had the idea to signify the added element that this digital tool brought to the brand with a simple plus sign put next to the Swoosh. We explored a few options, including using the word "Plus." When we nixed that idea, we focused on the plus symbol and experimented with scale, proximity, height, detailing, and so on. There were at least a hundred different options put forth. The eventual winner was a slightly rounded plus sign (hardly noticeable, but believe me, the curved edges are there). We couldn't have known it then, but we had just begun a trend in digital branding that continues to this day, with brands from Disney to Walmart adding plus symbols to represent their digital membership services. Well, we were the first. This was also one of the only times we dared tweak the Swoosh, but the significance of the project demanded that we made this special exception. We were building something brand-new—it was Nike, but it was also Nike *enhanced*. How to signify that part without overburdening the Swoosh and lessening its impact? The plus sign was the answer.

Our other task was designing an image that conveyed the collaboration between these two brands, while also showcasing the merging of two otherwise incompatible products as one complete product. The result of our effort became what we internally labeled "the butterfly." The image shows two upright black Nike running shoes with the soles touching. In the center of the shoes is a silver iPod nano with the earbud cords wrapped sinuously around the shoes themselves, as if they're tying the two incompatible products together; they seamlessly interact with each other and the athlete like an ecosystem. Light, kinetic, clean.

We were also on the hook for creating athlete images, showcasing the product on a person. This was tougher than it sounds, since we're talking about a puck-like sensor that is *inside* a shoe, and an iPod Nano that, had we focused on the screen, would have eliminated the athlete. Our solution to this was to focus on the athlete using the product, but without really showing the product itself. To do that, we superimposed over the image of the athlete in midstride the digital metrics that a runner would see on the iPod screen: their pace, their distance, and so on. It was the perfect way to get both priorities—the athlete and the product—into a single image. It also set something of a precedent too, since today brands like Peloton, Strava, and Soul Cycle use the same method to visually communicate an athlete's personal fitness data over their images. But, again, Nike was the first.

Radical Creative Collaboration

The night before the launch event, many members of the team were running laps at Chelsea Piers in New York City. I wish I could say that this was to get rid of some last-minute jitters, but no. With the clock ticking, we had to make absolutely sure that every Nike+ demo product worked flawlessly and as advertised. We were about to exhibit revolutionary technology, and the results had to match our rhetoric. Roughly one hundred journalists were going to be on hand to demo the product, and if one or two or fifteen didn't work, that was going to be all the headlines would say the day after.

After all, trying to *describe* Nike+ Running to journalists was going to be a challenge. We had set up demo stations where we could individually walk each media member through the experience, because there was no vocabulary that existed in the world yet for it. Every aspect of it was new. There was the sensor that went into your shoe and under your sock liner. It had to sync with your iPod. You could add friends, or program challenges. You could start your PowerSong, which would give you that extra motivational boost. This was all new, and the only way we could make the media believers was if we showed them it worked. Every person that met with a journalist that day had to make the future accessible and inspiring to everyone.

It was May 24, 2006, and that meant the weather in New York could still get cold. And guess what? It was freaking cold. Although the Chelsea Piers facility is all indoors, there was no heat, and our team wasn't dressed for either the weather *or* for running. No matter. At 2:30 a.m. most of the team was running laps around Chelsea Piers in their work clothes. Each time one of the team ran a lap, they'd push the button on the iPod for the performance feedback and then hold down the button for the PowerSong to come on. All of the demo products were working flawlessly. It was a moment of magic for both the Apple and the Nike teams, who had come together to create technology that had never existed before. Just a truly inspiring collaboration. There were tears in the eyes of many.

But we weren't out of the woods yet. The demo products worked, thankfully, but there were other obstacles to overcome before the curtain rose. The launch event at Chelsea Piers was a huge undertaking, like preparing for the Super Bowl. The brief called for creating a space that had to serve a lot of different needs within a tightly scripted experience for the media and analysts. There was the stage and presentation area, a product and inter-active zone for members of the press to experience Nike+, and finally a large area for sportswear and running retailers to meet with the Nike Sales force and book potential orders. The main stage area was a large amphitheater space, where the CEOs of each brand were to appear and have a conversation (similar to Jobs's famous product launches), as well as copresent the Nike+ concept.

As Ricky Engleberg, marketing director on the project, said, "Watching rehearsals of the press event was what I imagine the '92 Dream Team practices felt like." From hearing Steve Jobs give feedback on whether an analogy worked in the script or not, to watching the reaction of the amazing athletes we had invited to the event who were trying out the innovation for the first time, it was truly a once-in-a-lifetime experience."

And then there was the famous Jobs attention to detail. The head of Apple was clear that when it came to the cobranding of the experience, anywhere that a Swoosh showed up, an Apple logo must show up equal in size right next to it. I directed the team to make sure that this was followed to a tee. There was one problem. The sea of desks where the media would be invited to give Nike+ a trial run were branded only with the Swooshes. On the day of rehearsals, Jobs noted this and sent word that this branding detail would need to be fixed before the start of the event. No exceptions. The fact that each table had a total of three iMacs on them, all with Apple logos, didn't matter. I called the team together and told them we needed to change the branding to the Apple-Swoosh combo, and we needed to do it before the launch event start time. They had forty-eight hours to create forty Apple-Swoosh logos out of cut vinyl, then repaint the table the night before the show. So in addition to the lap runners testing the demo products, we had another team fixing the media desks. But the result was worth it. The visual power of seeing the Apple side by side with the Swoosh conveyed to all the guests, media especially, that what was about to happen brought together the absolute best of both brands.

When the curtain lifted, the all-nighters had made the difference, and the launch event was a thrilling success. The seventy-five thousand square feet of brand power we had put on display in Chelsea Piers had the desired effect, and media accounts exceeded expectations. Scott Denton Cardew, who was an art director on my team, had worked straight through multiple nights leading up to the event. After the launch event started, when his role in the preparations was finally finished, he went for a full English breakfast, a whiskey, and then a few pints of Guinness—breakfast of champions. And then he slept for a week.

The Nike+ with iPod—the result of the radical creative collaboration between two innovation titans in their field—not only helped launch a wearables movement, but also ushered in an era of connected devices that seamlessly interact with one another. Consumers for the first time could see personal health and fitness metrics—pace, distance, calories burned, and so on—without the help of a medical professional or trainer. In time, the iPod would be replaced with the iPhone, then only a year away from launch, further improving the seamless integration between consumer and data. By 2012, 7 million users had joined the Nike+ community.

In 2008, the success of Nike+ convinced us that the technology existed to put on the largest race in human history, appropriately called the Human Race. In the cities that were participating in formal race events, runners could use the Nike site to register and track and rate their performance against anyone else in the world. But—and this was key—for those who weren't in one of those cities, the Nike+ (now an app) would still allow them to participate in the race—whether in a sponsoring city or in their own neighborhoods—and log their performance alongside everyone else.

By the end of the twenty-four hours, a million runners had collectively covered 802,242 miles—or thirty-two trips around the circumference of the earth. It was of particular pride to us at

Nike that so many of these runners came from the cities where the major event had been held, fulfilling our ambition to focus on marketing efforts on helping people in inner-city communities out of their homes and onto the track. For myself, I remember looking at the digital leaderboards after the race and being more bummed than I probably should have been that Matthew McConaughey beat me. Following up on the success of the Human Race, in 2015 we had the vision of making August 27 the "Fastest Day Ever." We challenged everyone around the world to run their fastest mile on the same day. By using Nike+ Data and Google Street View, we were able to give runners everywhere personalized videos of their running routes. All this was possible because of our vision to design a product that wasn't aimed at the elite runner but rather at the would-be runner who just needed that extra bit of motivation to lace up the shoes. The technology served as a tool to organize a movement around running, by making it easier for runners to get personalized data in real time as well as connect them to others all over the world. Running may remain a solo endeavor, but it's no longer lonely when you're part of a movement.

Make It Count

On a YouTube video from 2012 there's a comment from user Fluffy Penguins that reads: "This is either a masterpiece or just a video about a dude stealing sponsor money."

Who says it can't be both, Mr. (or Ms.) Fluffy Penguins?

The film in question, named "Make It Count," begins with hands unboxing a Nike+ FuelBand. The product itself is wrapped around an elliptical groove, and in the center of the ellipse are the words: "Life is a sport. Make it count." The hands take out the FuelBand, hold it for a second, then the scene cuts to a man running out of a nondescript door in some city. And I mean running. He bolts down the sidewalk and out of the frame. Cut to black with the following words on-screen:

"Nike asked me to make a movie about what it means to #makeitcount." The text scrolls down, a la *Star Wars*. "Instead of making their movie, I spent the entire budget traveling around with my friend Max. We'd keep going until the money ran out. It took ten days."

The remaining four minutes of the film (which I can't possibly do justice describing with words) shows filmmaker Casey Neistat traveling around the world with Max. They start in New York and fly to Paris. From Paris they go to Cairo. Then...well, then it gets tricky to decipher their path, but we see London, Johannesburg, Zambia, Nairobi, Rome, Doha (or, as Casey says to the camera, "back in Doha"), Bangkok, and, probably a few other cities. What's carried throughout the film is that Casey is running from one end of the frame to the next, picking up from him running out of his office door, in all these locations. He's continually running, never stopping, always on the move. He's also doing back flips off random platforms, jumping from incredible heights into bodies of water, and doing handstands. Then, the money gone, the final shot sees Casey running back to his office door (from the opposite direction).

Throughout Casey's travels, quotes appear on-screen, that all carry a common theme:

> **"Life is either a daring adventure or nothing at all."**
> —*Helen Keller*

"Buy the ticket, take the ride."
—*Hunter S. Thompson*

"You only live once but if you do it right once is enough."
—*Mae West*

"Above all, try something."
—*Franklin D. Roosevelt*

"I never worry about the future. It comes soon enough."
—*Albert Einstein*

"One who makes no mistakes makes nothing at all."
—*Giacomo Casanova*

"Do one thing every day that scares you."
—*Eleanor Roosevelt*

"If I'd followed all the rules I'd never have gotten anywhere."
—*Marilyn Monroe*

"Action expresses priorities."
—*Gandhi*

The amazing thing about this film is that what the viewer sees is what actually happened: Casey had been handed the money and the brief, and then he...took off. He did something nobody expected, spent the money, and came back with a finished project that was about him flying around the world with no plan wearing a FuelBand. And he gave it back to us as a finished product and said, "It's done, here you go."

Well, that's almost true. One tweak that came later concerned the quotes that Casey sprinkled throughout the film. He needed one more and asked Nike's advice. Nike's only condition was that the quote had to be in the public domain, and that anything said more than a hundred years ago was probably safe. Which made Casey think of Abraham Lincoln and found this quote: "It's not the years in your life, it's the life in your years." Perfect.

So, we got what we got. But it was brilliant as only Casey Neistat can be, and a story that only Nike could tell. The film is impressive in the way it shows how life is a sport, and you need to make it count. At the time, it became Nike's most viewed YouTube film ever, and one that earned its views virally versus being paid through a traditional advertising media model. It might have one of the biggest ROIs for a piece of film in Nike history.

And it was the perfect way to introduce the world to Nike's new innovation, the FuelBand.

How to Start a Movement

In 2012, Nike launched the revolutionary Nike+ FuelBand, an all-new activity tracker worn on your wrist and connected to your phone, that allowed its wearers to track their physical activity, daily steps, and the amount of energy burned across multiple sports. It was the most democratic sports activity sensor to date, in the sense that exercise and fitness was now a shared activity across multiple platforms. When we launched Nike+ Running with Apple in 2006—before Facebook became the dominant social media platform, before Twitter, and well before Instagram—we saw that sharing their runs that had been recorded digitally was a powerful way for runners to feel validation from friends and fellow runners. Suddenly going for a run seemed like it didn't count unless you tracked it with Nike+.

It was that insight—that the product gave consumers the

power to make their fitness moments count—that led to imagining the next phase in Nike wearable technology. Davide Grasso, who was the CMO at this time, put it succinctly to the team when he declared: "Let's start a revolution." What he meant was that the market seemed ready to embrace a product that would forever transform the way consumers looked at their fitness data. We saw an age when even the beginner runner knew their fitness stats off the top of their head. They would have a deeper understanding of their own physical activity and health than their doctors did five years earlier.

It was this call to launch a movement that struck a chord inside Nike. Davide asked the team to actually research and learn from other revolutions, from political to social to cultural, to find common threads and tactics that helped them succeed. How could we draw inspiration from these historical movements to create a marketing plan that would lead to a Nike+ FuelBand revolution?

The first step, we realized, is that we needed a call to action, a slogan that wouldn't only inspire, but also motivate consumers behind a common cause. The initial thought was to go with "Make Everything Count." It was a good description of the breadth of metrics that the FuelBand tracked, but it was too wordy. We landed on "Make It Count" for two reasons. One, we liked the idea of the line sounding like a commitment, a genuine call to action. It sounded like "I will make THIS count." The second reason is because of its connection to "Just Do It." "It"—not "everything"—was already part of Nike's DNA. So, "Make It Count" became the line.

In our research on revolutions, we found a TED Talk from entrepreneur Derek Sivers on how to start a movement that greatly helped us visualize the direction of our plan. In the talk, Derek shows one guy dancing dynamically among a bunch of seated people at an outdoor music festival. Derek narrates over the footage explaining that this first person is just a lone nut. He's not really started anything yet, and people just think he's maybe a bit off. But then someone joins him because the lone nut has made it OK to dance. The original dancer doesn't ignore the new one; he welcomes the newcomer to the dance heartily. The one-time lone nut now has his first follower. Moreover, the follower has legitimized the lone nut in the eyes of others, and makes joining him easier. After all, they're at a music festival. They're there to dance. They *want* to dance. As more people join in, the whole dynamic of the scene has changed: Now it's weird *not* to be dancing. Eventually the whole crowd is dancing. Derek sums it up that it takes not just a lone nut, but a first follower to start a movement. This served as inspiration for defining our FuelBand marketing vison.

Recruit. Rally. Roar.

David Schriber, the marketing leader for the launch, broke the plan down into "Recruit. Rally. Roar." We had the first two words coming out of the TED Talk: "Recruit" meant we had to find a bunch of people to be the first brave souls to do something noteworthy. Not only that, they had to be good leaders and embrace anyone who joined them. So we created a list of potential ambassadors who we knew could share their experiences with the FuelBand to their own audiences across a wide spectrum of fields: sports, film, music, dance, and gaming.

"Rally" was turning the call to action into something concrete. In other words, "Make It Count" works as a rally cry only if there is action behind it. In this case, we didn't just want consumers buying FuelBands; we wanted them sharing their daily fuel activity scores. The act of sharing, we knew, would elicit friendly (or perhaps fierce, depending on the consumers) competition, and competition has the magic of generating its own momentum. With games and rivalries, contests and races, just springing up spontaneously, the movement would spread and pull in others who didn't care about the tech but just wanted in on the action. We also knew we could amplify this level of sharing through our own social media channels and hashtags, allowing us to highlight Fuel scores on screens in our retail spaces. You could track, say, NFL quarterback Andrew Luck as he went through a hard day working out, and see if you could keep up.

"Roar" wasn't really pulled from Sivers's talk, but was more something David made up to mean celebration. Once enough consumers were using the FuelBand, we could create and sponsor events tailored specifically for those users, allowing them to celebrate with each other.

One of the first people we recruited was Casey, who before he made "Make It Count," put together a "teaser film" as a sort of prelude to the official launch. The film was intentionally cryptic, just showing everyday movement from normal people to start building this idea that "sports" are everywhere and anywhere. This first film ended with a shot of the back of an NYC cab with graffiti on it, alluding to Nike+. This started the rumor, as we'd hoped, that Nike was coming out with a new wearable device. The film also shared "Make It Count," our call to action, which became the second most tweeted hashtag on New Year's Day in 2012, after #happynewyear. We also asked 130 Nike athletes to tweet their athletic resolutions and goals. It being an Olympic year, there was a lot to tweet about. More people joined in, and before you knew it, the movement was on. Of course Casey's lasting contribution was the masterpiece film that was part of the official launch, in which he captured the ethos of "Make It Count" and the promise and power of the FuelBand so perfectly.

But Casey's film wasn't the official "commercial" of the campaign; it was meant to be a viral effort, built for YouTube and to be spread via social media and sharing. For the commercial film, we stayed with the ideas Casey explored in his work, and which we had been building in our campaign efforts, that sports are not defined by rules or games; they are defined by movement. The film's genesis started with an internally produced mood film—where clips of videos showed activity that either counted because they were moving, or didn't because they weren't. There were clips grabbed from famous movies, shows, YouTube videos, and sports coverage. We kept this general feel and look for the actual film itself, which proved to be quite the challenge. This was arguably the most difficult film to create from a legal and copyright standpoint since we'd secured the rights to use the Beatles' "Revolution" back in 1987. We had scenes from *Indiana Jones* alongside those from *The Wizard of Oz*, a Monty Python sketch, and the film *Amadeus*. Each scene was chosen for the movement of the characters. We had a Popeye cartoon, Bruce Lee, and *The Big Lebowski* all within a few seconds of one another. (By the way, the Dude is there as an example of nonmovement.) There isn't an original shot in the entire minute-long ad; it's all taken from films, television, YouTube, or sporting events—all of it cut to create a dynamic montage of movement. The film ends with "Life Is Sport. Make It Count" followed by a shot of the FuelBand—with Mozart (played by Tom Hulce in the iconic pink wig) giving the final flourish.

The team worked round the clock to get the rights to use the footage from these iconic scenes and characters. As it was coming down to the wire, we could not track down Roger Hill, the actor who played Cyrus from the 1979 film *The Warriors*. Because of his famous line "Can you count, suckas?" Hill's scene opens the film, as it kicked off the idea of counting, so cutting it out was not an option. With time running out, someone finally found Hill, who had become a librarian, and we were able to get his approval.

We showed the film at a big media event hosted by Jimmy Fallon, where we officially launched the FuelBand. (I was literally reviewing the final edit from my iPhone within an hour of the event's opening.) While the event was going on, we sold out of the first few thousand units online in minutes. Soon enough, all the bands sold, and it would be weeks before we could put more in the market—a great problem to have. The movement was building.

The Roar

We'd recruited, we'd rallied, and now it was time to roar. We felt our best chance for the most impactful roar moment would come at the South by Southwest Conference in Austin. The Texas town was an active one with a big running community, not to mention that SXSW, in addition to being a tech showcase, was also part music festival. The cornerstone of our efforts was an outdoor sport court of the future: a space where we could have great musical performances and sports all rolled into one—augmented with experiential stories of the FuelBand.

At the center of the sport court was a hundred-foot-long electronic billboard that was constructed at the sidewalk level. The billboard displayed the "Fuelstream," a sort of leaderboard for all the contests and competitions we had going on, powered by conference attendees wearing the FuelBands. The board also listed our scheduled events, including when the next sneaker launch was to drop. What made the billboard the stand-out display at the conference was that it responded to movement. If nothing was moving in front of it, the billboard would turn red, but the moment that someone moved in front of it, a silhouette in shades of orange to yellow to green moved with them. The shade depended on the speed of the movement. So, for instance, a walker's silhouette appeared orange on the billboard, but a sprinter's flashed green. Once visitors understood the dynamics, it was great fun to watch them manipulate the colors of the board by their movement—and that played right into our movement about movement. People mobbed it day and night.

But the showstopper was our indoor music venue, which was also sensitive to movement. All the walls inside shifted from red to green depending on how much the crowd was moving. We had Girl Talk, Major Lazer, and Sleigh Bells performing on the stage, and as they got the crowd going, the room lit up like a Christmas tree. This maelstrom of movement could also be seen from the outside. We had designed a lighting system that was directed at Frost Tower, the tallest building in the city, and right outside the music venue. As the crowd inside lit up the walls with their dancing, the lights outside kept pace, replicating the light show on the building itself. It looked as if the tower itself was dancing, flashing red, yellow, orange, and green—the show could be seen for miles.

The final element in our "roar" wasn't as innovative, but was no less effective in celebrating the movement we had created with the FuelBand. We had asked the Nike apparel team to work up a T-shirt design that had across the chest in Nike Futura typeface: "I'M WITH THE BAND." This single T-shirt idea became a driver for the whole event experience. The pun meant that if you had a FuelBand, you had access to everything that Band members get—a play, of course, on the music element of SXSW. A Band member got special food, backstage passes, cool giveaways, access to celebrities and athletes, and, most important, the ability to cut all the lines. If you had a FuelBand, you would get VIP access to everything Nike had to offer at SXSW. Attendees sporting the T-shirt got access to our movie showings, musical performances, and our art exhibit. Each venue had a prominent sign that said "WITH THE BAND," and you would simply enter through the back door and hang out in our giant outdoor "green room."

SXSW wrapped on March 18. We took one last photo of our digital wall, which displayed the FuelBand saying "GOAL," and dropped the mic. One reviewer tweeted, "Nike won SXSW. Not a tech company. Not a band. Nike."

Providing Purpose

Good brands create memorable moments; great brands create movements. But any movement needs to begin with an aspirational vision: What do we want to achieve? Put another way, since brand movements are tied to products, the better question is: What do we want this product to achieve? Not *do*, but *achieve*. What can it facilitate? How can it improve the consumer's life? Find the answer to those questions, and you have the vision for your movement.

Marketers too often lose sight of the purpose of their product by focusing on what it does. It has the latest tech, it has the best fabric, it has the best engine, it has the best interface. These things might be true, but they say nothing to the person who really wants to understand something far more basic: How will this product help me? And by helping one person, it can help many people. But don't stop there. Don't leave it to the individual customer to be converted as a believer in your product; *help them convert others*. Be active and purposeful in building a cause around the product.

From one into many. From one lone nut—or ambassador—into an entire festival of dancers. From one reluctant runner into an entire city joined together, triumphantly climbing the steps to the Philadelphia Museum of Art. Movements are community led; they flourish when those within them believe they are a part of something greater, something that helps not only them but everyone around them. And that share a feeling of progress, that together we are unleashing our own potential, that is the fuel that keeps them going.

Discover the potential in your product, and you will help consumers discover the potential in themselves.

PRINCIPLES FOR "SPARK A MOVEMENT"

1. AN AUDACIOUS FUTURE

Movements are about change. The goal should be attainable, but also audacious. Audacity is, after all, far more inspiring than timidity. It should make dreamers sit up and skeptics scoff. It's the dreamers you want; leave the skeptics on the couch.

2. A CATALYST FOR ACTION

Movements need an inspirational, charismatic leader. Likewise, a leader must be both relatable and work as a catalyst to action. As a brand, your consumer needs to feel inspired by the leader and, just as important, see themselves in the leader.

3. TOOLS FOR EMPOWERMENT

Successful movements are tied to tools of empowerment, the means by which people can achieve the audacious goal. Too often brands think technical superiority drives consumer affinity. Although people care about *what's in* the product; they care more about what *they can do* with the product.

4. MOVEMENTS NEED MOMENTS

Use a time or place to let people see that they are part of something that is both meaningful *and* growing. They began alone, isolated, and stuck sharing a dream but without the means of realizing it. Now they are part of something bigger, something important, and something that has made them better than they were before.

CHAPTER 8

CLOSE THE DISTANCE

On July 13, 2016, NBA stars Carmelo Anthony, Chris Paul, Dwyane Wade, and LeBron James opened the ESPYs with one of the most powerful moments in the show's history.

"Generations ago, legends like Jesse Owens, Jackie Robinson, Muhammad Ali, John Carlos and Tommie Smith, Kareem Abdul-Jabbar, Jim Brown, Billie Jean King, Arthur Ashe, and countless others, they set a model for what athletes should stand for," said Paul. "So we choose to follow in their footsteps."

The crisis that had brought the four athletes to the stage at the Microsoft Theater in Los Angeles was injustice against Black Americans. The week prior, Alton Sterling and Philando Castile had been shot and killed by police in separate incidents, sparking protests across the country. At least, that was the immediate issue; there were other issues, deeper tragedies that went back... well, centuries, that American society had never been able to reconcile.

"The system is broken, the problems are not new, the violence is not new, and the racial divide definitely is not new, but the urgency for change is definitely at an all-time high," said Anthony.

One to the next, each athlete talked about their role in the ongoing crisis, and how they were standing there to help others feel the urgency to stand up themselves.

"Tonight we're honoring Muhammad Ali, the GOAT," said James. "But to do his legacy any justice, let's use this moment as a call to action to all professional athletes to educate ourselves, explore these issues, speak up, use our influence and renounce all violence and, most importantly, go back to our communities, invest our time, our resources, help rebuild them, help strengthen them, help change them. We all have to do better."

We do, indeed. That was my thought as I watched these four Black Americans follow in the footsteps of someone who has been a source of inspiration for me my entire life, Ali. I was only two months into my role as chief marketing officer at Nike, and listening to these men speak, I suddenly felt both a sense of urgency and courage. Urgency, because these players were setting down a challenge for everyone to step up. It was time to amplify our athlete's voices, as Nike has done so well in the past, to bring attention to the struggle of Black America and a legacy of systemic racism. The opportunity was now.

But also courage, because I was filled with a profound sense of responsibility in that moment. Or, perhaps, a rediscovery of what had always been my responsibility. Nike had used its voice to amplify the cause of justice in America and around the world, but here was a moment when, more than ever, those who could had to take a leadership role in effecting change. Now, these four athletes reminded me that it was time to do so, that the moment was upon us and action was urgent.

Here was an issue whose relevance to sports was staring us in the face. Where did sports intersect with racial injustice? How were these two concepts related? Answer: Anthony, Paul, Wade, and James. They stood up for those who couldn't stand themselves.

They were athletes, four of the greatest to ever play the game, and they were telling us that this issue was relevant to sports. Right then, I decided to use their example as a catalyst to find the deeper insights within sports to reveal the hard truths about our society.

No doubt spurred by the ESPYs speech, the next day, and for many days after, my team and I pondered how we would accept the challenge just set down.

We were being asked to lead. Nike would answer. It was time to stand up.

Stand Up, Speak Up

In October 2004, Luis Aragonés, the coach of the Spanish national football team, with journalists and a camera crew looking on, was attempting to pump up one of his players, when he said: "Tell that negro de mierda [black shit] that you are much better than him. Don't hold back, tell him. Tell him from me. You have to believe in yourself, you're better than that negro de mierda." The player Aragonés was referring to was France's Thierry Henry.

Unfortunately, racism in international football was nothing new, with fans often being the worst offenders. There's even been a term for the chant that some fans use against Black players on the opposing team: They're called "monkey chants," because of the way the fans make monkey noises. But player-on-player racism had also been rising at this time, with several incidents over the preceding years in which Black players were called the N-word by players and coaches of the other team. Aragonés's phrase when talking about Henry was enough to make the French footballer say, "Enough is enough."

And that was when Nike got involved.

Partnering with Henry, Nike launched the "Stand Up, Speak Up" campaign in January 2005 across Europe, aimed at sparking a movement against the racist culture that had infected the sport for so long. Other players, like Rio Ferdinand, Wayne Rooney, Ronaldinho, Cristiano Ronaldo, and Adriano, also joined the movement. The centerpiece of the campaign was a thirty-second film that showed Henry and the other players holding up printed signs one by one, that said:

"I love football."

"I love the challenge."

"I love"

"The sound of the ball"

"Hitting the back of the net."

"The sound of the fans"

"Screaming with joy."

"And yet"

"We are still abused"

"For the color of our skin."

"We need your voices"

"To drown out the racists."

"Wherever you hear them"

"Say no."

Then, the only words spoken in the entire film: "Stand up. Speak up."

The central insight that unlocked the film was that there existed a "silent majority" of nonracists, those whose love for the beautiful game, no matter the player's race, matched only their disgust at those who tried to degrade it with their racist taunts. The film was aimed at them, telling them that the players, the best players in the world, stood with them. That to save the game they loved, they had to fight for it. They wouldn't be alone in that fight. Henry and the others would stand with them. The film was shot in five different languages and released all over the continent.

But, as we saw in chapter 7, movements aren't made by single commercials. More needed to be done to unleash the silent majority and change football. Which is why the campaign also sold black-and-white interlocking wristbands with the words "Stand Up, Speak Up" engraved on them. Proceeds from the wristbands went to support the Stand Up, Speak Up fund, which donated the money to charities and nonprofits all over Europe dedicated to combating racism in sports. Players wore the wristbands on the pitch, and within a few years five million had been sold.

At the time, I was the vice president of Global Brand Design, and responsible for driving the brand identities and experiences for Nike football, and other sports categories, around the world. The "Stand Up, Speak Up" campaign would influence how I approached future moments to use sports to drive social and cultural transformation. The commercial itself works brilliantly by talking directly to the fans themselves, bringing them into the movement, and providing a direct call to action. The key insight was that the racists were ruining the sport these fans loved, but also that the athletes themselves needed help in pushing back. Much of the racism occurring in the sport was behind the scenes, away from the pitch, and the athletes were just supposed to "take it." The commercial exposed the fans to the hard truths of the sport: that players of color were often treated less than by other players and coaches. The "beautiful game" had a very ugly side to it. As a business, European football cannot ignore its customers, and if its customers demanded change, then it would force change. Enter the movement of antiracists across Europe who would help restore the beautiful game.

Drawing on these lessons is how we at Nike responded to the moment raised by the four players at the ESPYs.

Push the World Forward

The "Stand Up, Speak Up" campaign, and others like it—especially the 1995 film "If You Let Me Play," which addressed increasing girls' participation in and empowerment through sports—provided Nike with a firm foundation on which to continue addressing topics of justice as they intersected with sport. Our action in this field wasn't new, in other words. In fact, before the ESPYs, I had held my first Global Marketing offsite event as CMO in Paris, France, which brought together the brand leaders of all the Nike geographies, sports categories, and functions. The offsite coincided with the NBA Championship series between the LeBron-led Cleveland Cavaliers and the Golden State Warriors. Game 7 of the series was played at 1:00 a.m. Paris time, and I—as well as a lot of the team—stayed up to watch it all. The game, which the Cavs won, went down in history as one of the greatest, with LeBron making a play known today as "the Block" to seal the victory. With less than two minutes to go and the game tied, Warriors forward Andre Iguodala grabbed a rebound and raced down the court for what appeared would be an easy layup. LeBron, however, caught Iguodala at the basket and blocked the layup attempt in a magnificent display of speed and agility. The Cavs would go on to win Cleveland's first major sports title since 1964.

Inspired by the Cavs victory, I quickly spent the next few early-morning hours reworking my presentation to reference moments from that incredible game. If you couldn't tell by now, I love to draw leadership lessons from sports, and that game was just *so* good. My talk got a little assist, when we released a piece of creative featuring an iconic black-and-white image of LeBron as a teenager with the words "Always Believe" that morning across social media.

Perhaps it was the excitement of the moment, the sense that we all had witnessed something historic, that pushed us during that offsite to supercharge Nike's efforts to drive themes of equality within our storytelling. We wanted to use sport as a vehicle to empower people and communities to see the confluence of sports with America's quest for equality. Thus, starting with the presentation that morning, the mantra "Push the World Forward" became our internal call to action that would become a strong area of focus within our marketing brand plan for the following year and beyond. It would be our statement of purpose, and we would keep going back to it and see if we were living up to it.

And then the shootings of Sterling and Castile happened, and America exploded.

The Reason

On July 7, 2016, those who visited the Wieden & Kennedy website expecting to learn about the agency's award-winning work found a black screen with some white text instead. The text read:

Why your Black co-worker seems especially bitter today...

Why your Black co-worker seems especially sad today...

Why your Black co-worker seems especially quiet today...

We are processing.

We are asking ourselves what to do.

We are hurt because it feels like watching our
own selves get gunned down.

We are telling ourselves, "do not let this make you
live in fear, do not let this make you hate."

But we're scared for our lives, our family's lives, our friend's lives.

We're mad that the protests aren't working. Why the video
recordings aren't working.

We're conflicted, in a place between crippling empathy for this man and his family and contempt at a
world that seems not to care enough.

We are disgusted at police but telling ourselves,
"you can't hate all police."

We are wondering the point of a moment of silence.

We are wondering if we ourselves will make it back home today.

We are wondering what to do, what to do, what to do.

Just an FYI, not for sympathy. Just acknowledging this
because it should be acknowledged. #AltonSterling

The words had been written by Wieden & Kennedy copywriter
Kervins Chauvet, who is Black. As he explained later:[10]

Waking up that morning, I learned what a heavy heart felt
like. Weighed down by questions that no answers could

possibly justify and anger that no one who didn't share my melanin could fully understand. The complexity of the feeling left me enraged and hopeless all at once. Like many of us on that morning, I showered and dressed myself with that feeling. Rode the bus to work with that feeling. Sat down at my desk, opened my laptop and stared down at my screen with that feeling. What to do? This will probably go down as the single most important thing I have ever written.

Chauvet had written the words for internal consumption, strictly within the Wieden & Kennedy offices, but Dan Wieden himself decided that those words would stand for the entire company, and they were posted on the website. The only change was that the hashtag at the end was changed to #blacklivesmatter. "The Reason," as the text became known as, generated plenty of conversation throughout social media and all over media. Even the *Washington Post* wrote an article on it the following day.[11]

To those who didn't work as closely (or at all) with Wieden & Kennedy, it may seem surprising, if still appreciated, that this creative agency had put forth one of the first and certainly one of the most powerful messages during those painful confusing weeks following the shootings of Sterling and Castile. But to those of us at Nike, Wieden & Kennedy's leadership on equality was anything but surprising. For the past year, Dan Wieden's team had been working on improving awareness and the processes of addressing inequality in the workplace through a series of "Courageous Conversation" workshops. More, the agency had been proactively presenting ideas to Nike that centered on stories of equality through sports. These concepts became the inspiration for a story that the brand would launch during the Summer Olympics in Rio de

Janeiro and which, ultimately, led to the development of Nike's "Equality" campaign, which would launch a year later.

Unlimited Together

People, people
We the people would like you to know
That wherever you go, we're right by your side

With echoes of the "Star-Spangled Banner," Chance the Rapper's "We the People" was the song Nike used to anchor its "Unlimited Together" film. Against projected footage of the USA Men's and Women's Basketball Teams on urban buildings, Chance sings this soulful ode that uses well-worn phrases from America's cultural tapestry to provide a song that both challenges and unifies. It is uplifting, but it's also a reminder that so many of America's most-touted achievements are in fact illusory to so many of "we the people." The basketball teams themselves serve as the connecting theme—the place that sports plays in the fabric of society—that showcases how Americans of all colors still are on the same side; that we still must play together.

The work on "Unlimited Together" started before the ESPYs, but its launch not long after those athletes called for change couldn't have been better timed. Early in development, I remember having the desire to make sure that however we used our voice to enter the fight against inequality, it needed to break from conventional notes, and that relying on traditional concepts of American greatness against the odds wouldn't cut through. We could love what America is supposed to stand for while also inviting more Americans to stand up.

Early on in the process, without visuals or a script, I listened to the vocals of Chance the Rapper's original song for the first time. It was clear. We didn't need anything else in that moment to move forward. Out of all the concepts that the creative teams had explored, Chance's soulful but also hopeful "We the People" was the one. The Wieden & Kennedy New York office developed the "Unlimited Together" campaign, and it was the first time that both the USA Basketball Men's and Women's Teams would be featured together in a film. The concept drew inspiration from two previous Nike commercials, tonally from an ad featuring Marvin Gaye from 2008, "United We Rise," and visually by the Nike Air 180 commercial from 1991. But Chance gave the film its soul. His lyrics provided the right tone we had wanted for the campaign—which was even more amazing because it was Chance's first stab at it.

A Change Is Gonna Come

The Fifty-Ninth Annual Grammy Awards aired on February 12, 2017. In the days leading up to the date, I was in Berlin. In between meetings, my face buried in my iPhone, I reviewed edits to the new Nike film that would serve as part of our response to the challenge put down by the four athletes at the ESPYs eight months earlier. We had chosen the Grammys as the launch event because it presented an opportunity to reach an audience beyond sport. The new film had to stand on its own as a storytelling vehicle to firmly set down Nike's voice in this most critical of moments, when the nation, still reeling from the upheavals over the summer and now further divided by a presidential election, was questioning whether its foundational principles still held true.

The journey to this moment, seven months in the making, had been one of the most exciting and profoundly moving of my professional career. As the team sat with the images and emotions from the previous summer, we saw a country divided by racial strife. Yes, the ESPYs had shown four of the greatest basketball players in the world coming together to stand against racial injustice, but we at Nike and Wieden & Kennedy couldn't limit our story to basketball. It had to be about sports, in all their forms, manifestations, and cultural impact.

In 1994, South Africa had just ended the criminal policy of apartheid and elected Nelson Mandela, a man who had been imprisoned for twenty-six years, as president of a united country. But South Africa was united only in name, and many Blacks had a particular hatred of the country's rugby team, the Springboks, because it was historically the sport for white Afrikaners. In 1995, South Africa was host for the Rugby World Cup, and Mandela, surprising both Black and white alike, threw his full support behind the Springboks. What Mandela saw, as others would see only later, is that the World Cup, this sport of rugby, was a moment around which the whole country could unite. He set aside decades-old animosities to embrace a united team and a united country. He called upon his empathy to remember that he wasn't president of one half of the country; he was president of all the country, and that included those who both played with and rooted for the Springboks. That was the power of sports; that was the beautiful magic sports have on people and communities. The country might remain divided outside the field of competition, but on that pitch, in that stadium, South Africa was one team, and they would win or lose as one team.

South Africa won the Cup, and the outpouring of national

pride that erupted in the streets and across the country, white and Black celebrating together, showed not only the power but also the wisdom of Mandela's actions. He would later say: "Sport has the power to change the world. It has the power to inspire. It has the power to unite people in a way that little else does. It speaks to youth in a language they understand. Sport can create hope where once there was only despair. It is more powerful than governments in breaking down racial barriers. It laughs in the face of all types of discrimination."

The question we had to answer, though, was *why*. Why did sports have this power? What was the insight that made Mandela see the purpose in bringing his country together for...a game? As we pondered this question, we realized that the world of sports, the one that plays out on the field or on the court, mimics our own in some crucial ways: discipline, hard work, dedication, raw talent, and, last, the idea that we all must follow a set of rules to ensure that the game is played fairly. But does this last attribute of sports really carry over in our real world? In some cases it does, but in many others it doesn't. We expect that the ball should bounce the same for everyone in sports; shouldn't we also expect that in our communities?

It was this key insight which unlocked the "Equality" campaign. The film wasn't going to respond to a single incident, such as the shootings of the previous summer. Those tragic deaths launched a rejuvenated effort to achieve racial equality in America. This was a story that stretched back decades, and was intimately tied to sports and, especially, those Black athletes who had fought for equality and inclusion.

For this reason, the creative team chose Sam Cooke's "A Change Is Gonna Come," drawing on the success of "Unlimited Together," also anchored in a song. But whereas Chance the Rapper's "We the People" was a hopeful cry for the country to live up to its founding ideals, "A Change Is Gonna Come" is forceful; it is a song of hope to those who still hurt and a warning to those who inflict pain.

> It's been a long, a long time coming
> But I know a change gonna come

Cooke's lyrics did not mourn what was; they announced what would be. A fact made clear when the great Alicia Keys gave vivid life to the iconic civil rights song. But then we moved on to the words, the message we would use to tell our story of Equality. The script had to be anchored in sports but also draw on empathy for those who live and have lived by a different set of rules. It had to declare why we are drawn to sports, the significance and power of what sports provide—a sense of excellence, of competition, and, most of all, fair play. And the insistence that these qualities must transcend sports; they must carry over beyond the lines on the court and field and into our world. With the words ready, a voice-over by the actor Michael B. Jordan provided the message:

> Here within these lines, on this concrete court. This patch of turf. Here, you're defined by your actions. Not your looks or beliefs. Equality should have no boundaries. The bonds we find here should run past these lines. Opportunity should not discriminate. The ball should bounce the same for everyone. Worth should outshine color.

In the expert hands of director Melina Matsoukas and cinematographer Malik Sayeed, the images the viewers see, in black-and-white, are of an urban basketball court, whose lines are being extended by those with spray-paint cans—a nod to the street activism that had defined so much of the previous summer's protests. A man is watching youth play ball. It's LeBron. The scene shifts to a tennis court, and we see Serena Williams. Another shift: a soccer pitch, and Megan Rapinoe. And on it goes, with Kevin Durant, Dalilah Muhammad, Gabby Douglas, and Victor Cruz all coming into frame. Other iconic American buildings intersperse the film: an inner-city church and a courthouse.

The spray painting continues and the lines extend from the court, outward into the streets and sidewalk, into the community, across the nation—where the rules that govern competitive play should govern how we live as well. Jordan then says, referring to the athletic arenas: "If we can be equals here..." To which LeBron finishes, "...we can be equals everywhere." Then Alicia's last soulful blast of "Change gonna come. Yes it will."

The film came together in time for the Grammys. It was broadcast live all over the world, and it helped launch a global campaign that might have begun with a film but didn't end there. On the night of the broadcast, Nike changed all its social media profile pictures to the word "Equality" in white letters against a black background. Nike also included other products to spread the message, including a T-shirt with the word "Equality" in the Nike typeface—Futura Extra Bold—all in caps. Since it was a statement of purpose, there was a period at the end of the word.

Over the next year, LeBron poured himself into promoting the campaign. During a game in 2018, he even wore one white and one black limited edition sneaker, each with the word "Equality" embroidered on the heel. LeBron summed up the campaign as powerfully as anyone: "Basketball is our vehicle, but Equality is our mission."

So far in this chapter we've looked at empathy mostly through the medium of film. But as we've seen elsewhere, film isn't the only way to elicit emotion to stir action, and Nike has found great success in using environments and products to even the playing field.

Empathy in Action

In 2010, the World Cup was held in Johannesburg. The global event brought a spotlight to both the beauty (as well as the poverty) of the capital of South Africa, a country where 350,000 kids play soccer almost daily. Many, however, lack the basic necessities of life, not to mention poor facilities and safe places to play their favorite game. In addition to its poverty, South Africa also has the highest rate of HIV/AIDS infection in the world. As we looked toward Nike's campaign to be launched during the World Cup, our attention was on these deficiencies and problems. We wanted to go beyond merely celebrating football for the world. We saw an opportunity to bring attention to the plight of South Africans. We also wanted to engage South Africans and understand their world and what mattered.

Learning the many problems that afflicted this country and city, the question we asked ourselves was: How could we use football to improve education and services for HIV/AIDS for South African youths? From these conversations, we started a partnership with Project Red, which works to raise awareness to end HIV/AIDS through other brands. The result of this partnership was called Lace Up Save Lives. When someone around the world bought a pair of (NIKE)RED laces, Nike contributed money to support programs that offer education and medication on the ground in South Africa. The program was backed up by incredible ambassadors like the legendary footballer Didier Drogba from the Ivory Coast.

But we took this program a step further, again with an understanding of the real needs of South Africans—especially the youth, whose playing fields, if they had them at all, were made of hard dirt, often in areas that were unsafe. To provide a safe space for South African kids to play football, we designed and built the Nike Football Training Centre in Soweto, South Africa. I wanted our efforts to involve the local community from the beginning to ensure that the architectural design was authentically South African.

It wasn't enough just to design functional structures. The community had aspirations beyond that, and they wanted the new Soweto Center to be a place where the spirit of their community and the dreams of their youth could flourish. So storytelling became a part of the architecture and environment, infusing those spaces with emotion and a sense of cultural history. Nike collaborated with local Soweto artists and drew from stories of legendary football clubs around the world to build into the Center a sense of place and purpose, a space that the local community could see and visit with pride.

When it was done, the Soweto Center served twenty thousand young footballers every year. Today the Center has gone beyond football and become a multipart training facility that looks to increase female sports participation in South Africa. It includes a running track, a skate park, a dance studio, and workshops to promote Soweto's creative community. This is an example of the power of radical creative collaboration and how in this case, sports, education, and medication can intersect to lift up underserved communities.

Creating social impact through design not only applies to architecture but product innovation too. Nike's recent Pro Hijab innovation is an example of seeing, listening, and learning and, in turn, delivering a breakthrough. Not long ago, there were no sport-performance hijabs available to athletes to compete in, not even at the Olympic level. You had elite-level fencers and boxers wearing hijabs with traditional fabric. When the material would get wet, it would get heavy and stiff, which ultimately led to obstructed hearing and discomfort. This could result in false start penalties for those fencers who wore a hijab during competition. The hijab also didn't interact with the uniforms, which further hindered performance, thus giving an unfair advantage to the competition. So Nike designers listened to the voices and stories of these underserved athletes and created a lighter, softer, and more breathable garment. As Zeina Nassar, a German boxer, said after competing in the Pro Hijab, "Suddenly, I could hear, I wasn't as hot, and it felt like my body was able to cool itself down better and faster."

While these examples of empathy in action may not be directly related to the racial injustices that have plagued America, they are no less impactful for seeing how brands can respond to the unseen and unmet needs that exist in the world.

Full Circle

In February 2011, the Nike Black Employee Network (BEN), one of several employee networks Nike has built over the years, held its inaugural Sneaker Ball. With February being Black History Month, the BEN wanted to have an event that celebrated the inter-section of Black culture and social change with sports. Thus, the

Sneaker Ball was born. During the event, I was called to the stage by Howard H. White, the longtime Brand Jordan sports marketing legend. Howard was there to present me with the "H" Award, an honor in his name, given to the Nike leader for their commitment and contributions to the Black employee community within Nike. The honor was something of a "full circle" moment for me, considering that I had joined Nike nineteen years earlier as part of the brand's first minority internship program, and was the only Black member of the Image Design team during that summer in 1992. My journey wasn't finished, but to be honored by my colleagues in such a way was one of the more memorable moments of my professional life.

In the early stages of my Nike career, in addition to my design duties, I was also part of the original team that created the Nike Black History Month posters—years before most major brands chose to celebrate the month. These weren't your typical sports-centered posters that revolved around superstar athletes. They were far more artistic in design and reflective in purpose. For example, one 1996 poster showed a figurative drawing of a person, painted in brown, against a yellow background. But this was only the top half of the poster. The bottom half was a reflection, the silhouetted person in yellow, against a brown background. Words like "equality," "peace," "justice," and "integration" cover both halves of the poster, both right side up and upside down, serving as a reminder that there are two sides to every issue. These posters were distributed within the brand, but also to schools, organizations, and publications, and were meant to spark both discussion and learning on topics that mattered to the Black community.

Working on the posters was just the beginning of a number of opportunities that were either presented to me or I found through my own initiative. These issues don't stop at the edge of the court or field, nor do they at the doors to the office. When I first joined Nike, the concepts of Diversity, Equity, and Inclusion (DEI) were just beginning to form across the internal brand cultures of America. While the level of diversity within brands might have been lacking at that time, I sensed opportunities to change that trajectory within my roles at Nike. As my leadership platform and profile grew, and I found myself in positions to influence recruiting and hiring decisions, I made a point to improve the representation of marketers and designers of color within the brand. But I didn't do it alone, nor did I learn the concepts of being a leader who strives to create a diverse workforce simply on my own. I had help, plenty of help, and whatever progress I was able to make in creating teams that reflected the consumers we served, I owed to those who inspired and partnered with me. Three leaders in particular stand out for helping to multiply my ability to make a difference during this time.

I like to say that Pamela Neferkara "unlocked my leadership." As a senior leader within the marketing organization of the Jordan Brand, Pamela was instrumental in moving Nike's relationship with its consumers to online platforms, where it almost exclusively exists today. She also brought her perspective as a rare Black female senior leader to work every day. As I got to know Pamela, she asked me to become a member of the advisory group for BEN. I was reluctant at first, citing my workload as the reason. Internally, I questioned whether my perspective, as a mixed-race man, would be as valued. But Pamela wouldn't have it. She kept asking, and finally I embraced the moment and responsibility. It kicked off a fifteen-year run of leadership for the Black community of Nike marketers and designers.

Jason Mayden "pushed me on to take the stage." As a gifted designer and an equally gifted speaker and motivator, Jason was a powerhouse in BEN, and he helped push the creative rebranding of the Network to new levels. Initially, he and I developed a strong connection over our shared passion for the sweet science, otherwise known as boxing. Now that I was one of the advisory leaders for the network, Jason would often ask me to kick off events and get in front of the audiences, such as the annual Sneaker Ball. He would make these "requests" in such a way that I couldn't say no. Sometimes he would fuel my presentations by giving me a Martin Luther King Jr. quote to read for my opening remarks. Jason's talent was to make me feel that it was my duty and my destiny to rise to the moment. Such is the gift of great motivators.

Jonathan Johnson Griffin "multiplied my skills." In the mid-1990s, the Black History Month posters represented the extent of our work to commemorate and celebrate Black Americans. Over time, however, we branched out, creating a limited edition Air Force 1 sneaker, for example. Then I met a young designer named Jonathan Johnson Griffin, also known as JJG, who felt we could do much more than just a shoe. At this point I was well into my role of leading Nike's creative storytelling around the world. Together, JJG and I talked about a bigger vision: creating a story around an entire collection of products, all celebrating and commemorating the achievements and excellence of Black athletes. The collection would represent the whole Nike family: Converse, Jordan, and Nike Basketball through three monumental Black athletes, Julius Erving, Michael Jordan, and Kobe Bryant. These Black History Month shoes would be worn on the court at the NBA All Star game, but would also be available for everyone. JJG pushed me to expand my field of vision and embrace a cause that deserved so much more than a poster.

Beyond the partnership and inspiration these unique individuals provided me, they all challenged me to see in myself what they saw, and pushed me to unleash the leadership qualities I needed to cultivate. Through their example and belief, I was able to accelerate my journey as a leader of not just a business and a brand, but as someone who could advance the goals of diversity, equity, and inclusion. I always remembered that when I found myself in a position to elevate and support others who needed to be seen and heard, especially those individuals who oftentimes were the only ones in the room who looked like themselves. Because I had leaders who unlocked my talents as a diverse leader, I learned how to draw out the talents of others. Their example was also a lesson in making sure that as you climb the mountain, you bring along others who don't necessarily have a voice that is heard or work that is seen. Thanks to these individuals, I was able to aspire to a leadership role beyond the brand and business.

Dream Crazy

I was in a private dining room at the Joan Benoit Samuelson Building on Nike's Beaverton campus. With me were other members of the marketing and business teams. We were waiting to have lunch with Colin Kaepernick, who, this close to the start of the NFL season, was still without a team. We wanted to sit down with Colin to discuss where he was and what he wanted to accomplish. As ever, Nike seeks to amplify the voice of the athlete, on and off the field, and Colin's voice, to say the least, had grown considerably in the past year. At the start of the 2016 season a year earlier, Colin took a stand against racial injustice and police brutality against the Black community by kneeling during the national anthem. Since then, Colin, a one-time Super Bowl quarterback who had been released by the 49ers in the off-season, had only increased his activism. The unique challenge (from a traditional marketing point of view) was that he was currently unemployed—in the sense that as an athlete, he wasn't "playing."

Although one would never have guessed that when he walked in, fresh off a morning workout at the Bo Jackson Fitness Center on campus. It was the first time I met him. Even I, who was no stranger to meeting professional athletes, was impressed with his physical presence. Clearly, this was a guy who hadn't lost a step. In fact, he looked to be in the best shape of his life. The other thing I noticed immediately was that Colin came with no entourage—no agent, no PR person, no handlers. It was just him and his friend who was also his trainer. Colin sat down next to me as we started to eat.

For someone who had been at the center of a media firestorm for the past year, Colin was remarkably composed and reserved—but passionate. Passionate about getting back on the field, but also focused on his fight against racial injustice and the continued development of his "Know Your Rights" camps, which seek to empower underprivileged youths from Black communities. If the past year had been hard on Colin's football career, it hadn't quieted his voice. As we listened, he emphasized that he didn't want our storytelling efforts to be about him; it had to be about his cause. Not the man who knelt, but *why* he knelt.

I can't speak for the others at the lunch that day, but I can talk about my own feelings and thoughts. I can talk about how when I saw Colin for the first time face-to-face, I felt a connection to his story. I too am a biracial man who was adopted and raised by white parents, and spent a lot of my childhood searching for my own identity. Like a lot of kids growing up in my neighborhood, I had my sports heroes, the athletes I admired and emulated, whose success allowed me to find inspiration and generated a sense of pride in my own racial identity. These Black athletes of the 1970s and 1980s used their heroic performances to instill pride in the communities from which they came, not just the city whose uniform they wore. They played for those who didn't have a voice, whose communities were wracked with poverty, injustice, and prejudice.

The confluence between sports and culture has achieved tremendous progress for society over the decades, from the days of Jackie Robinson to Colin Kaepernick. To dismiss that connection, to "focus on football," is to ignore one of the primary reasons sports is at the heart of American culture, whose practitioners have used their platform for all varieties of inspiration. I didn't understand the full importance of this as a child, but there was a reason I was drawn to these great men and women. They weren't just larger than life because they could play better than most; they swelled my pride and imagination—and yes, love of sports—because they were full of passion and purpose whether they were wearing a jersey or not. Forty years later, a Black athlete takes a knee to protest police brutality and pays a professional price for doing so. Perhaps someone without empathy for the Black experience in America might not have heard what Colin was telling us that day. But I was there, and I saw my younger self, a kid searching for his identity who would have seen this star quarterback take that knee, and realized he did that for others like me.

The empathy that all of us felt at the table that day for Colin and his purpose was the first step in designing a message to support him and the cause. After this pivotal lunch, I spent the weekends that football season with our creative partners at Wieden & Kennedy brainstorming concepts that would shed light on Colin's message. We had to communicate through the platform of sports and ensure that sports' role wasn't lost to a social-justice message only. We reminded ourselves over and over again that any idea that wasn't using sports to reveal a greater truth in culture was one we shouldn't follow.

We explored multiple concepts, taglines, and visual motifs. For inspiration, we even looked at a letter a young Colin wrote to himself in the fourth grade, explaining how he was going to play in the league one day. The letter was poignant, but not quite right for where Colin was at that moment. Nothing stuck. The ideas either were not directly related to sports and the role they should play, or to Colin, who didn't want the focus on him but rather on the cause. It must be said that at no time in our brainstorming together did we consider using the controversy in highlighting Colin's message. Our only concern was crafting a message that addressed racial injustice through the lens of sport. Our aim was to take the conversation that Colin had started to a place where we could move people to act. What we found, however, was that our concepts would address *some* of the issues we needed to include, but not all of them. We weren't going to go out with anything that wasn't 100 percent true to Colin's message. And in the end, we simply ran out of time. As the weeks of the season went by, I decided to table the creative conversations and revisit them at a later time.

Eight months later, I started my new role as VP of Global Brand Innovation. It was bittersweet. It would mean leaving behind a body of work that was deeply personal. I would be supporting my successor, DJ Van Hameren, as well as Gino Fisanotti, KeJuan

Wilkins, VP of Nike Communications, and Alex Lopez, a long-time leader within Nike Advertising, as they looked to finally discover the message for Colin over the next three months.

Fortunately, they didn't lack momentum. Twenty eighteen was the thirtieth anniversary of Just Do It. Our internal discussions on the coming campaign to commemorate the occasion centred on childhood, the dreams we have when we're young, and the importance of believing in one's self. The focus would be on positioning Just Do It to the next generation of rising athletes. We packaged this idea in a creative brief and consumer proposition and got to work with the Wieden & Kennedy creative directors, Alberto and Ryan. For the Wieden & Kennedy team, it was an ideal assignment, because it opened up the world of imagination and dreams.

The creative minds at the agency came back with the words "Dream Crazy." What after all are a young person's dreams if not "crazy," at least by adult standards? It flowed perfectly into Just Do It as well, retaining the clarity of purpose and simplicity of that thirty-year-old motto. The W&K team also produced a mood film to convey the concept to us at Nike. The film was powerful, as were the words that accompanied it, but it still needed something more to truly cut through.

And that was when the idea of using Colin as the voice-over was raised. The film would focus on youth—a kind of callback to the ideas of Colin's childhood that we had explored during the previous fall season—but it wouldn't be about Colin, at least not directly. It would be about doing what you know is right in your heart, doing what you know you must do, embracing the crazy idea that stirs your soul and not caring what others think. It was about sacrifice, and standing against the world, because you know it's the right thing to do. This insight, however, doesn't end when you're young, even if that's where we must nurture it. It continues as one enters the adult world, and those "crazy dreams" run up against the cold, hard reality of real choices, and even sacrifice. What then? Are you too old to dream crazy? Colin certainly didn't think so, and so the final lines of the film were added, emphasizing that the dreams that ignite our spirits, that make us reach beyond our own material desires, are worth the sacrifice.

Finally, in September 2018, after a year exploring the best way to acknowledge Colin's cause (and sacrifice), the "Crazy Dreams" campaign was launched on Opening Day in the NFL.

The film opens with a skateboarder sliding down a railing. He falls, badly. He does it again, and falls again. Badly. This happens for a third time. The scene shifts to a wrestling mat, showing a wrestler with no legs. Meanwhile, Colin's voice-over provides the message:

If people say your dreams are crazy

If they laugh at what you think you can do

Good.

Stay that way.

Because what nonbelievers fail to understand is that calling a dream crazy is not an insult.

It's a compliment.

We see surfers; women boxers in hijabs. We see disabled basketball players in wheelchairs. Colin mentions brain cancer; he mentions refugees. We see LeBron in high school dunking a basketball, then LeBron, an adult now, speaking at the opening of his "I Promise" school.

And then, the conclusion: Colin, on a street corner, turns to look at the camera, with his voice-over providing the theme of the campaign: "Believe in something, even if it means sacrificing everything."

Although the media made it the Colin Kaepernick campaign, the film is, in fact, a celebration of athletes who "Dream Crazy." Of course, the film caused controversy when it was released. But, as we look back four years later, as we look at how NFL games have opened with a commemoration for racial justice, we know that what was considered crazy was in fact only the beginning.

Close the Distance

The creative journeys recounted in this chapter all start from the same premise. We often find the most impactful insights when we expand our field of vision and see what formerly we didn't see. The essence of this is empathy, our willingness to listen to and understand those whose experiences differ from our own. As told in this chapter, many of those insights discovered through empathy led to transformational change. We were able to look deeper at a person or an issue than we had previously and find the hard truth buried within. When we went beyond simple observations and assumptions, we were able to tap our creative energies in ways that might otherwise have remained hidden.

As creative leaders, our role is to find those connective threads between what we sell and what the world needs. To use our talents, to call upon our empathy, to see that the world we inhabit isn't the world that others experience; to ensure that those ideas reveal a deeper insight about our world, and also lead to impactful story-telling. Indifference isn't an option if we are to push society forward. With our insights, and through our stories—told in images, in film, in architecture, and in products—we are able to close the distance between the disparities in our world and a more equitable future, and thus ensure that the ball bounces the same for everyone. When we tie this insight to our brand purpose, we are able to ignite conversations with our consumers that lead to collective action and result in positive change in the world around us.

PRINCIPLES FOR "CLOSE THE DISTANCE"

1. STRENGTHEN YOUR PERIPHERAL VISION

Go beyond simple observations and assumptions. Dig deeper to find the unseen needs that exist in underserved communities. By increasing our ability to see, hear, and feel, we can unlock access to a better future for everyone.

2. REVEAL THE HARD TRUTHS

Embrace the uncomfortable conversations to uncover the deeper truths within society and to reveal them in more profound ways. Use your platform to amplify the voices of others, not just your own.

3. PULL TOGETHER TO RISE HIGHER

Avoid entering into the creative process with the final answer. To build solutions that respect the community you look to serve, you must include them. Shape your ideas together. This will develop a sense of pride and ownership in the future.

4. BE MORE THAN A PRODUCT

Go beyond transactions. Use your product as an invitation and a catalyst to a more equitable future. Strive to serve the moment as well as a lifelong journey of progression and transformation for the community.

5. LIVE THE PERSONAL IN THE PROFESSIONAL

Creating more diverse representation by the numbers isn't enough. It's crucial to empower diverse individuals to bring their life experiences into their work experiences. By leveraging one's life perspective, you can affect the lives of countless others.

6. DESIGN DREAMS

It's not enough to serve only functional needs. The underserved communities you look to support have aspirations, too. Infuse the solutions you create with emotion through the stories and dreams from the community itself.

CHAPTER 9

LEAVE A LEGACY, NOT JUST A MEMORY

Portland artist Emma Berger didn't ask anyone's permission. She just started painting. And when she was done, the boards surrounding the Apple Store in downtown Portland, Oregon, showed the face of George Floyd, as well as his final words: "I can't breathe." The protests that broke out all over the nation following that tragic day came to Portland, and in the turmoil the all-glass façade of the Apple Store was smashed. The Apple managers put up boards to protect the store from further damage, but they also painted the plywood black, to show that they stood with the protesters and supported their fight for justice. The black boards offered the perfect canvas to Berger, who painted not only Floyd, but also Breonna Taylor and Ahmaud Arbery, two other victims of racial injustice.[12]

And Berger's creation offered me the perfect moment to show my daughter, Ayla, the power that artists and designers play as visual storytellers. In August 2020, I took Ayla, then a high school senior and an aspiring creative director who is now studying design in college, to see the Floyd mural. By the time we got there, other artists had added to Berger's canvas, which had become a destination for those wishing to bring their own bit of art to the growing display. In particular, someone, or many, had spray-painted the numbers "846" across the mural in several places, signifying the amount of time (8 minutes and 46 seconds) the police officer had had his knee on Floyd's neck before Floyd died.

My first reaction to the mural was that it was much larger than I had imagined, spanning the entire block of the street in downtown Portland. But it wasn't just the Berger memorial that stunned me. Other artists had created artwork on the protective boards in front of other buildings in the surrounding area. Beauty from tragedy: the power of art to transform a space into something that not only instills meaning but also elicits a powerful emotional response.

I could tell Ayla was as moved as I was. We talked about how the artists' creativity had revealed hard truths about our society in profound ways. This wasn't art that was pinned to the wall of a museum; this was art in its natural element, an organic display of grief, anger, but also hope. Art where it was *supposed* to be, tied to a moment, but also timeless in its ability to generate passions. The Floyd mural—and others like it around the country—wouldn't have the same impact if they were seen from behind a glass enclosure, or a velvet rope, where ushers are asking you to not take pictures. The mural was moving because it was where it was meant to be, a visual response to a violent act.

We create art to reflect the world that we see, as if reality passes through our creative prism and is projected onto a canvas. One can identify the reality, but now it has been transformed into something that also reflects the artist. I explained to Ayla how those artists, by using their imagery and words, are able to stir emotions within us and inspire us to action. To see in the projected image, that echo of reality, the world that we want to live in.

We have seen, and my daughter has been witness to, the power of creativity across a multitude of disciplines in recent years; from art and architecture, to writing and filmmaking. This ongoing creative output has reached into the hearts and minds of people, unifying them through a common cause such as fighting against racial injustice, calling attention to health care inequities, stopping Asian hate crimes, and voter suppression. Creativity has served as a catalyst by inviting people into the conversation through inspiration, provoking reflection, and empowering action.

The visit also gave me a chance to share my feelings about Floyd's murder directly with Ayla. Being born and raised in Minnesota and attending the Minneapolis College of Art and Design, not far from the tragedy, I saw the divide between law enforcement and the Black community then, and it pains me to see it now. Seeing the expression of that pain represented in art reminded me why I do what I do. From my earliest memories I have been drawn to the power that both sports and art have to elicit the most intense of human emotions, and perhaps for this reason I was drawn to a life of being a creator of work that stirred those same emotions in others. I followed those passions, as my daughter, Ayla, is following hers today.

Standing there with her, I was reminded of the wall mural my parents had made for me as a child to encourage my artistic talents. Well, "made" is probably too strong a word. They left one wall in the bedroom that I shared with my two brothers completely blank, only adding a wooden border, which became the canvas on which I poured my early artistic imagination. My childhood mural was meant for the time and place in which it was created; it showed the budding talent and vivid imaginations of a teenager, which I now saw reflected back on me in Ayla's artistic passions. My daughter might have gotten her artistic passion from me. But where did *I* get it?

A Source of Passion

As this book neared completion, I came face-to-face with the answers to questions I had pondered over my entire professional and personal life.

On a Saturday afternoon in April 2021, I received a message through 23andMe from a woman I didn't know.

> Hi there! Wow, I was not expecting to see that I have an uncle on here that I wasn't aware of. I see so much resemblance between your picture and my mom. Do you have any contact with that side of the family?

An hour later, after a bit of social media "research," it was clear I wasn't this woman's uncle. I was her brother. Her mom was my birth mother, someone I never dared imagine I would know or meet in this life.

That initial inquiry opened the doors to me finding not just my maternal family, but also the paternal side of my family. Within days, I had answers to a lot of those life questions so many people simply take for granted. My mind was reeling, flooded with revelation after revelation. I had gone from knowing literally nothing about my birth parents—why I looked the way I did; where I might have gotten some of my passions and characteristics—to suddenly knowing about as much as anyone can know without having grown up with them. Most people take this journey over a lifetime, their field of vision expanding from knowing these two people as "Mom" and "Dad" to knowing who those two people were in life. I received it all in a matter of weeks.

I was also struck by the irony of the situation. In recent years, I had been cautioning that soon brands grown only by data-driven marketing would squeeze all the emotion out of consumer relationships. Now, here I was, experiencing some of the most intense emotional power I had ever felt thanks to a data-driven, scientifically based website. 23andMe—a service powered by machine learning, algorithms, and data—had led to this meaningful (and instantaneous) moment of human connection. Suddenly I had answers.

Answers like knowing where I inherited my passion for sports, especially basketball. In the mid- to late 1990s, I worked on display designs for the Nike Store inside the Mall of America in Minneapolis. Perhaps because the store was in my hometown—and perhaps because if you're going to have a store in the largest mall in the world, it better live up to its destination—I had a special affinity for this particular Nike location. Nearly thirty years later, I would learn that my birth dad had made that store his destination of choice, often hanging out there for hours as the rest of his family shopped in other areas of the mall (typical dad shopping). He loved Nike, especially the Jordan Brand. He saw the displays his son had designed, even as (I would also learn later) he tried to find me during those years. He never found me, but he saw my work. I was with him.

Meanwhile, my birth mother was a flight attendant for Northwest for twenty years. During her layovers around the world, she would pass the time at art museums—Paris, London, Rome. She loved art, a passion she had inherited from her own mother, my grandmother, who enjoyed painting. In my online conversation with my sister (the one who had originally reached out to me), she sent along one of my grandmother's paintings, and I recognized a true talent as well as a source for my own artistic passion. As for my sister, she is a graphic designer, just like I had been when I graduated from the Minneapolis College of Art and Design to start my career. Our shared passion was a symbol of the connection we shared. We were part of each other even though we had never met.

I eventually took my own family to meet the relatives they never knew existed. My first embrace with my birth mother is a moment that can't be described with words, but I felt a deep connection immediately. The following day, during a reunion with my birth father's side, my new aunt gave me a series of mementos, one of which was an original class photo from the 1955 University of Minnesota graduating class. She points to the lone Black student within the grid of white portraits. There's my grandfather, the only Black man in his mortuary class to graduate that year. Breaking barriers. After college, my grandfather continued to defy convention and opened up a funeral home business on the white side of town in Minneapolis. This was a man who never played it safe, professionally or personally.

We all have talents, some hidden within us. Sometimes they come out naturally over the course of a lifetime, while others reveal themselves only in an environment that draws them out and allows them to flourish.

My own artistic passions started when I was young. I know now I was born with some of it, having inherited the gifts my birth grandmother passed on to my mother. But that's not the end of the story. Perhaps those gifts would have matured on their own, coming out in ways that passions tend to do with children. But there's no guarantee that I would have stuck with it, or felt that art was worth sticking to. How many of our childhood passions do we leave in childhood, deciding that we better put our energies toward more "useful" activities? The other half of the story is that my adoptive parents, with limited resources, nurtured my early passion for art at a young age. They did all they could to help me start my artistic journey.

Ayla, my daughter, knows where she got her passion. She also knows that her parents have tried to nurture her talent throughout her childhood, giving her the tools and support she needed to develop those passions into something that one might call a "useful" activity. And her education continued, as did mine, when we both went to the Floyd mural and saw together the incredible emotive power that true art can create.

We may inherit tremendous gifts and talents from our ancestors, and these talents may get us our start down a road that leads to joy and fulfillment. But we can never stop developing that talent and those gifts; we can never stop striving to improve the way we do what we do. We can never think that there are no more questions to be answered. The world is full of tragedy and injustice, but it is also full of hope, and it's hope that makes us believe that we can always be better.

Continuing a Journey of Creativity

And for this reason, upon retiring from Nike, I founded Modern Arena, a brand advisory group that strives to build solutions that live at the intersection of business growth and brand strength, while delivering social impact. Through Modern Arena, I began to advise a diverse set of start-ups and entrepreneurs that hope to contribute to a better and healthier world. From New Zealand, there is AO-Air, a start-up that seeks to reinvent the traditional mask—that safety accessory we all got to know very well in 2020—with its uncomfortable ear loops and less-than-airtight seal around the nose and mouth. AO-Air masks use tiny fans to provide a continuous flow of clean air without the restrictive, claustrophobic seal. Founded before the pandemic, AO-Air's mission has become even more important today, with studies showing that its masks are fifty times more effective than the market-leading solutions—and have an innovative form to match that function.

"What should we do today?" That's the tagline of another Modern Arena client, Shred. A mobile app, Shred connects users to outdoor adventures all around them (or to places they're traveling to), and to each other, making it easy to do something fun and active without a lot of online research. Users can also use Shred to book with the company providing the activity, reducing the inconvenience of booking online. Nothing better captures how you can get outside yourself than with trying something entirely new, pushing aside your fears and making the leap. We learn so much about the outside world—and ourselves—when we escape our comfort zones and go in search of adventure.

To outside observers, the connection between these two otherwise very different brands may seem distant at best. But, looking deeper, we see that both are actually in pursuit of similar goals: to improve the well-being of people. The products empower everyone to enhance their own lives, giving them the tools that improve their mental and physical health, while also building human connections. As Shred says, its mobile app "empowers people to spend more time experiencing life's best moments."

It may seem like I am very far away from Nike these days, but, I don't feel that way at all. In fact, I'm closer than you might realize. In the fall of 2021, alongside my work as a brand advisor, I became the branding instructor at the University of Oregon's Lundquist College of Business. Of the many "full-circle" moments I've experienced in my life, teaching at the institution where the

Nike cofounders had worked as coach and student athlete stands as one of the most poignant for me. Of course, I'm not there to revolutionize the athletic footwear industry. Each week I stand in front of fifty graduate students who have dreams of becoming the future general managers in the sports product industry. Through lectures, discussions, and workshops, we talk about the power of a brand, especially the importance of building the type of equity that leads to a strong emotional connection in the consumer's mind. How do you ensure that your intentions as a brand—what you want to be known for—match the consumer's perception? Why do you exist as a brand and what is the benefit you provide? Using the very concepts and ideas in this book, my ultimate hope is to impart to these young, diverse minds that creating a strong brand identity and having a positive impact on the world are not mutually exclusive. I'm happy to report that, so far, my students appreciate the connection, far more than I did when I was at that point in my life.

As brand leaders, we have so many ways to use our knowledge and our passion to help change the world. My passion and interests have brought me before such varied audiences as Summit Series, which holds events for a diverse membership of leaders, from entrepreneurs and academics to authors and artists. Through its Summit Impact initiatives, the organization leverages its global community to generate a positive impact on our world, with a focus on the environment and sustainability, houselessness, and civic engagement.

Following conversations with my friend and the cofounder of Summit, Jeff Rosenthal, I joined the board of directors of Summit Impact, and have had the honor of presenting to its membership on the theme of cultural impact through brand leadership.

I have found myself before an incredible group of Black creatives who are part of the One Club for Creativity, a free online portfolio school for students who aspire to work in advertising.

We were able to discuss the art of storytelling within the realm of social impact, in particular the arena of racial justice. For an industry that greatly lacks diversity, they can use their voices and showcase their unique perspectives to provide the necessary insight to unlock truly exceptional storytelling. Their task, I urge them, shouldn't be just to meet the demands of the business brief, but to use that brief to push the world forward in a positive way.

Through these endeavors, and especially with my teaching position at the University of Oregon, I have had to refine the lessons that I have learned throughout my career, first as an intern, then as a designer, then as a marketer. As my work has brought me before such an eclectic array of start-ups, entrepreneurs, students, and organizations, I have had to refine my ideas to make them both accessible and timely. But as I put the hours into this varied work, a structure began to form, slowly at first but also inexorably toward a defining central idea. Namely, that a brand builds a creative advantage through the fostering of a strong culture of creativity which leads to the consistent ability to construct powerful emotional bonds with its consumers. This is how some of the most iconic brands in the world have built a legacy of emotional attachment with their consumers. Some call this brand loyalty, but loyalty fails to account for the *mutual* connection that flows between brand and consumer. I don't preach brand loyalty; I talk about the power of human connection, the way in which a brand can *matter* in someone's life and can impact positive change.

A brief example may help illustrate the point.

In the winter of 2021, I had the opportunity of speaking to a group of innovators and entrepreneurs of color that are part of Andreessen Horowitz's Talent X Opportunity Fund. This remarkable organization provides funding, training, and mentorship that helps these entrepreneurs build durable, successful companies around their innovations. In our discussion, I talked about what it takes to build a "Brand Personality," a distillation of the ideas and lessons I've addressed in this book and packaged in a way that is action oriented.

"Now more than ever," I said, "it's important for a brand to be more human in this age of automation." Then I discussed the importance of building a brand's characteristics in a way that makes it unique in the world, and how to leverage the touchpoints through which consumers associate those traits with the brand in their minds. "It's our job to express different tones to our brand voice," I continued, "and play different notes in different moments. When we experience a brand that says the same thing over and over again, they can become boring or, worse, annoying, and the consumer ends up tuning them out." But it's that first line that stands out as we close this book. And I'd like to condense it even further. "It's important for a brand to be human." *To be human.* Humans experience emotions. Humans create art. Humans provide and receive inspiration. Humans take risks. Humans empathize. Humans tell stories. Humans build movements. Humans work as a team. Humans make memories. And humans close the distance.

Your brand is more than a collection of products and services. It is more than mission statements and algorithms. Your brand is bigger than the marketing or innovation departments. Your brand is human. And it is by being human that your brand will build emotional bonds with other humans. It is by being human that you can leave a legacy, not just a memory.

Back Where I Began

I now end this book where I began it, at the Minneapolis College of Art and Design. Now on the board of trustees and the chair of the Innovation Committee, I once more found myself in front of an audience. I was there (virtually) to address the faculty and students at the kickoff of the 2020 school year with an all-school assembly, touching on many of the themes I have explained in this book. The power of empathy. The role of curiosity in finding inspiration. The need to step outside oneself to understand the experiences of others. I talked about closing the distance, urging the students to see their art and design as catalysts for change, to appreciate the power of the artist and designer to elicit emotion. They were certainly ideas I was concerned about thirty years earlier, but my understanding of the power of art and design and its ability to move people and create change had evolved over the decades. I gave the talk I wished I had heard as an undergraduate, just starting out, full of confidence and ambition, but also wildly inexperienced in both the profession and world I was about to enter.

Importantly, these weren't entrepreneurs and start-up owners. These weren't marketers or brand leaders. They were students, perhaps just as confident and full of ambition as I had been, and perhaps more receptive to a message of change than I and my peers would have been in 1988, when I was a freshman. My message to them, as my message is here, was that now more than ever the power of storytelling through words and images, through film and architecture, through products and services, is needed to move an audience to embrace change. To use their creative talents to make art that reflects their reality and also seeks to build a better one. To expand their vision beyond what they can see today or tomorrow, and look beyond the weeks, the months, and the years to create art that lasts because it makes a difference. To create so that you leave a legacy of excellence and purpose.

So much of this book has been about looking at the past, at the work we remember today because of its excellence and its ability to create emotion in us. That work—the films, the images, the buildings, the campaigns, the products, and the moments—stays with us because it connected with us on an emotional level that was powerful enough to withstand the effects of time. So much lesser work is forgotten. Perhaps it made an impact at first, a laugh or a tear, but its ability to stay with us lessened as the clock moved forward until it became just another grain of sand on the beach. The power to move people, to capture their hearts and send their spirits soaring, is not easy to achieve—nor should it be. We humans, after all, may be entertained for a moment by the trite or the superficial, but we don't return to them. We move on quickly, forgetting whatever that particular piece of storytelling was attempting to convey.

But that which stays with us, that which connects, will always connect because it touches us on a level that is impossible to ignore or forget. We don't just remember it; we will always *feel* it, not simply as a momentary bit of entertainment, but as something that revealed a little bit of ourselves and a little bit of our world. It left its mark. The lessons and ideas presented in this book were designed to create that type of work, the type that overcomes our cynicism, envelops our senses, moves us to action, brings us to tears, or pushes us to be better than we had been.

Brand leaders must remember that our job, our purpose, (alongside driving demand and business growth) is to find that emotional connection with humans. That requires maintaining the balance between the left- and right-brain thinkers within our teams and emphasizing that the art of marketing is a conversation between two people—brand and consumer. Let's continue to tap into the creative ingenuity of the human mind, and cultivate the power of human-to-human interaction. Make them see you. Make them hear you. Make them feel you.

As I look ahead to the work that is before me, I am inspired by the progress we have made as a profession and as a society. I see those students sitting in the very seats my peers and I sat in, and I am humbled by their concern for the world. I see those entrepreneurs and start-up owners across the screen from me, and I am reinvigorated by their ambition and sense of purpose. I see the eyes of my daughter as she assesses the life before her and the world she is to enter, and I am overwhelmed with pride by her passion and love—a passion and love which I now know goes back generations.

Be human. Design emotion. Leave your legacy.

ACKNOWLEDGMENTS

This book is about creating strong emotional bonds, and none could be more important to me than the one I have with my wife, Kirsten. Your support and partnership throughout the writing process helped to turn my thoughts and musings into something real and meaningful. A special thanks to my Nike teammates who sat together in the Mike Schmidt building years ago. I thought I was going to see a Jackie Chan movie with all of you and it turned out that my future wife and I were the only ones who showed up. You set us up. We watched the movie and have been together ever since that day. Thanks for seeing our potential. That's the definition of teamwork.

Next, a special thank you to my son Rowan and daughter Ayla for constantly dreaming with me and asking the question "What if?" Seeing your imagination every day serves as my biggest inspiration. Thanks for being my ultimate travel partners and for putting up with my obsession with a lifestyle of design and my constant need to point out the brilliance (or lack thereof) in our everyday surroundings. Years ago, as we began the process of designing a home, Rowan, then twelve years old, told me that Frank Lloyd Wright said a house should be built into a hill, not on top of, so that the house and hill can become one. Thank you for that gem and every one since. And Ayla, you have chosen to explore a career path of art and design. I hope you find the same lifetime of creative exploration, collaboration, and fulfillment that I have been privileged to experience.

Like any creative endeavor, writing a book, though often seen as a solitary experience, requires a roster of talented players, moving as one team. I was extremely fortunate in the team that formed around me, guiding me as I embarked on a project that was somewhat outside my area of expertise.

First, I have deep gratitude for my writing collaborator, Blake Dvorak, who helped shape my lessons and anecdotes into stories that reveal greater truths. You took the ball as a kid, growing up next door to the great Chicago Bull Steve Kerr, and developed an expertise in seeing the hidden meanings in sports and life pursuits. Thanks for passing the ball with me.

Writing a book for the first time requires a willingness to listen and learn, and a coach to motivate you and tell you when you need to raise your game. Kirby Kim was more than a literary agent to me, he was the ultimate coach in the process. Kirby, his colleague Will Francis, and the Janklow and Associates team always put me in a position to advance the ball. You saw a story worth telling in that visual timeline pdf I sent you of my life and career, and by doing so, you took a chance. I only hope that the final product lives up to your standards.

Next, I want to thank my editor, Sean Desmond from Twelve Books, who saw the potential in the ideas of a rough proposal. You pushed me past the marketing and business jargon to find my voice and create a story that could be both inspiring and practical to a broader audience. Thanks also to Bob Castillo, Megan Peritt-Jacobson, and the extended team at Twelve Books. Your patience, discipline, and expertise proved invaluable to me throughout this process, especially when the going got tough.

A thank you also to Rowan Borchers and the team at Penguin Random House UK. Your energy and passion for the ideas in this book were felt from the beginning.

The seeds for this book were sown long ago, in the meeting rooms, design studios, arenas and stadiums, cafes, and cars that made up my workplace for thirty years. Thank you to all the daydreamers, especially my former Nike teammates, for their generous recollections, advice, and support on this book. A special shout-out to Ron Dumas, Ray Butts, Gino Fisanotti, Pam McConnell, Jason Cohn, David Creech, Ean Lensch, Heather Amuny-Dey, Mark Smith, David Schriber, Ricky Engleberg, Pamela Neferkara, Gary Horton, Musa Turig, Alex Lopez, Michael Shea, Scott Denton-Cardew, Valerie Taylor-Smith, Leo Sandino-Taylor, Vince Ling, and Dennie Wendt. In your own way, each of you helped me fulfill the journey of this book.

A big thanks to the Wieden and Kennedy family, with a huge debt of gratitude to Karrelle Dixon, Alberto Ponte, and Ryan O'Rourke. You always creatively challenged us to push through our comfort zone. Who else would pitch a global campaign called "Risk Everything"? We often did, and I don't regret a single moment.

Taking those creative risks with your brand voice, again and again, takes a level of fearlessness to go beyond what is safe. To that point, a very special thank you to Davide Grasso and Enrico Balleri for the partnership during a prolific moment in time and for always representing the true nature of radical creative collaboration.

I also want to recognize and thank Bob Greenberg and the RGA team and Ajaz Ahmed and the AKQA team for the close partnership during the "digital revolution" of Nike marketing. Commonplace now, but it took a level of vision, innovation, and collaboration to ignite the movement.

There are individuals who contributed to this book indirectly through their influence on the early stages of my career. Jan

Jancourt, my college typography professor, challenged me to raise my game and see the difference between good and great. Laurie Haycock Makela encouraged the young version of me to break out of the safety of a design grid and take some bold risks.

To my parents, Gary and Jacqui Hoffman, who put that wood frame around the edges of that white wall in my childhood bedroom, creating a mural for me to fill with my imaginations and dreams, and for always supporting my creative pursuits, no matter how audacious. And of course, thanks for the use of your van during the magical summer of 1992.

Finally, a thank you to my newly discovered birth families. As an adoptee, I had questions about where my traits and passions came from. Their contributions to me and this book started long ago, even if we have just recently come together. Creativity and its power to build deeper relationships and change the world for the better is forged through both, nature and nurture. May we continue to build both through emotion by design.

ENDNOTES

1. https://www.nytimes.com/1997/04/30/sports/using-soccer-to-sell -the-swoosh.html
2. https://www.elartedf.com/ginga-essence-brazilian-football-years/
3. https://www.marketingweek.com/career-salary-survey-2020-marketing -diversity-crisis/
4. https://www.nasa.gov/missions/science/f_apollo_11_spinoff.html
5. https://rocketswire.usatoday.com/2020/01/29/hakeem-olajuwon-said -kobe-bryant-was-his-best-low-post-student/
6. https://www.esquire.com/sports/a30668080/kobe-bryant-tribute -20-years-after-draft/
7. https://www.si.com/nba/2018/05/30/origin-lebron-james-chosen -1-tattoo
8. https://www.adweek.com/performance-marketing/this-agency-used-a -weather-balloon-to-fly-nikes-new-vapormax-shoe-into-space/
9. https://nypost.com/2015/10/27/why-thousands-of-people-are-running -with-kevin-hart/
10. https://cargocollective.com/kervs/following/all/kervs/The-Reason
11. https://www.washingtonpost.com/news/on-leadership/wp/2016/07/08 /this-advertising-agency-turned-its-entire-home-page-into-a-powerful -blacklivesmatter-message-2/
12. https://katu.com/news/local/mural-honors-george-floyd-in-downtown -portland

INDEX

Index

Index

Index

Index

Index

Index

Index

Index

Index